*International Crises
and the Role of Law*

THE UNITED NATIONS
OPERATION IN THE CONGO
1960–1964

*International Crises
and the Role of Law*

THE UNITED NATIONS OPERATION IN THE CONGO 1960–1964

BY

GEORGES ABI-SAAB

OXFORD UNIVERSITY PRESS

1978

Oxford University Press, Walton Street, Oxford OX2 6DP

OXFORD   LONDON   GLASGOW
NEW YORK   TORONTO   MELBOURNE   WELLINGTON
IBADAN   NAIROBI   DAR ES SALAAM   LUSAKA   CAPE TOWN
KUALA LUMPUR   SINGAPORE   JAKARTA   HONG KONG   TOKYO
DELHI   BOMBAY   CALCUTTA   MADRAS   KARACHI

© OXFORD UNIVERSITY PRESS 1978

Published under the auspices of the American Society of International Law

British Library Cataloguing in Publication Data

Abi-Saab, Georges
    The United Nations operation in
    the Congo, 1960–1964. – (International
    crises and the role of law).
    1. United Nations – Armed forces – Zaire
    2. Zaire – History 1960– 3. Zaire –
    Politics and government – 1960 –
    I. Title   II. Series
    341.5'8   JX1981.P7
    ISBN 0–19–825323–0

PRINTED IN GREAT BRITAIN BY
COX & WYMAN LTD, LONDON, FAKENHAM AND READING

To the memory
of
John McMahon

FOREWORD

IF we want law and legal institutions to play larger and more effective roles in coping with international conflict, we shall need to understand more clearly the roles they now play. This book is one significant step in the search for such understanding. It is the product of a keen and experienced mind looking closely at one international crisis to learn more about the ways in which law affected—and failed to affect—decisions that were being made.

Under the auspices of the American Society of International Law, a group of us set out, individually and collectively, to learn more about the roles which law plays in the making of decisions at a time of crisis—a crisis which involves issues of war and peace. That legal considerations do play various roles in many important government decisions is clear. It is also clear that many other factors—military, political, economic, psychological, historical, cultural, social, and so forth—also have effect on such decisions. Little is to be gained through argument over the comparative importance in any one decision of the different contributing elements. That law played a ten per cent role or a sixty per cent role tells us nothing about how to increase that role. What one needs to know is not *how much* did law affect a given decision, but *how*. What are the different ways in which law and legal institutions affect what happens in international affairs? This book is part of the quest for useful categories of thought to help us all to understand better how international law works and how it fails to work. It is part of the search for practical insight that may lay a foundation for measures designed to expand or strengthen the roles which law plays.

Work of the American Society of International Law in this sphere was made possible by a generous grant of the Old Dominion Foundation (a predecessor to the Andrew W. Mellon Foundation). This monograph has been commissioned and is published under the auspices of the American Society of International Law. Although the author retains full responsibility for the text, an earlier draft of the text was reviewed and discussed by a panel of members of the Society in furtherance of the project. As chairman of the panel, I would like to express our appreciation to the Foundation, to the Society, and particularly to its Executive Director, Professor Stephen M. Schwebel, for supporting and guiding this project from conception to fruition.

Harvard Law School   ROGER FISHER

PREFACE

THERE are many ways of treating the legal aspects of the Congo crisis and of its handling by the U.N. One current approach is to evaluate U.N. action by the gauge of law as understood and interpreted by the writer. Another common approach, especially for the common lawyer, is to examine what has been done with a view to tracing the impact of experience on law, reformulating it in the light of practice or 'precedent', and thus treating law as an *output* of action.

This essay, however, follows the reverse process, by trying to trace the role of law as an *input* of decisions and action. In other words, it inquires in what ways and to what extent, if at all, legal considerations, as understood by the decision-maker at the time of decision, had a bearing on the ensuing decision. This implies trying to reconstitute, as far as possible, the decision-making process, including the legal vista facing the decision-maker, bringing out in each case the state of the legal debate on the points at issue, as well as the other factors bearing on the decision, and relating both these types of considerations to the decision taken, thus identifying, as far as available evidence permits, the role of law in relation to each analysed decision.

This approach explains why the study passes quickly or even silently over certain aspects of the crisis while paying greater attention to others which may seem of lesser importance, but which shed more light on the role of law in the decision-making process.

The study focuses on two categories of decisions. The first includes the initial and most important one, from which all the others flowed, namely the decision of the U.N. to undertake a peace-keeping operation in the Congo. The analysis of this decision not only provides the necessary background for the understanding of subsequent developments both of the crisis and of the U.N. role in it; it also sheds light on the general set-up of the U.N. during that period, especially in respect of its growing political role and of the evolving relationship between its deliberative and executive organs.

But once the U.N. was in the Congo, decisions were continuously called forth by a highly dynamic and changing situation. The second category of decisions studied includes three clusters of decisions which the U.N. had to take to face up to unexpected developments or particularly persistent obstacles. They are the decisions relating to the controversy over the deployment of the Force in Katanga in August 1960; to the constitutional crisis which broke out in September 1960; and finally to the ending of the Katanga secession.

In the study of each of these clusters, it is not proposed to analyse each decision in isolation but rather as a point on a curve, a part of a continuous process. This approach is closest to reality, for the decisions in each cluster build on each other and constitute part of the U.N. response to the same problem.

The decisions studied are all U.N. decisions; they are mostly Secretariat decisions taken either exclusively or jointly with other organs. With the exception of some of the decisions relating to the ending of the Katanga secession, they were all taken during the tenure of Dag Hammarskjöld and can be said to be either his or largely influenced by him. This explains the prominent place given in the study to the ideas and role of the late Secretary-General.

Graduate Institute   GEORGES ABI-SAAB
of International Studies
Geneva

ACKNOWLEDGEMENTS

In view of the approach adopted in the preparation of this study, no special effort was made either to undertake original historical research or to partake in the doctrinal controversies on the different legal facets of the Congo Operation (the purpose being not to identify the 'correct' or 'better' interpretation of each legal issue discussed, but —regardless of it being rightly or wrongly perceived by the decision-maker—to assess its bearing on the decision).

The reconstruction was mainly done on the basis of contemporary U.N. debates and documents. Much insight was gained, however, from consulting the verbatim records of the U.N. Advisory Committee on the Congo. I am particularly indebted to the late Ralph Bunche and to Mr. F. T. Liu for having granted me permission to examine these otherwise classified records and to quote certain passages from them. I am also grateful to the numerous persons who had a role to play in the Congo Operation as U.N. officials, diplomats, or politicians, from whose recollections and impressions I profited; my gratitude is not diminished by the fact that they must remain nameless. Though I have tried to refer only to published materials, the background knowledge gained from these two sources helped me to choose among the possible interpretations of what is often stated in a bland and elliptic language that which came nearest to the understanding by the actors of the points at issue and which reflected the relative importance and urgency they attributed to them at the critical time.

For historical background I relied heavily on Catherine Hoskyns's *The Congo since Independence*. I also relied very heavily, and for obvious reasons, on Brian Urquhart's authorized biography of Dag Hammarskjöld, and for one particular episode in Conor Cruise O'Brien's *To Katanga and Back*. I am most grateful to these authors whose works rendered such an interpretative study possible. Unfortunately, Ambassador Rajeshwar Dayal's *Mission for Hammarskjöld* (1976), came out after the completion of the study. I am consoled, however, by the fact that it does not invalidate the main lines of analysis here adopted.

I would like also to express my appreciation to all those who helped me in the course of the preparation of the study, and in particular to my friend and former student Malek Gabr and to my wife Rosemary who was of constant help in manifold ways, especially as reader and critic.

CONTENTS

ABBREVIATIONS

Congo 1960   J. Gérard-Libois and B. Verhaegen (editors), *Congo: 1960*, vol.
              I (Dossiers du Centre de Recherche et d'Information Socio-
              Politique C.R.I.S.P., Brussels, 1961)

Gavshon   Arthur L. Gavshon, *The Last Days of Dag Hammarskjöld* (Pall
              Mall Press, London, 1963)

Hoskyns   Catherine Hoskyns, *The Congo since Independence: January 1960–
              December 1961* (O.U.P., London, 1965)

O'Brien   Conor Cruise O'Brien, *To Katanga and Back: A Case History*
              (Hutchinson, London, 1962)

Urquhart   Brian Urquhart, *Hammarskjöld* (Knopf, N.Y., 1972)

GAOR   General Assembly Official Records

ONUC   Opération des Nations Unies au Congo. The initials of the
              Operation used in all languages

SCOR   Security Council Official Records

A/   General Assembly documents

S/   Security Council documents

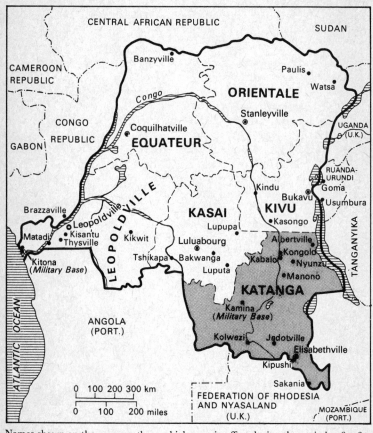

Names shown on the map are those which were in effect during the period 1960–64

Map of the Congo

I

THE INITIAL DECISION TO UNDERTAKE A PEACE-KEEPING OPERATION IN THE CONGO (JULY 1960)

THE major decision which brought the U.N. into the Congo and which conditioned all its subsequent activities and decisions was taken formally by the Security Council. But in fact the Council did no more than authorize the Secretary-General to execute the plan he had submitted to it for consideration. Thus, if the Security Council provided the formal sanction, the political initiative and proposed content of the decision came from the Secretary-General.

The formulation of this decision exemplifies very clearly the role of law as a tool of social engineering. It aimed at designing a type of collective action which was considered an apt response to a certain political crisis, liable to defuse its explosive potential.

1. CONCEPTS OF THE SECRETARY-GENERAL CONCERNING THE ROLE OF THE U.N. IN A DIVIDED WORLD

To understand the reasons that led to devising the peace-keeping operation it is necessary to examine the political premisses on which it was built.

The doctrine of preventive diplomacy

In the Introduction to his Annual Report to the 15th General Assembly for the Year 1959–60, Dag Hammarskjöld describes the role of the U.N. in the field of maintenance of peace and security as he saw it. He starts by admitting that '[w]ith its constitution and structure, it is extremely difficult for the United Nations to exercise an influence on problems which are clearly and definitely within the orbit of present day conflicts between power blocs'.

But this does not mean the denial of all 'possibilities of substantive action by the United Nations in a split world'. It merely 'defines the main field of useful activity of the United Nations in its efforts to prevent conflicts or to solve conflicts'. This field covers 'conflicts arising within the non-committed areas'. They offer opportunities for solutions which avoid an aggravation of big Power differences and can remain uninfluenced by them. There is thus a field within which international conflicts may be faced and solved with such harmony between the power blocs as was anticipated as a condition for Security Council action in San Francisco. Agreement may be achieved because of mutual interest among the big Powers to avoid having a regional or local conflict drawn into the sphere of bloc politics.

This 'community of interests which is created by the desire of everybody to limit areas of conflict, to reduce the risk of conflict' provides 'a basis for joint action for solution or at least localization, of conflicts' and can be used as a 'lever' for widening 'the scope for possible diplomatic and political action by the Organization'.

The possible diplomatic and political action of the Organization in this context is what Dag Hammarskjöld describes as 'preventive diplomacy' or 'preventive action'. It can be beneficially deployed in 'conflicts which are initially only on the margin or outside the bloc conflicts, but which, unless solved or localized, might widen the bloc conflicts and seriously aggravate them'.

[P]reventive diplomacy . . . is of special significance in cases where the original conflict may be said either to be the result of, or to imply risks for, the creation of a power vacuum between the main blocs. Preventive action in such cases must in the first place aim at filling the vacuum so that it will not provoke action from any of the major parties, the initiative for which might be taken for preventive purposes but might in turn lead to counteraction from the other side. The ways in which a vacuum can be filled by the United Nations so as to forestall such initiatives differ from case to case, but they have this in common: temporarily, and pending the filling of a vacuum by normal means, the United Nations enters the picture on the basis of its non-commitment to any power bloc, so as to provide to the extent possible a guarantee in relation to all parties against initiatives from others.[1]

'Executive action' and the 'executive tasks' of the Secretary-General

'Preventive diplomacy' describes the action of the U.N. by its aim or purpose which is to forestall the extension, through intervention and counter-intervention, of the cold war to conflicts outside or on the periphery of the contending blocs; and this by the strict localization or 'international neutralization' of these conflicts through the intervention of the U.N. itself. Such an intervention requires what Hammarskjöld calls 'executive action'.

In the Introduction to his Annual Report to the 16th General

1   A/4390/Add. 1.

Assembly he contrasts the great attention given in the Charter to the purposes and principles with the little which is said about executive arrangements.

[T]he executive functions and their form have been largely left to practice ... The forms used by the Security Council [and] by the General Assembly are varied and are to be explained by an effort to adjust the measures to the needs of each single situation. However, some main types are recurrent. Sub-committees have been set up for fact-finding or negotiation on the spot. Missions have been placed in areas of conflict for the purpose of observation and local negotiation. Observer groups of a temporary nature have been set out. And, finally, police forces under the aegis of the United Nations have been organized for the assistance of the governments concerned with a view to upholding the principles of the Charter. As these, or many of these, arrangements require centralized administrative measures which cannot be performed by the Council or the General Assembly, Members have to a large extent used the possibility to request the Secretary-General to perform special functions by instructing him to take the necessary executive steps for implementation of the action decided upon.[2]

'Peace-keeping' forces and operations

The devolution of wide 'executive responsibilities' on the Secretary-General took place especially in connection with the establishment and direction of international police forces, i.e. in peace-keeping operations, where the General Assembly (and later on the Security Council) 'found that the most adequate way to meet the challenges which it had to face was to entrust the Secretary-General with wide executive tasks on the basis of mandates of a general nature'.[3]

Thus in the Suez crisis, the General Assembly—'[b]earing in mind the urgent necessity of facilitating compliance with its resolution 997 (ES-I) of 2 November 1956' concerning the cease-fire and the withdrawal from Egyptian territory—'[r]equest[ed], as a matter of priority, the Secretary-General to submit to it within forty-eight hours a plan for the setting up, with the consent of the nations concerned, of an emergency international United Nations Force, to secure and

---

2 A/4800/Add. 1.

3 A/4390/Add. 1. Such mandates have been granted under article 98 of the Charter which reads: 'The Secretary-General shall act in that capacity in all meetings of the General Assembly, of the Security Council, of the Economic and Social Council and of the Trusteeship Council, and shall perform such other functions as are entrusted to him by these organs. The Secretary-General shall make an annual report to the General Assembly on the work of the Organization.'

supervise the cessation of hostilities in accordance with all the terms of the aforementioned resolution'.[4] The U.N. Emergency Force (UNEF) was officially established by the General Assembly on the basis of the plan and recommendations submitted to it by the Secretary-General in two successive reports.[5] It was thus left to the Secretary-General to design the Force, to define its functions, and to lay down the modalities and principles governing its functioning, in addition to the task of negotiating its recruitment and deployment and the overall responsibility for its operation.

It is true that the first two resolutions adopted by the General Assembly in the Suez crisis gave the Secretary-General some indications; but these were very scanty. Similarly, he built on the prior experiences of the U.N. in the establishment of observer groups (especially UNTSO in Palestine); but again these were much more limited than the proposed Force both in their scope and in the functions entrusted to them. Thus in great measure, UNEF can be said to be the brain-child of Dag Hammarskjöld.

It was characteristic of Hammarskjöld's preoccupation with rational system building to distil the lessons of the UNEF experience in a Report which he submitted to the General Assembly in 1958, and in which he tried to identify those of the solutions and principles evolved which were of general significance and thus applicable to

4 G.A.Res. 998 (ES–I) of 4 Nov. 1956 (submitted by Canada). The resolution referred to therein is G.A.Res. 997 (ES–I) of 2 Nov. 1956 (submitted by the U.S.) urging all parties 'to agree to an immediate cease-fire', and all parties to the armistice agreements (i.e. Israel) 'promptly to withdraw all forces behind the armistice lines'. During the same meeting, the General Assembly adopted another resolution, submitted by nineteen Afro-Asian members, authorizing 'the Secretary-General immediately to arrange with the parties concerned for the implementation of the cease-fire and the halting of the movement of military forces and arms in the area' and requesting him 'to obtain compliance of the withdrawal of all forces behind armistice lines'. G.A.Res. 999 (ES–I) of 4 Nov. 1956.

5 G.A.Res. 1000 (ES–I) of 5 Nov. 1956 and G.A.Res. 1001 (ES–I) of 7 Nov. 1956. The first of these resolutions, following on the recommendations of the First Report of the Secretary-General of 4 Nov. 1956 (A/3289), established a U.N. Command and appointed a Chief of the Command, authorizing him to start the recruitment for the Force in consultation with the Secretary-General. The second resolution (1001 (ES–I)) approved the guiding principles for the organization and functioning and the definition of the functions of the Force which were proposed by the Secretary-General in his Second and final Report of 6 Nov. 1956 (A/3302). It also established an Advisory Committee, to be chaired by the Secretary-General. Both resolutions specifically authorize the Secretary-General to take all administrative measures and executive action necessary for their implementation.

future operations.[6] It was upon these that he called in setting up the Congo Operation; an Operation in whose creation and direction he played an even greater role than in the case of UNEF.

2. INITIATIVES OF THE SECRETARY-GENERAL AT THE OUT- BREAK OF THE CONGO CRISIS

The doctrine of 'preventive diplomacy' particularly applies, and 'executive action' is especially needed, in 'situations in which the liquidation of the colonial system has led to acute conflict'.[7] It is an appropriate technique to stabilize post-colonial situations in Asia and Africa behind the shield of the U.N. This institutional intervention, which aims at temporarily filling the power vacuum created by col- onial disengagement, gives the newly independent States time to develop their own solutions to ensuing conflicts and problems and to engage in 'nation-building', while protecting them from becoming a theatre of competition and intervention on the part of the contending blocs.

The Congo crisis provided the test, one is tempted to say the acid test, of this theory; and the Secretary-General found in it both a challenge and an opportunity to provide a practical demonstration of the validity of his doctrine.

Africa and the U.N.

1960 was Africa's year in the U.N., culminating in the admission of seventeen new Members, sixteen of which were from Africa. From the close of the 1950s, Dag Hammarskjöld paid special attention to the prospects and problems of African independence and saw in them an opportunity for the U.N. to play a constructive role in both the political and the economic fields. This role is very clearly described in the Introduction to his Annual Report to the 15th General Assembly, the opening section of which is entitled 'Africa and the United Nations':

The Organization must further and support policies aiming at independence, not only in a constitutional sense but in every sense of the word, protecting the possibilities of the African peoples to choose their own way without undue influences being exercised and without attempts to abuse the situation. This must be true in all fields, the political, the economic, as well as the ideolog- ical—if independence is to have a real meaning.[8]

6 A/3943, 9 Oct. 1958.
7 A/4800/Add. 1.
8 A/4390/Add. 1.

From 21 December 1959 to the end of January 1960 Hammarskjöld undertook an intensive African tour which took him to twenty-four countries, territories, and regions. Among them figured the Belgian Congo, in which he visited both Leopoldville and Stanleyville. He thus had a first-hand view of the last stages of the hurried process of decolonization in the Congo and was fully aware that, given its lack of preparation for independence and its size and natural wealth, the Congo was heading for exceptional transitional difficulties.[9] Late in May 1960, he asked Ralph Bunche to go to the Congo to represent the U.N. in the independence ceremonies and 'to stay on in the Congo for some time after independence, to be of such assistance as might be required of [him] by the new government, bearing in mind ... that there might well be trouble in that new country'.[10] In other words, Hammarskjöld sensed the coming storm in the Congo and wanted to establish a 'U.N. presence'—by then a well-sharpened device in his tool-set of preventive diplomacy[11]—in the person of Dr. Bunche, in order to steady the situation and to enable him, and through him the U.N., to act quickly in case of crisis.

The outbreak of the crisis

At the time of independence, the Congo suffered from a severe shortage of local skills: there were only a handful of Congolese University graduates; there was not a single Congolese doctor or engineer, not a single commissioned officer in the *Armée Nationale Congolaise* (A.N.C., the former *Force Publique*) and no senior staff in any field. In these circumstances, the solution which was envisaged by the Treaty of Friendship and Co-operation between the Republic of the Congo and Belgium (which was signed but never ratified by the Congo) was that most of the Belgian administrators and technical personnel would continue to discharge their functions after independence.

Political activities in the Belgian Congo had been rather subdued and the possibility of independence was hardly discussed until the late fifties. It was only after the riots in Leopoldville early in 1959 that Belgium hurriedly consented to the principle of independence and the political institutions of the new State were negotiated in a Round

9 Urquhart, 381, 388–9.

10 R. Bunche, 'The United Nations Operation in the Congo', in Cordier and Foote (eds.), *The Quest for Peace* (1965), 119 at 123.

11 Urquhart, 388. On the evolution of the concept and practice of 'U.N. presence', see J. Lash, 'Dag Hammarskjöld's Conception of his Office', 16 *International Organization* (1962) 542–66.

Table Conference held in Brussels in early 1960. The result was the *Loi Fondamentale* which was promulgated by the Belgian Parliament and which was to serve as the Congolese constitution.

At that moment, political formations proliferated in the Congo. On the one hand there were movements chiefly based on regional and ethnic affinities, the most important of which was the *Alliance des Ba-Kongo* (ABAKO) led by Joseph Kasavubu. These movements were in favour of federal structures guaranteeing for them a large degree of autonomy within the new State. On the other hand, there were the nationalist movements, basically the Lumumba-led *Mouvement National Congolais* (M.N.C.), which aspired to forge the Congo into one nation and consequently favoured a unitary state structure.

The first elections were held in May 1960. The M.N.C. and its allies won a relative majority. The formation of the first government took a tortuous path in which the Belgian representatives could not resist the temptation of intervening and as a result aggravated the distrust of the nationalists. Finally, a compromise was reached with Kasavabu elected by the Parliament to the Presidency and Lumumba charged with the formation of the Government. Because of the desire to include in it as many political movements as possible, the Cabinet which eventually emerged on 24 June was very heterogeneous, without being all-embracing.[12] The fragile *entente* between Kasavubu and Lumumba, the precarious equilibrium within the Cabinet, and the threatening attitude of Moïse Tshombe, the President of the Katanga provincial government (who had tried to secede just before independence but was prevented from doing so by the Belgians),[13] were all ominous signs of things to come.

The Republic of the Congo acceded to independence on 30 June 1960 and the storm broke out much earlier and with more intensity

12 For more details on the pre-independence period, see Hoskyns, 1–84; W. J. Ganshof van der Meersch, *Fin de la souveraineté belge au Congo* (1963).

13 See Hoskyns, 81; R. Lemarchand, *Political Awakening in the Congo: The Politics of Fragmentation* (1964), 246. Tshombe was the leader of the *Confédération des Associations Tribales du Katanga* (Conakat). In the pre-independence elections to the Katanga Assembly Conakat won twenty-five seats and its allies another thirteen, while its competitors, the *Association des Ba-Luba de Katanga* (Balubakat) and M.N.C.(K) (for Kalonji) won twenty-two seats. The latter complained of electoral malpractices and refused to participate in the Assembly until their complaints were examined. As the *Loi Fondamentale* required a majority of two-thirds of the Assembly for the election of the President, Tshombe could not get elected until the Belgians amended the *Loi Fondamentale*; which they did without consulting the other Congolese leaders, although the *Loi Fondamentale* was the result of collective negotiations with them in the round-table conference (see Hoskyns, 70–1).

than expected. It took the shape of a mutiny by the A.N.C. against its Belgian officers. This in turn led to the breakdown of law and order in the country, harassment of, and some atrocities against, Belgian civilians, and the intervention of Belgian metropolitan troops stationed in the military bases which Belgium had retained in the Congo by virtue of the Treaty of Friendship and Co-operation (a treaty which had not been, and was never to be, ratified by the Congo Government, and which, in any case, did not grant Belgium any right of intervention without the express request of the Congolese Government).[14]

Soon after the mutiny and before the Belgian intervention, the Congo Government made a request to Bunche, on 10 July, for military technical assistance, with a view to reorganizing and retraining the A.N.C.[15] But after hearing of the Belgian intervention (which started in Katanga on that very day) and especially after the Belgian attack and occupation of the Port of Matadi[16] and the declaration of independence of Katanga, both occurring on 11 July, the Congolese authorities became convinced of the need for a friendly outside military presence to counterbalance that of Belgium. On 11 July Kasavubu and Lumumba flew to Luluabourg to calm the soldiers and convince the Belgian civilians not to leave.[17] In their absence, three ministers—Gizenga, Bomboko, and Nyembo—appealed to the American Ambassador in Leopoldville the following day for 3,000 American troops to help restore law and order. The Americans, however, advised them to turn to the U.N.[18]

14 Ibid. 85–97.

15 This request was decided after Bunche 'had explained in detail the possibilities and limitations of U.N. military assistance' in a Cabinet meeting of 10 July, 'at which it became clear that the Congolese Government urgently wanted help from the U.N. but had no clear idea either of what was required or what might reasonably be expected', Urquhart, 393; Bunche, loc. cit. 124.

16 Ralph Bunche had strongly warned Belgian representatives against military intervention and its likely results (see Urquhart, 393). It is to be noted that by the time the intervention started the situation was in the process of calming down (see Hoskyns, 98). The attack on Matadi was called by the *Daily Telegraph* of 21 July 1960 a 'reprisal raid', which it probably was. This raid was followed by the deployment of Belgian troops in all the major cities of the Congo, including the capital.

17 In order to reassure the Belgian civilians, Lumumba consented to the presence of the Belgian troops in Kasai for two months, under certain conditions (for the exchange of letters between him and the Belgian Consul on this matter, see *Congo 1960*, 411). But this was by no means a general acceptance of the Belgian intervention, especially in the light of the subsequent attack on Matadi and the Katangese declaration of independence which took place later that day.

18 Hoskyns, 114; Urquhart, 395.

From Luluabourg, Kasavubu and Lumumba sent their first cable (of 12 July) to the Secretary-General, urgently requesting U.N. military assistance. But unlike their previous request for military assistance of a technical nature, they specified that '[t]he purpose of the requested military aid is to protect the national territory of the Congo against the present external aggression which is a threat to international peace'.[19] The following day (13 July), having heard of the appeal made by the three ministers for American troops, they sent a second cable to the Secretary-General to clarify the nature of their request:

(1) the purpose of the aid requested is not to restore the internal situation in Congo but rather to protect the national territory against acts of aggression posed by Belgian metropolitan troops. (2) The request for assistance relates only to a United Nations force consisting of military personnel of neutral countries and not of United States as reported by certain radio stations. (3) If requested assistance is not received without delay the Republic of the Congo will be obliged to appeal to the Bandung Treaty Powers. (4) The aid has been requested by the Republic of the Congo in the exercise of its sovereign rights and not in agreement with Belgium as reported.[20]

At the same time, they sent a cable to Mr. Krushchev asking him to follow the situation 'hour by hour' and declaring that they might call on the Soviet Union for help.[21] But as with the reference to the 'Bandung Treaty Powers', the cable to Krushchev did not solicit or reflect any firm commitment; it only meant to keep open a final possibility in case all else failed. Probably, it was also conceived as a lever inciting the U.N. and the Western powers to exert pressure on Belgium to withdraw.

The convening of the Security Council under article 99 of the Charter

The Secretary-General's contribution was not limited to the articulation of a political doctrine and the establishment of a U.N. presence

19 S/4382, 13 July 1960.

20 Ibid. The reference to the 'Bandung Treaty Powers' shows how little the new Congolese leaders knew about international relations, a fact which became progressively clear in their relations with the U.N. (see *supra*, p. 8, n. 15) and which explains many of the misunderstandings and disputes which were to follow. Urquhart (400 n.) writes: 'The U.N. was a total novelty to the Congolese. Already on 10 July, Bunche had to explain to Lumumba that the U.N. would not be in the Congo to fight anyone; and the district administrator in Thysville had asked him *"l'ONU c'est quelle tribu?"*.'

21 Hoskyns, 127–8.

in the Congo—a presence which made it an available and credible alternative to big power intervention. His major contribution was to devise a blueprint for U.N. action in response to the crisis which was legally and constitutionally compatible with the Charter, politically acceptable to all concerned, and materially capable of fulfilling its objectives. This is the social engineering aspect of the Secretary-General's activity, which is most relevant to the role of law in this context. But for such action, the authorization of one of the two major organs of the U.N. was necessary; and, in order for this authorization to be forthcoming, the problem had to be presented to the authorizing organ in a manner conducive to general agreement.

This is why, once he received the two cables of President Kasavubu and Prime Minister Lumumba, the Secretary-General took the initiative of asking the President of the Security Council urgently to convene the Council.[22] His letter to the President does not refer specifically to article 99 of the Charter.[23] However, the first sentence literally reproduces the language of that article.[24] Moreover, in his initial statement before the Council, the Secretary-General said that he used his powers under article 99.[25] This initiative, which was formally exercised for the first time in the history of the Organization, was not a mere procedural step; it meant to emphasize the gravity of

22 Hammarskjöld had already planned to consult with the African representatives and members of the Security Council on the first request of assistance (see *supra*, p. 8, n. 15) which he did with the former in the morning of 12 July and with the latter in a luncheon at his office on 13 July. But by that time, the second request had reached him and thus became the subject of consultations (see Urquhart, 394, 396).

23 Article 99 reads: 'The Secretary-General may bring to the attention of the Security Council any matter which in his opinion may threaten the maintenance of international peace and security'. The political importance of this article goes much beyond the procedural question it directly treats. It has been interpreted as providing the legal basis of the political functions of the Secretary-General which are directly devolved on him by the Charter as distinguished from those which are conferred on him by the deliberative organs. (See M. Virally, 'Le rôle politique du Secretaire Général des Nations Unies', 4 *Annuaire Français de Droit International* (1958) 360–99). Dag Hammarskjöld gave great importance to article 99 as a legal basis for his political initiatives. See his Introduction to the *Annual Report to the 14th General Assembly, for the Year 1958–1959*, A/4132/Add. 1; and his Oxford Lecture on 'The International Civil Servant in Law and in Fact', reproduced in W. Foote (ed.), *Dag Hammarskjöld: Speeches* (1962), 329 at 335; see in general Lash, loc. cit. This article is based, among others, on a lengthy interview with Hammarskjöld on 20 April 1960, a substantial part of which was devoted to his understanding of article 99.

24 S/4381.

25 SCOR, 873 Mtg., 13 July 1960, para. 18.

the situation, by reflecting the Secretary-General's conviction that it fell under Chapter VII of the Charter.[26]

By taking the initiative, the Secretary-General could more easily channel the debate in the direction he wanted, which was to reach a decision on U.N. action without making it depend, as a condition precedent, on a clear legal characterization of the situation. For the characterization of the Belgian intervention as aggression would not have been accepted by the Western members of the Council as it would have entailed not only condemning Belgium but would have also opened the way to applying collective measures against it. On the other hand, characterizing the situation as a mere breakdown of internal law and order would have indirectly justified Belgian intervention and would not have been acceptable to either the Socialist or the Afro-Asian members of the Council.[27]

For Hammarskjöld, then, it was important to avoid this pitfall in order to reach the type of practical action which would command the acceptance of all the members. For him the real alternative was not between the different characterizations but between action or no action.[28] Even if condemnation were obtainable, it would not have led to positive action by the U.N. in the absence of a machinery for collective measures, nor would it have had any moderating influence on Belgium to bring to an end its intervention. Thus, it would not have served a useful purpose and would not have enabled the Organization to play a constructive role in the crisis.

26 According to Lash (loc. cit. at 551 n. 39) Hammarskjöld·considered that the explicit invocation of article 99 necessarily implies a finding by the Secretary-General of the existence of a situation falling within the scope of Chapter VII, i.e. article 39.

27 This explains the preliminary controversy in the Council over the title of the agenda item: Hammarskjöld having formulated it by reference to his letter to the President, while Sobolev (U.S.S.R.) wanted to add to it a reference to the telegrams of Kasavubu and Lumumba (which asked for U.N. help against Belgian 'aggression'). Hammarskjöld explained that the telegrams were addressed to him and did not mention the Council; and although the Congo, then a non-member state, could have seised the Council under article 35, paragraph 2 of the Charter, no such intention was manifested in the telegrams. Finally Hammarskjöld's formula was maintained. (SCOR, 873 Mtg., 13 July 1960, paras. 1–16). Obviously, the characterization of a situation by a party who seises the Council does not bind the Council, but it sets the tone of the subsequent debate. Later on, the Secretary-General would invoke the absence of reference to the telegrams in the title of the item as a proof that their terms were not controlling either the characterization of the situation or the terms of the mandate. SCOR, 920 Mtg., 13–14 Dec. 1960, para. 76; see also SCOR, 973 Mtg., 13 Nov. 1961, paras. 1–41.

28 Urquhart, 389.

Of course, the partisans of the two characterizations voiced their opinions during the debates in the Council.[29] But as they had before them a concrete plan of action on which they could all agree regardless of the characterization they adopted, the importance of the characterization was reduced from the main battle ground to a mere registration of positions. The Council, following the Secretary-General's suggestion, did not opt explicitly for either characterization. This allowed each member to vote for the proposed action while safeguarding its position. But it left open to each to interpret the decision in the light of its own characterization, a fact which accounts for most of the subsequent legal difficulties encountered by ONUC and the Secretary-General.

Proposed action

The Secretary-General drew the lesson from the handling of the Suez crisis in the General Assembly, which set the pattern for preventive diplomacy through peace-keeping. The British delegate had declared:

By entering the Suez Canal area, we would only be seeking to protect a vital waterway, and it is also the only practicable line of division between the combatants ...

The first urgent task is to separate Israel and Egypt and to stabilize the position. That is our purpose. If the United Nations were willing to take over the physical task of maintaining peace in the area, no one would be better pleased than we. But police action there must be, to separate the belligerents and to stop the hostilities.[30]

Taking him at his word, the General Assembly—on a proposal of Lester Pearson, the Canadian Foreign Minister—decided to create

29 Thus, e.g., Mr. Ortona (Italy) considered that 'we are facing not intervention but a temporary security measure' (SCOR, 873 Mtg., 13 July 1960, para. 121) and Sir Harold Beeley (U.K.) that 'Belgian troops have performed a humanitarian task for which my Government is grateful and for which the international community should be grateful' (ibid., para. 130). In the same vein, the Belgian representative, Mr. Loridan, declared that: 'The Belgian Government can only interpret the statement just made by Mr. Hammarskjöld as recognition of the material necessity for Belgian military intervention in the Congo, and indeed an implicit acknowledgement for [its] legality' (ibid., para. 196).

On the other hand, Mongi Slim (Tunisia) characterized the Belgian intervention as an 'unwarranted act of aggression' (ibid., para. 87), a point Mr. Sobolev (U.S.S.R.) emphasized from the beginning (ibid., para. 2). He even proposed an amendment to the Tunisian draft, which would have added to it the following paragraph: 'The Security Council ... condemns the armed aggression by Belgium against the Republic of the Congo' (ibid., paras. 198–201). But the amendment was not adopted.

30 GAOR (ES–I) Plenary, 561 Mtg., 1 Nov. 1956, paras. 102 and 111.

an international police force, thus depriving the Anglo-French oper-ation of its self-confessed justification.

Similarly, in the Congo crisis, the Secretary-General starts his initial statement to the Security Council by stating:

The difficulties which have developed in the Congo . . . are connected with the maintenance of order in the country and the protection of life. But the difficulties have an important international bearing as they are of a nature that cannot be disregarded by other countries.

He then refers to the Belgian intervention:

The Belgian Government has in the Congo troops stated by the Government to be maintained there in protection of life and for the maintenance of order. It is not for the Secretary-General to pronounce himself on this action and its legal and political aspects, but I must conclude from the communications received from the Government of the Congo that the presence of these troops is a source of internal, and potentially also of international, tension. In these circumstances, the presence of Belgian troops cannot be accepted as a satis-factory stopgap arrangement pending the reestablishment of order through the national security force.

He then interprets the cables of Kasavubu and Lumumba in terms of a request for a more acceptable stopgap arrangement through the U.N., thus indirectly setting aside the question of 'aggression':

It is in this light that I personally wish to see the request for military assistance, which has been addressed to me by the Government of the Congo. Although I am fully aware of the problems, difficulties and even risks involved, I find that the stopgap arrangement envisaged by the Government of the Congo is preferable to any other formula.

This leads him to the further conclusion that: 'It would be under-stood that, were the United Nations to act as proposed, *the Belgian Government would see its way to a withdrawal*.'[31]

Thus, in both cases, without formally condemning an act which is obviously a violation of international law and the Charter, but which is allegedly fulfilling a necessary function (protecting a vital waterway or protecting the lives of nationals threatened by the breakdown of law and order in another country), preventive diplomacy aims at creating conditions which permit such actions to be terminated by getting the U.N. to fulfil the functions which allegedly incited them. In a way, this is what is meant by 'filling the vacuum'. U.N. decisions, while asking for the cessation of those actions, are less concerned with the condemnation of their illegality, because they need to marshal the

31 SCOR, 873 Mtg., 13 July 1960, paras. 19–27 (emphasis added).

widest possible consensus (including the acquiescence of the target
State or States) on the proposed U.N. action.

The Security Council adopted the Secretary-General's recommendation—formally submitted in a Tunisian draft—in its resolution of 14 July 1960, which reads:

The Security Council,
Considering the report of the Secretary-General on a request for United
Nations action in relation to the Republic of the Congo,
Considering the request for military assistance addressed to the Secretary-
General by the President and the Prime Minister of the Republic of the Congo
[S/4382],

1. *Calls upon* the Government of Belgium to withdraw its troops from the
territory of the Republic of the Congo;
2. *Decides* to authorize the Secretary-General to take the necessary steps, in
consultation with the Government of the Republic of the Congo, to provide
the Government with such military assistance as may be necessary until,
through the efforts of the Congolese Government with the technical assistance
of the United Nations, the national security forces may be able, in the opinion
of the Government, to meet fully their tasks;
3. *Requests* the Secretary-General to report to the Security Council as appropriate.[32]

The crucial part of this resolution concerning U.N. action in the
Congo, operative paragraph 2, reproduces almost verbatim a phrase
from the Secretary-General's initial statement.[33] Thus, the tailoring
of U.N. action to meet the situation, and of the mandate of the
Secretary-General to execute it, were in effect undertaken by the
Secretary-General himself.[34] It is true that this was done on the basis
of an emerging pattern from previous experience; but in this case there

32 S/4387.

33 SCOR, 873 Mtg., 13 July 1960, para. 22. Later on, the Secretary-General
declared in the Security Council: 'The resolution of 14 July (S/4387) was in response to
my proposals and the main operative paragraph was in fact, for all practical purposes, a
quote from my statement.' SCOR, 920 Mtg., 12 Dec. 1960, para. 76. Cf. First Report
S/4389, 18 July 1960, para. 3; Lash, loc. cit. at 547.

34 Another aspect of the social-engineering approach of the Secretary-General was
his contingency planning in case the authorization for his proposed action was blocked
by a conflict of characterization. According to Urquhart (398), if the Tunisian draft
resolution, based on his own proposals, were to run into opposition, 'Hammarskjöld
was prepared to propose a short resolution simply putting U.N. troops in the Congo',
i.e. to avoid completely the characterization of the situation or the definition of the
mission of the U.N. troops. Finally, 'if this also failed, he was ready to take steps to
ensure that the question was transferred to an emergency session of the General
Assembly, where there would be no doubt a majority vote in favor of action'. However,
in view of the great controversies which arose out of the ambiguities of the first Security

were many new elements; in particular the mandate of the Secretary General was both much wider and vaguer than in previous cases.

3. THE MANDATE AND ITS INTERPRETATION

Unlike the General Assembly Resolutions in the Suez crisis which created UNEF (thus conferring on it the legal status of a subsidiary organ of the General Assembly[35]) and appointed its Commander, the Resolution of the Security Council did not even mention the word 'Force'. It merely authorized 'the Secretary-General to take the necessary steps, in consultation with the Government of the Republic of the Congo, to provide the Government with such military assistance as may be necessary ...' The nature and modalities of the assistance to be given to the Congo Government were thus largely left to be determined by the Secretary-General himself. However, this does not mean that the Secretary-General was the sole master of the Operation. For the resolution was adopted against the background of his initial statement, in which he specified that he intended to create an international peace-keeping force on the basis of the principles distilled from the UNEF experience.[36]

Moreover, the Secretary-General was keenly aware that he had to work with and under the continuous surveillance of the Security Council.[37] This was one of his constant preoccupations and the reason why he endeavoured from the very beginning to articulate explicitly the formal pattern of his relations with the Council and the lines of division of labour between them. Thus, in his initial statement, after inviting 'the Council to act with the utmost speed', he added:

I would welcome consultations followed by renewed meetings for a fuller elaboration of the mandate which I recommend to the Security Council to give me now. As a matter of course I will report to the Council as appropriate on any action taken on the basis of the authorization which I hope the Council will give me tonight.[38]

Council resolution based on the Tunisian draft, one can imagine with the benefit of hindsight the havoc that would have been wrought had the first of these alternatives been followed.

35 See *supra*, p. 4.

36 SCOR, 873 Mtg., 13 July 1960, paras. 18–29.

37 According to Urquhart (394), Hammarskjöld told Piero Spinelli in Geneva on 11 July—that is before receiving the Congolese request for military assistance— that '[t]he Congo operation ... would be the most difficult and complex one ever undertaken by the U.N., not least because the Security Council would be involved in it from the very beginning'.

38 SCOR, 873 Mtg., 13 July 1960, para. 29.

However, once the authorization was granted, the initiative of providing an interpretation and a fuller elaboration of the mandate shifted once again to the Secretary-General, who stated in his First Report to the Council:

The resolution of the Security Council was adopted in response to my initial statement to the Council ... Therefore, that statement may be regarded as a basic document on the interpretation of the mandate ... However, ... important points were left open for an interpretation in practice. In submitting this first progress report, I want not only to bring to the knowledge of the Council what so far has been achieved, but also what lines I have followed concerning the implementation of the authorization.[39]

This statement is followed, in the first section of the Report entitled 'The Mandate', by a fuller elaboration of three major points which he had briefly enunciated in his initial statement. These are 'the main purpose of the introduction of a United Nations Force in the Congo ... the relationship between this action and a withdrawal of Belgian troops ... and the legal principles ... which should apply to the operation'.[40]

The role and functions of ONUC

In his First Report, the Secretary-General provided a more explicit characterization—in fact an *ex post facto* clarification of his understanding—of the situation justifying U.N. action; and one wonders whether the initial elliptic attitude was not intended by its ambiguity to facilitate consensus:

It was implied in my presentation that it was the breakdown of those instruments of Government, for the maintenance of law and order which had created a situation which through its consequences represented a threat to peace and security justifying United Nations intervention on the basis of the explicit request of the Government of the Republic of the Congo. Thus the two main elements, from the legal point of view, were on the one hand this request and, on the other hand, the implied finding that the circumstances to which I had referred were such as to justify United Nations action under the Charter. Whether or not it was also held that the United Nations faced a conflict between two parties was, under these circumstances, in my view, legally not essential for the justification of the action.[41]

Here, the Secretary-General characterizes the crisis as a 'situation' in the meaning of article 34 of the Charter which, in contrast to a

39 S/4389, 18 July 1960, paras. 1–4.
40 Ibid., para. 3.
41 Ibid., para. 5.

'dispute', need not involve parties and can even be of an internal character as long as it affects international peace and security.[42] This implies a distinction between the two aspects of the crisis and an exclusive concentration on the first, i.e. the breakdown of law and order, which alone can be considered as a 'situation'. This was sufficient, it is true, to justify U.N. action under the Charter. But it also made it possible to set aside the question of Belgian intervention, while stating that action in relation to the first aspect would lead to the disappearance of the second.

Thus, according to the initial understanding of the mandate, the function of ONUC was to be limited to assisting the Government in the maintenance of law and order; the Operation would have no direct functions in relation to the withdrawal of Belgian troops, though indirectly it would provide Belgium with a way out.

The principles

The mandate consisted not only of the functions of the Operation, but also of the principles to be followed in performing these functions. These principles were briefly mentioned in the initial statement and further developed in the First Report, though basically by reference to the Secretary-General's Report on the UNEF experience.[43] They are:

(1) *The principle of the autonomy of the Force and the Operation:*
Although the United Nations Force under the resolution is dispatched to the Congo at the request of the Government ... and although it may be considered as serving as an arm of the Government for the maintenance of order and protection of life ... the Force is necessarily under the exclusive command of the United Nations, vested in the Secretary-General under the control of the Security Council ... The Force is thus not under the orders of the Government nor can it ... be permitted to become a party to any internal conflict ...

[One consequence of this autonomy is that the] authority granted to the United Nations Force cannot be exercised within the Congo either in competition with representatives of the host government or in cooperation with them in any joint operation. This naturally applies *a fortiori* to representatives and military units of other Governments than the host Government.[44]

42 On the distinction between 'dispute' and 'situation', see Y. Liang, 'The Settlement of Disputes in the Security Council: The Yalta Voting Formula', 24 *BYBIL* (1947) 330 at 349; E. Jimenez de Arechaga, *Voting and Handling of Disputes in the Security Council* (1950); L. Goodrich, E. Hambro, and A. Simons, *Charter of the United Nations* (3rd edn., 1969), 271.

43 A/3943, 9 Oct. 1958.

44 The allusion in the mention of Governments other than the host Government is clearly to Belgium (see *infra*, p. 21).

[Another consequence is that the Force] should have freedom of movement within its area of operations and all such facilities regarding access to that area and communications as are necessary for a successful accomplishment of the task.

(2) *The principle of non-intervention in internal affairs:*
United Nations Units must not become parties in internal conflicts [and] ... they cannot be used to enforce any specific political solution of pending problems or ... influence the political balance decisive to such a solution.

(3) *The principle of non-use of force except in self-defence:*
... men engaged in the operation may never take the initiative in the use of armed force, but are entitled to respond with force to an attack with arms, including attempts to use force to make them withdraw from positions which they occupy under orders from the Commander ... The basic element involved is clearly the prohibition against any *initiative* in the use of armed force.[45]

This presentation of the mandate by the Secretary-General in his initial statement and First Report constitutes a logical and coherent blueprint. Thus, the *political role (or aim) of the U.N.* in the crisis is to fill the vacuum created in the Congo by the breakdown of the instruments of law and order. This in turn would make it possible for Belgium's unilateral intervention to come to an end and would pre-empt other interventions and counter-interventions which would inevitably extend the cold war to the heart of Africa.[46] But this general political role is pursued through a more specifically defined *mandate* to provide assistance to the Republic of the Congo in the field of security administration. The assistance takes the shape of a peace-keeping Force whose *function* is to assist in the maintenance of law and order and the protection of life. However, this function has to be performed according to certain modalities and within certain limitations laid down in a set of legal *principles*.

This general scheme is almost entirely due to Dag Hammarskjöld. It provides a further illustration not only of his primordial role in devising the mandate but also of his strategic position in the process of its interpretation.

4. THE PROCESS OF INTERPRETATION: THE GENERAL FRAMEWORK

The application of general rules to specific situations necessarily

---

45 S/4389, paras. 7–15.
46 Cf. Introduction to the *Annual Report to the 15th General Assembly for the Year 1959–1960*, A/4390/Add. 1.

implies two operations: the interpretation of the rule and the legal characterization of the factual situation to which it is applied. In general this process of day-to-day interpretation by application does not raise any problems and in most cases goes unnoticed. However, a need arises for a more authoritative process of interpretation if the factual situation is of a type which was unforeseen at the time of the formulation of the rule or if the interpretation on which action is based is challenged.

Both these hypotheses are of frequent occurrence in relation to the execution by the Secretary-General of general mandates conferred on him by the Security Council or the General Assembly. This is because, given the divergent ideologies, interests, and outlooks between member States, consensus on action is very hard to achieve, except on deliberately vague formulae glossing over points of potential disagreement which would have blocked the initial U.N. decision to act. These points, however, cannot be dodged in practice; sooner or later the executing organ has to face them in the course of implementing the mandate. Similarly, the factual situations very frequently develop in a manner unforeseen in the mandate and can no longer be adequately handled within its clear confines. But even when both the situation and the mandate and consequently the course of action to be taken seem clear to the executing organ, certain members of the Organization may construe them differently. A conflict of interpretation then ensues between these members and the executing organ. Both types of difficulties may materialize in the same case, as happened in the Congo crisis.

The U.N. Charter does not provide a system of authoritative interpretation.[47] Nor is there a procedure of judicial review to settle controversies as to the legality and constitutionality of contested decisions or actions (except for the voluntary procedure of requesting an advisory opinion from the International Court of Justice). In these conditions, the system does not guarantee that a final and legally unchallengeable decision would be reached in all cases. This state of affairs, which protects to the maximum the sovereignty of member States, is compatible with the 'forum' or 'static conference' functions of an Organization where each member can in the final analysis stand on its position, without unmanageable practical results. But it is

47 See the statement of Committee IV/2 of the San Francisco Conference on the interpretation of the Charter, 13 *UNCIO*, 709.

incompatible with the more dynamic functions of an Organization undertaking 'executive action'.[48]

In U.N. practice, mandates to undertake executive action have been granted either to a group of States, to the Secretary-General, or to subsidiary organs. In the case of an authorization given to a group of States, the risk is great that it will be used or abused as a vehicle for the realization of the national interests of these States rather than for the realization of the purposes of the Organization. In these cases, challenges to the legality of the mandate itself, as well as of its implementation, are to be expected.[49].

In case of a mandate entrusted to the Secretary-General, the danger of abuse, though not impossible, is less likely, for he is an organ of the Organization and is supposed to act as the guardian of its purposes and principles. Still, this does not prevent conflicts of interpretation from arising. Of course, in such cases, the Secretary-General can always go back to the authorizing organ to ask for an interpretation. But, given the veto, once a controversy over the implementation of a mandate arises in the Security Council, it is equally difficult to obtain an authoritative interpretation of this mandate as it is to put an end to it. For in both cases a positive vote is needed.[50] The same situation applies *mutatis mutandis* to the General Assembly where a two-thirds majority vote is necessary for interpreting or putting an end to a mandate, although this may in practice be less formidable an obstacle than the veto. Thus, the constitutional and political context of the U.N. is favourable to the continuation of a mandate once it is granted, even when its implementation is challenged, but less favourable to arriving at authoritative hierarchical interpretations or variations.

This may be the reason why the Secretary-General initially sought a vague and wide mandate in the Congo. For while submitting to the hierarchical authority of the Council, by frequently reporting and going back to it for guidance, this mandate enabled him to retain a very wide margin of freedom in its implementation and in adapting his action to changing situations.

48 The contrast as well as the terms used are drawn from the Introduction to the *Annual Report to the 16th General Assembly for the Year 1960–1961*, A/4800/Add. 1.

49 For a discussion of this possibility, see Second Report on UNEF, A/3302, 5 Nov. 1956, paras. 4–5. The only example in practice is that of Korea. The dangers of this possibility become clear, if one remembers that the U.K. and France had suggested using their intervening troops as a U.N. Force in the Suez area (ibid.).

50 Later on, a legal device was used to reduce the autonomy of the executing organ. It consisted of creating the Force for a fixed and relatively short period. Thus, a positive vote, i.e. a new resolution, was periodically needed to prorogue its mandate.

II

THE DEPLOYMENT OF THE
U.N. FORCE IN KATANGA

ONCE the initial decision to undertake a peace-keeping operation in the Congo was taken by the Security Council—by conferring a mandate to that effect on the Secretary-General—a continuous stream of decisions was called forth by the unfolding events of a highly dynamic crisis. Unlike the first, these decisions were taken by reference to, and in application of, the mandate. They constitute an interpretation and an elaboration of its different facets in relation to specific and largely unforeseen situations.

The deployment of the U.N. Force in Katanga encountered the first serious obstacle to the implementation of the mandate. It required overcoming different and contradictory types of objections and resistance on the part of Belgium, the Katanga provincial government, and the Central Government. The decisions taken by the Secretary-General in dealing with these different sources of resistance illustrate very clearly the style of action of Dag Hammarskjöld as well as his concept of the political role of ONUC and of the legal parameters within which it had to be performed. In other words, they illustrate both the process of interpretation as well as the substantive interpretation he gave to the basic principles conditioning the U.N. Operation in the Congo.

1. BELGIUM

The Belgian legal position

From the beginning, the Belgian Government tried to present its military action as a humanitarian intervention, an action it 'was compelled to take to protect its nationals and in the interests of the Congo and of the international community at large.'[1]

From this premiss—and following the example of the U.K. and France during the Suez crisis[2]—Belgium tried to obtain retroactive legitimization of its action by the U.N., through having its intervening troops accepted as part of, or operate in collaboration with, the U.N.

---

1 SCOR, 873 Mtg., 13 July 1960, para. 196.
2 See *supra*, p. 20, n. 49.

Force which would be sent to the Congo. Thus, in the initial discussion of the crisis in the Security Council, the Belgian representative declared that: 'Belgium requested and hoped for United Nations military aid *to collaborate* in the restoration of security and the protection of human life ... in the Republic of the Congo where security is at present ensured only by Belgian troops.'[3]

This line of argument was of course totally unacceptable to the Congolese government and to the Members who defended its cause in the Council; it was also at variance with Hammarskjöld's own concept of the Operation[4] and was not taken up even by Belgium's allies in the Council. But it was the line that Belgian commanders tried to follow on the terrain; though it was consistently resisted by U.N. troops which avoided (probably under strict orders from the Secretary-General) any situation where they would have to co-operate, or perhaps more important, where they would seem to co-operate with the Belgian intervening troops.[5]

But if collaboration with the U.N. Force was not forthcoming, a second line of justification was for the Belgians to establish the continuity between the activities of their troops and those of the U.N., by having the latter relieve the former. This would have demonstrated the identity of purpose of the two operations; hence the declaration of the Belgian representative in the initial Security Council debate:

When the United Nations forces have, as the Belgian Government hopes, rapidly moved into position and are able to ensure the effective maintenance of order and the security of persons in the Congo, my Government will proceed to withdraw its intervening metropolitan forces, *which are at present alone capable of ensuring the accomplishment of these aims.*[6]

3 SCOR, 873 Mtg., 13 July 1960, para. 195 (emphasis added). The French original is even clearer in indicating the Belgian intention: '... la Belgique demandait et souhaitait une aide militaire de l'Organisation des Nations Unies, en vue de collaborer au rétablissement de la sécurité et la sauvegarde de la vie humaine ... sécurité qui est assurée, en ce moment, par les seules troupes belges ...' Cf. S/4752/Annex II (27 Feb. 1961).

4 See First Report S/4389, para. 12.

5 This is in spite of the meddling of General Alexander, the then British Commander-in-Chief of Ghana's armed forces, in the early stages of the deployment of the Force, which created some confusion as to the functions of the U.N. Force and its relations with the Belgian intervening troops. See S/4445/Annex II (19 Aug. 1960) and S/4451 (21 Aug. 1960). See also H. I. Alexander, *African Tightrope* (1965), 33–49; Hoskyns, 135–9; Urquhart, 400 n.

6 SCOR, 873 Mtg., 13–14 July 1960, para. 196 (emphasis added).

This line of reasoning implies the legal characterization of Belgian action as humanitarian intervention; and it was those who adhered to this characterization in the Security Council, who also insisted on the necessity of subjecting the Belgian withdrawal to the prior deployment of the U.N. Force.[7] On the other hand, those who considered the Belgian intervention as 'aggression' insisted on the immediate withdrawal of the Belgian troops, regardless of the deployment of the U.N. Force.[8]

The Secretary-General, as we have seen, avoided taking a clear position on the legal characterization of the situation in the initial debate. In his First Report, four days later, he put the emphasis on the breakdown of law and order in the Congo rather than on Belgian intervention. He interpreted the mandate on that basis and treated the question of Belgian withdrawal as a separate, though related question.[9]

This could be taken as an espousal of the Belgian thesis; but more likely it was a tactical stand, to avoid pronouncing himself on the question of the timing of Belgian withdrawal, hence on the characterization of Belgian intervention, while pushing for the speediest possible withdrawal in his diplomatic efforts with Belgium.[10] His

7 See *supra*, p. 12, n. 29: e.g. Sir Harold Beeley (U.K.) described the relationship between the deployment of the Force and the withdrawal of Belgian troops as an 'interlocking process' (SCOR, 879 Mtg., 21 July 1960, para. 27). Mr. Lodge (U.S.) explained that he voted for the resolution, on the understanding that the withdrawal of Belgian troops in accordance with paragraph 1 was 'contingent upon the successful carrying out by the United Nations of paragraph 2' (SCOR, 873 Mtg., 13–14 July 1960, para. 235). Cf. the Italian representative (ibid., para. 245); the French representative (ibid., para. 143). Sir Harold Beeley (U.K.) explained his abstention by the fact that the link between the first two paragraphs was not made explicit in the resolution (ibid., para. 133, 240). See also, for the understanding of the Belgian Government, S/4419 (6 Aug. 1960).

8 See *supra*, p. 12, n. 29. The U.S.S.R. representative proposed to add the adverb 'immediately' to the first paragraph of the Tunisian draft resolution calling on Belgium to withdraw its troops (SCOR, 873 Mtg., 13–14 July 1960, para, 199), and after the adoption of the resolution, he declared his understanding that: 'The principal purpose of the resolution ... is ... to ensure the immediate and unconditional withdrawal of the Belgian troops ... without regard to any other provision in the resolution' (ibid., paras. 241–3). Cf. the Polish representative (ibid., para. 246); Slim (Tunisia) intimated, though only indirectly, a similar understanding (as he was anxious to get the resolution adopted) (ibid., para. 216).

9 See *supra*, p. 16.

10 Regardless of what Hammarskjöld thought the legal nature of the Belgian intervention was, his attitude on the question of withdrawal was in fact quite pragmatic. Thus, when he was asked by the U.S.S.R. representatives, on 18 July, to set a

approach at that stage was to assume that Belgium would apply the resolution in good faith, particularly the first paragraph addressed to it. In other words, his approach was not to assert officially his functions under the mandate in relation to this part of the resolution, while pushing unofficially for its rapid implementation.

The Secretary-General thus hoped that the Belgian intervention would quickly come to an end without his having to take a stand on its legal characterization or on the timing of its ending—a stand which would have complicated his diplomatic efforts. The U.N. would then be left with the task of helping the Congo Government in the maintenance of law and order (and in running the basic services after the exodus of the Belgian technicians) in the short run; while providing it with technical assistance to develop its own capacity in this as in other fields, in the long run.[11]

The Secretary-General's First Report was based on these assumptions. But in the short period between the release of the Report on 18 July and its discussion in the Security Council on 20 July, positions had polarized, and the approach of the Secretary-General as presented in his Report was overtaken by events.

The problem of withdrawal from Katanga

The question of the withdrawal of Belgian troops centred mainly on their withdrawal from Katanga. The Central Government was becoming increasingly impatient with the slow pace and fragmentary character of Belgian withdrawal and especially with their entrenchment in Katanga. They could not understand why the Organization they had called in to help and which had the means to do so, was not using more expeditious methods to effect this withdrawal.

Lumumba was keenly aware of the great danger of the Katanga secession consolidating into a *fait accompli* with Belgian support and

---

date for Belgian withdrawal, for example 'within three days', he replied 'that he could not take responsibility for such a decision, since the decisive point was whether or not human lives could be properly protected. He would not ... support a withdrawal of Belgian troops from any point unless ONUC headquarters in Leopoldville was prepared to assume responsibility for security' (Urquhart, 405).

11 Although the initial attention of the Security Council and the Secretariat was exclusively concentrated on the military aspects of the Operation, its civilian components grew very quickly both in volume and importance under the urgent and pressing needs of the situation. The civilian operation—as these came to be known—is not treated in this study. For the organization of this operation, see S/4417/Add. 5, 11 Aug. 1960.

under Belgian protection, while the Central Government and the U.N. stood passively by. On 18 July, the day the First Report was released, he 'presented Bunche with the first of a series of ultimatums, in which he declared that if all Belgian forces were not withdrawn within forty-eight hours the government would appeal for aid elsewhere, specifically to the Soviet Union.' In New York, Central Government's supporters were also increasing the pressure on the Secretary-General. On the same day, the U.S.S.R. representatives Kuznetsov and Dobrynin requested from Hammarskjöld that a time-limit be set for the withdrawal, for example 'within three days'.[12]

On the other hand, Belgium was most reluctant to withdraw from Katanga and from the bases of Kamina and Kitona. Its tactics were to separate the general question of withdrawal from that of withdrawal from Katanga. Several arguments were presented to that effect: that Belgian troops were in Katanga 'at the request of the authorities', that Katanga was the only part of the Congo where there was no problem of law and order, that withdrawal would cause an exodus of the European population, which in turn would lead to the collapse of the economy, etc.[13]

A wide spectrum of Belgian public opinion was strongly in favour of Katanga. In a broadcast on 21 July King Baudoin expressed similar feelings:

Like all revolts, this one has been carried out by a minority. Whole tribes led by sober and honest men have asked us to stay and help them build a real independence in the midst of the chaos which now reigns in what was once the Belgian Congo. Our duty is to give a favourable reply to all those who loyally request our co-operation.[14]

The second Security Council resolution

In view of this polarization of positions on the question of the withdrawal of Belgian troops from Katanga, it became impossible to set it aside in the Security Council debate. Once again the initiative of proposing a line of action to the Security Council came from the

12 Urquhart, 405. For Hammarskjöld's reply, see *supra*, p. 23, n. 10.

13 Second Report, S/4417 (6 Aug. 1960), para. 5.

14 Reproduced in Hoskyns, 141. The revolt referred to in the speech is that of the *Force Publique*, which was attributed by the Belgians to Lumumba. They thus represented the legal Central Government as the rebel, and the rebellious secessionist movement in Katanga as legal by contrast.

Secretary-General; his proposal sought to clarify three aspects of the mandate:

(1) To specify the Secretary-General's functions, as part of his mandate, in securing Belgian withdrawal:

Although the Security Council did not, as it has done in previous cases, authorize or request the Secretary-General to take specific steps for the implementation of the withdrawal—apart, of course, from the establishment of the Force—my representatives in the Congo have taken the initiatives they have found indicated for the coordination of the implementation of the Security Council decision on withdrawal. Although I do not consider it necessary, a clarification of my mandate on this point may be found useful by the Council.[15]

This proposal was intended to strengthen his position *vis-à-vis* Belgium; it may have also been motivated by the desire to meet half-way those who considered that the main, if not the only function of ONUC was to effectuate and supervise the withdrawal of Belgian troops.[16]

(2) To specify also that the mandate applies to the whole territory of the Republic of the Congo, including Katanga:

The resolution of the Security Council [S/4387], in response to the appeal from the Government of the Congo, clearly applies to the whole of the Territory of the Republic as it existed when the Security Council, only a few days earlier, recommended the Congo for admission as a Member of the United Nations [S/4377]. Thus, in my view, the United Nations Force, under the resolution and on the basis of the request of the Government of the Congo, is entitled to access to all parts of the territory in fulfilment of its duties.[17]

(3) To invite the specialized agencies on a formal basis to provide the Secretary-General with whatever assistance they can offer within the framework of the civilian Operation.[18]

Once again the Council faithfully followed the proposals of the Secretary-General, by adopting on 22 July a draft resolution submitted this time by Tunisia and Ceylon, which illustrated once more, if further proof was needed, the close collaboration in the design and

15 SCOR, 877 Mtg., 20 July 1960, para. 18. The reference to previous experiences is clearly to Suez. See *supra*, p. 4, n. 4.

16 e.g. Mongi Slim (Tunisia) SCOR, 878 Mtg., 21 July 1960, paras. 28–9; SCOR, 886 Mtg., 8 Aug. 1960, para. 256. See also the declaration of Kuznetsov (U.S.S.R.) quoted *infra*, p. 39, n. 49.

17 SCOR, 877 Mtg., 20 July 1960, para. 15.

18 Ibid., para. 14.

conduct of the Operation between the Secretary-General and the Afro-Asian members. It reads:

The Security Council,
Having considered the first report by the Secretary-General [*S/4389 and Add. 1–3*] on the implementation of Security Council resolution S/4387 of 14 July 1960,
Appreciating the work of the Secretary-General and the support so readily and so speedily given to him by all Member States invited by him to give assistance,
Noting that, as stated by the Secretary-General, the arrival of the troops of the United Nations Force in Leopoldville has already had a salutary effect,
Recognizing that an urgent need still exists to continue and to increase such efforts,
Considering that the complete restoration of law and order in the Republic of the Congo would effectively contribute to the maintenance of international peace and security,
Recognizing that the Security Council recommended the admission of the Republic of the Congo to membership in the United Nations as a unit,

1. *Calls upon* the Government of Belgium to implement speedily the Security Council resolution of 14 July 1960 on the withdrawal of its troops, and authorizes the Secretary-General to take all necessary action to this effect;

2. *Requests* all States to refrain from any action which might tend to impede the restoration of law and order and the exercise by the Government of the Congo of its authority and also to refrain from any action which might undermine the territorial integrity and the political independence of the Republic of the Congo;

3. *Commends* the Secretary-General for the prompt action he has taken to carry out resolution S/4387 of the Security Council, and for his first report;

4. *Invites* the specialized agencies of the United Nations to render to the Secretary-General such assistance as he may require;

5. *Requests* the Secretary-General to report further to the Security Council as appropriate.[19]

This resolution constitutes an authoritative interpretation by the Security Council of its first resolution, explaining and elaborating the Secretary-General's mandate in the light of the subsequent developments of the crisis. Its aim was basically to maximize the pressure on Belgium in order to speed up the withdrawal of its troops from all parts of the Congo, including Katanga. This was explicitly stated in the first paragraph, both by calling on Belgium to withdraw its troops speedily and by directing the Secretary-General to take all necessary action to that effect. But it was further specified in relation to Katanga by referring, in the preamble, to the recommendation by the Security

19 S/4405 (adopted unanimously).

Council of the admission of the Republic of the Congo to the U.N. *as a unit*, and by enjoining, in the second operative paragraph, all States—but clearly with Belgium in mind—to refrain from any action which might undermine the *territorial integrity* of the Republic of the Congo.

2. KATANGA

Preparation for entry

At the time of the adoption of the second resolution, the U.N. Force was being deployed and the Belgian troops withdrawn all over the territory of the Republic of the Congo, with the exception of Katanga and the bases of Kamina and Kitona.[20] At that juncture, the question of the secession of Katanga was generally considered as a mere by-product of Belgian military intervention, which would wither away once the Belgian withdrawal from the province was completed.

Armed with the new Security Council resolution as an added legal instrument of pressure on Belgium, and in response to the pressures on him from Lumumba (who arrived in New York on 24 July and met Hammarskjöld before the latter's departure to Leopoldville, on his way to South Africa), the U.S.S.R., and the Afro-Asian members, the Secretary-General started preparing for the deployment of the Force in Katanga. On his way to Leopoldville, he stopped for consultations in Brussels on 27 July.[21] Through this and subsequent *démarches*, he managed to obtain, on 2 August, a private and reluctant assurance of the acquiescence of the Belgian Government to the application of the resolution to Katanga—i.e. that Belgian troops would not resist the deployment of the U.N. Force there—though such assurance was not given on behalf of Belgian civilians nor of the Katangese.[22]

As Lumumba—whose increasing impatience was reflected in his joint communiqués with the Heads of African countries he was visiting—was expected back in Leopoldville shortly afterwards, and to forestall uncontrollable developments which could lead to a Korean-type situation in the Congo,[23] the Secretary-General decided to act

20 On withdrawal of Belgian troops, see S/4389/Add. 4, 26 July 1960. Kamina base is situated in Katanga.

21 Urquhart, 408.

22 Ibid. 413–15; Hoskyns, 160.

23 Urquhart, 414–15.

without further delay. On 2 August in Leopoldville Hammarskjöld addressed the Congolese Cabinet Committee for Cooperation with the U.N. He stated that the time had come 'to give effect to the Security Council's resolutions in Katanga also', and outlined the practical plan he intended to follow. It consisted of sending Dr. Bunche, on 5 August, to Elisabethville with the necessary staff 'to begin the initial negotiations concerning the withdrawal of Belgian troops to their bases, as a first step towards the full implementation of the Security Council resolutions'; to be followed the next day, 6 August, by the first U.N. military units.[24]

On 3 August he received, through the Belgian diplomatic mission in Leopoldville, a message from Tshombe, declaring the determination of 'the Katanga Government ... to resist by every means ... the dispatch of United Nations forces to Katanga', and offering to explain the position to Dr. Bunche 'at Elisabethville not later than tomorrow before calamitous incidents occur'. He reiterated, however, his 'readiness to consider any formula of cooperation with other *sovereign* States of the former Belgian Congo'.[25]

Bunche's mission to Katanga

In his reply of 4 August, the Secretary-General emphasized the obligatory character of the resolutions by drawing Tshombe's attention to articles 25 and 49 of the Charter which 'confer on the Security Council an authority applicable directly to Governments and *a fortiori* to subordinate non-governmental authorities of Member nations', as well as to the possibility of applying sanctions in case of resistance to Security Council resolutions. He also reiterated the principles governing the functioning of the Force, especially that of nonintervention in internal affairs. At the same time, he dispatched Dr. Bunche to Elisabethville, with the instructions to discuss with Belgian authorities the modalities for the withdrawal of their troops and their replacement by the U.N. Force. He also authorized him to have 'through the Belgian authorities ... such contact with leaders of the European community and with Mr. Tshombe and other representatives of the population as he may find necessary in order to prepare the ground for the withdrawal of the Belgian and the entry of United Nations troops', and if necessary to inform them 'on the legal

24 Second Report, S/4417, 6 Aug. 1960, para. 4.
25 Ibid. para. 6 (emphasis added).

basis of the United Nations action and of the consequences of resistance'.

The most important part of these instructions is the contingency plan which the Secretary-General put in the following terms:

Should you arrive at the conclusion that resistance by force represents a serious risk in view of the attitudes of leaders and that for that reason you have to advise against the entry of United Nations troops, I shall, upon receipt of your report, ask for the immediate convening of the Security Council to which I shall present a complete report on what has occurred, with a request for instructions.[26]

In Elisabethville, though cordially received, Bunche was subjected to a display of military preparedness and emphatically told by all those he saw, whether Belgians or Katangese (including Tshombe and especially Munungo, his Minister of Interior) that 'Katanga was determined to resist by force any attempt to bring in the United Nations troops'.[27] On these grounds, Bunche based his evaluation of the situation, i.e. he made a determination to the effect that the deployment of U.N. troops in Katanga would be resisted and would have had to be achieved by the use of force, thus compromising 'the impartial attitude and pacific status' of the Force. On his return to Leopoldville, on the afternoon of 5 August, he reported to the Secretary-General recommending not to undertake the entry operations intended for the next day, on the basis of the following:

(i) The unqualified and unyielding opposition of Mr. Tshombe, his Ministers and the Grand Chiefs, to the coming of United Nations troops; their repeated warnings that the United Nations troops would be opposed by all the force Katangans could bring to bear (the last such warning being at 11 a.m. on 5 August); and the demand that their position be conveyed to you fully and personally, since in their view the United Nations would have to bear the responsibility for the disaster that would occur if United Nations troops tried to enter Katanga;

(ii) The tangible evidence of opposition to the arrival of United Nations troops, in the Press, in the calls for 'mobilization', in the long columns of new recruits for the army marching in the streets, in the appeal to the 'warriors' and the possibility of a trap being prepared at Jadotville, should elements of the Force land there;

(iii) The quite convincing evidence of fanatical opposition at the airport on the morning of 5 August where I was able to avert most serious trouble only with the greatest difficulty;

26 Ibid. paras. 6–8.
27 Hoskyns, 163.

(iv) The fact that preparations for the operations were not based on an assumption of an arrival likely to encounter armed opposition and that such a contingency would make necessary much different planning if the operation were to be carried out successfully.[28]

To what extent did this determination correspond to the realities of the situation? According to Pierre Davister (a Belgian journalist sympathetic to Tshombe) Katanga's show of strength was a bluff. It consisted of a parade, at the airport, of five trucks, one armoured car (with an African soldier appearing from the turret, but strictly instructed not to touch anything), one crane, and a large number of oil drums to block the runway. Katanga's 'military force' amounted then to a few hundred *gendarmes* and volunteers, with all the military direction in the hands of Europeans.[29] An acute observer considered it 'likely that had the United Nations forces tried to enter they would have encountered a fair amount of opposition. Had they been pre-pared to parachute in and fire a few rounds the opposition would almost certainly have collapsed (particularly as the Europeans behind it could hardly afford to show themselves), but in the process there might have been casualties.'[30]

In 1964 Bunche justified his evaluation on the basis of another consideration, of a more general nature:

While it was apparent that Katanga had no military force of consequence at that time, Mr. Tshombe was appealing by every means to the people of Katanga to resist United Nations entry. It would clearly put the United Nations Force in an untenable position if it had to fight the people of Katanga to enter that province and to remain there, for this would give it the posture of an army of occupation ... I greatly doubt that a United Nations peace force could be stationed for very long in any country if, even in self defense, it would have to turn its guns on civilians rather than military forces.[31]

The third Security Council resolution

On the basis of Bunche's report, the Secretary-General gave the order to stop the entry of U.N. troops in Katanga and submitted the problem, in his Second Report, to the Security Council for exami-nation and instructions.

The Council met on 9 August, to find a solution to the dilemma the Operation was facing and which was described by the Secretary-

28 S/4417, para. 9.
29 P. Davister, *Katanga; enjeu du monde* (1960), 116–21.
30 Hoskyns, 164.
31 Bunche, loc. cit. 130–1.

General along the following lines: the Security Council resolutions were intended to apply to the whole territory of the Republic of the Congo. But Tshombe's attitude introduced an unexpected element of organized military opposition to the deployment of the Force in Katanga. To overcome such opposition would require a military initiative on the part of the Force, to which it was not entitled under the mandate as it stood.[32]

The alternatives open to the Council, if it wanted to maintain its objectives, were either to change the mandate and consequently the character of the Force—a change which the Secretary-General considered 'impossible both for constitutional reasons and in view of the commitments of the contributing Governments'[33] (which were made on the basis of a police and not a fighting Force)—or to find other means for the Secretary-General fully to implement the resolutions within the existing limits of the mandate.[34]

In fact, here as on previous occasions, the Secretary-General had in mind a solution to the dilemma for which he was seeking formal approval by the Council to strengthen his hand in its pursuit. However, as with the initiation of the Operation, this solution implied a certain legal characterization of the situation he had to deal with:

The difficulty which the Council faces in the case of Katanga does not have its root in the Belgian attitude regarding the problem as stated to me, as the Belgian Government acquiesces in the Security Council decisions ...

Nor is the problem a desire on the part of the authorities of the province to secede from the Republic of the Congo. The question is a constitutional one with strong undercurrents of individual and collective political aims. The problem for those resisting the United Nations Force in Katanga may be stated in these terms: Will United Nations participation in security control in Katanga submit the province to the immediate control and authority of the Central Government against its wishes? They consider this seriously to jeopardize their possibility to work for other constitutional solutions than a strictly unitarian one, e.g. some kind of federal structure providing for a higher degree of provincial self-government than now foreseen.[35]

32 S/4417, para. 10; SCOR, 884 Mtg., 8 Aug. 1960, para. 12.

33 S/4417, para. 10. In his oral statement, the Secretary-General used more circumscribed terms. He no longer implied that the Council could not change the mandate because of constitutional limitations on its powers; he invoked the limitations only *on his own* powers. (SCOR, 885 Mtg., 8 Aug. 1960, para. 12).

34 S/4417, para. 10.

35 Ibid.

In other words, if the problem was not one of Belgian intervention and resistance, nor of a Katangese wish to secede, but merely that of finding an appropriate constitutional framework to accommodate the different tendencies within the Congo, it was inescapably a purely internal one. But both these findings could be and were in fact questioned in the Council. This was especially the case in connection with the first assertion, for to several representatives, the problem did 'have its root in the Belgian attitude', and accordingly was an international problem.[36] Similarly, it was contended that if the Force was being deployed in the implementation of the mandate and if it were attacked in the process, it had the right to defend itself, without compromising its peaceful character or transforming the Operation into one of 'collective measures', of the type envisaged in article 42 of the Charter.[37]

However, here again, as the Secretary-General had proposed a course of action which—though deriving from his characterization of the situation and his concept of the role of the Force—was acceptable to most, divergencies on characterization were reduced to a registration of positions and did not prove to be an unsurmountable obstacle to agreement. The proposed course of action was 'to separate effectively questions of a peaceful and democratic development in the constitutional field from any questions relating to the presence of the United Nations Force'.[38]

In his oral statement before the Council, the Secretary-General described more specifically his proposal as applying maximum pressure on Belgium and Katanga by emphasizing the mandatory character of the resolutions and their application to Katanga, while at the same time giving them the assurance that the deployment of the U.N. Force in Katanga would not affect the outcome of the political controversy between Katanga and the Central Government; and this by a formulation of the principle of non-intervention in internal affairs specifically tailored to the situation.[39] This solution was included in yet another draft resolution sponsored by Tunisia and Ceylon and adopted by the Council on 9 August, which reads:

36 See *infra*, p. 41 and n. 53.

37 e.g. Slim (Tunisia), SCOR, 885 Mtg., 8 Aug. 1960, paras. 65, 69; Lewandowski (Poland), SCOR, 886 Mtg., 8 Aug. 1960, para. 101; Kusnetsov (U.S.S.R.), ibid., para. 227.

38 S/4417, para. 10.

39 SCOR, 884 Mtg., 8 Aug. 1960, paras. 22, 27.

The Security Council,

Recalling its resolution of 22 July 1960 (S/4405), *inter alia*, calling upon the Government of Belgium to implement speedily the Security Council resolution of 14 July (S/4387) on the withdrawal of its troops and authorizing the Secretary-General to take all necessary action to this effect,

Having noted the second report of the Secretary-General [S/4417] on the implementation of the aforesaid two resolutions and his statement before the Council,

Having considered the statements made by the representatives of Belgium and the Republic of the Congo to this Council at this meeting,

Noting with satisfaction the progress made by the United Nations in carrying out the Security Council resolutions in respect of the territory of the Republic of the Congo other than the province of Katanga,

Noting, however, that the United Nations had been prevented from implementing the aforesaid resolutions in the province of Katanga although it was ready, and in fact attempted, to do so,

Recognizing that the withdrawal of Belgian troops from the province of Katanga will be a positive contribution to and essential for the proper implementation of the Council resolutions,

1. *Confirms* the authority given to the Secretary-General by the Security Council resolutions of 14 July and 22 July 1960 and requests him to continue to carry out the responsibility placed on him thereby;

2. *Calls upon* the Government of Belgium to withdraw immediately its troops from the province of Katanga under speedy modalities determined by the Secretary-General and to assist in every possible way the implementation of the Council's resolutions;

3. *Declares* that the entry of the United Nations Force into the province of Katanga is necessary for the full implementation of this resolution;

4. *Reaffirms* that the United Nations Force in the Congo will not be a party to or in any way intervene in or be used to influence the outcome of any internal conflict, constitutional or otherwise;

5. *Calls upon* all Member States, in accordance with Articles 25 and 49 of the Charter of the United Nations, to accept and carry out the decisions of the Security Council and to afford mutual assistance in carrying out measures decided upon by the Council;

6. *Requests* the Secretary-General to implement this resolution and to report further to the Council as appropriate.[40]

Tshombe's conditions

The pressure brought to bear on Belgium and Katanga through the adoption of the resolution produced the expected result. This was facilitated by the realization on their part that the danger they most feared—that the deployment of the U.N. Force would automatically

40 S/4426. The resolution was adopted by 9 votes, with 2 abstentions (France, Italy).

bring with it Central Government administration and control over Katanga—had vanished as a result of the conditions and assurances explicitly made in the resolution.

Thus on 9 August, the day the resolution was adopted, Tshombe sent a cable to the Secretary-General expressing 'the desire to study with a delegation from the United Nations the problem which exists in Katanga within the framework of the resolutions of the Security Council'. The Secretary-General replied by a cable on 10 August, proposing 'to discuss personally with [Tshombe] the modalities of the deployment of the United Nations troops in Katanga', but stating flatly that 'there can be no question of conditions or of an agreement, since such arrangements would be contrary to the constitutional rules which determine our relations'. He described the purpose of the meeting as having 'a frank exchange of views with you by which I may be guided in my instructions to my representatives and by which you may be given assurances concerning the rights which the United Nations protects'.[41]

By 'the constitutional rules which determine our relations', Hammarskjöld refers in fact to two consequences of the principle of the autonomy of the Force and the Operation as understood by him. The first is that the mandate is not negotiable with any government or authority and its interpretation is of the exclusive competence of U.N. organs. Any discussions that the Secretary-General may undertake in this respect must be limited to facilitating the implementation of the mandate by working out the modalities and by eliminating possible obstacles. But they can never amount to renegotiating the mandate or to imposing on the Secretary-General a certain interpretation of it. The other consequence has a more limited scope; it is that the executing organ does not conclude agreements with parties which are legally at fault in the situation, although the ultimate aim is to get them to change their behaviour.[42] This is of course in addition to the fact that

41 S/4417/Add. 4, 10 Aug. 1960.

42 The same consideration explains why in spite of continuous and tough negotiations between Belgium and the Secretariat concerning the withdrawal of the former from the Congo, the results never took the form of an agreement, even when they dealt with complex and highly technical subjects such as the take-over by ONUC from Belgian troops of the two bases of Kamina and Kitona. It is true, that in Korea, the U.N. Command did sign an armistice agreement with the North Koreans. But apart from the legally different nature of the two operations, this was a military agreement concluded by the U.N. as a belligerent party, and its conclusion determined by the vicissitudes of the battle field. Later on in the Congo. ONUC would be led to sign similar military agreements with Katanga (see *infra*, p. 154).

such an agreement could be interpreted as a recognition by the U.N. of Katanga.

The U.N. publication of this round of exchanges starts not with Tshombe's cable but with the Secretary-General's reply to it. Thus it is not clear whether the reference to 'conditions' and 'agreement' in the Secretary-General's cable was in response to something mentioned or alluded to in Tshombe's initial cable. In any case, the very day Tshombe sent his cable, he declared in a press conference that he would admit U.N. forces in Katanga on ten conditions:

(1) that U.N. troops in Katanga do not include contingents from communist or communist-oriented countries (by which he specially meant Ghana and Guinea);

(2) that the U.N. confirms its formal engagement not to interfere in the internal political or administrative affairs of Katanga;

(3) that all access routes to Katanga which the Government decides to keep open be jointly guarded by U.N. and Katanga forces. Other access routes should be completely prohibited. The U.N. would not hinder the control by Katanga of persons and merchandise entering Katanga; the U.N. would in no case oppose measures of prohibition of entry ordered by Katanga authorities;

(4) that the U.N. would in no case permit the use of its means of transport to introduce into Katanga any personnel sent by Leopoldville;

(5) that the U.N. would not hinder the exercise by the Katanga Government of the powers of police and justice;

(6) that the U.N. would not intervene in administration, finance or customs;

(7) that the U.N. would not oppose the organization and training of the Katanga forces of order. These forces would remain armed. It is understood that the arms of the old *Force Publique* are Katangese property. The same concerning the Kamina base, whose installations should be transferred intact to the Katanga Government;

(8) that Katanga reserve its right to call on experts of its choice in military, administrative, and financial matters;

(9) that until the final elaboration of the Congolese constitution and its acceptance by Katanga, the *status quo* would be maintained on the basis of the Katanga constitution. Katanga would remain free to enter in negotiations or refuse to do so with any government of the former Belgian Congo or of a part thereof;

(10) that the U.N. would oppose throughout the Congo the con-

stitution and armament of any paramilitary formations affiliated to political parties.[43]

3. THE CENTRAL GOVERNMENT: THE CONTROVERSY OVER THE MEMORANDUM ON IMPLEMENTATION

Hammarskjöld had proposed in his cable of 10 August to arrive at Elisabethville on 12 August, accompanied by a number of aides and two companies of the Swedish battalion; an offer which was accepted by Tshombe the same day.[44] On his way to Elisabethville, the Secretary-General issued a 'Memorandum on Implementation of the Security Council resolution of 9 August 1961, operative paragraph 4';[45] a document which brought into the open the controversy brewing between Hammarskjöld and Lumumba.

Analysis of the Memorandum

(1) The paragraph referred to in the title of the Memorandum reads:

The Security Council,

. . .

Reaffirms that the United Nations Force in the Congo will not be a party to or in any way intervene in or be used to influence the outcome of any internal conflict, constitutional or otherwise.

To interpret this paragraph, guidance was sought in 'attitudes upheld by the Security Council in previous cases where elements of an external nature and of an internal nature have been mixed'. The most important of these was the handling by the Security Council of the Lebanese question in the summer of 1958. In this case, the Security Council, at the request of the Government, sent an observer group to report on whether or not there was intervention from abroad, as alleged by the Government, in the civil war which was going on in the country. These observers were deployed on the side held by the Government as well as on the other side, and moved freely from one side to another.

It was perfectly clear that the Security Council considered itself as concerned solely with the possibility of intervention from outside in assistance to the rebels. All observation activities were limited to that problem and the

43 *Congo 1960*, 751.
44 S/4417/Add. 4, 10 Aug. 1960.
45 S/4417/Add. 6, 12 Aug. 1960.

Security Council never raised the question of intervention in support of the constitutional Government or in support of the other party.

Any request for assistance by either party would have been rejected by the U.N. Similarly, in the Hungarian case, 'decisions were directed solely against the intervention of foreign troops in support of the Government, without any stand being taken on the relationships between the Government and the insurgents'.

[The import of these precedents to Katanga] ... means that the United Nations is directly concerned with the attitude taken by the provincial government of Katanga to the extent that it may be based on the presence of Belgian troops, or as being for its effectiveness, influenced by that presence ... Therefore ... if the Belgian troops were withdrawn and if, pending full withdrawal, a Belgian assurance were given to the Secretary-General that the Belgian troops would in no way 'intervene or be used to influence the outcome of' the conflict between the provincial government and the Central Government ... the question between the provincial government and the Central Government would be one in which the United Nations would in no sense be a party and on which it could in no sense exert an influence.

[I]t follows that the United Nations Force cannot be used on behalf of the Central Government to subdue or to force the provincial government to a specific line of action. It further follows that United Nations facilities cannot be used, for example, to transport civilian or military representatives, under the authority of the Central Government, to Katanga against the decision of the Katanga provincial government. It further follows that the United Nations Force has no duty, or right, to protect civilian or military personnel representing the Central Government, arriving in Katanga, beyond what follows from its general duty to maintain law and order. It finally follows that the United Nations, naturally, on the other hand, has no right to forbid the Central Government to take any action which by its own means, in accordance with the purposes and principles of the Charter, it can carry through in relation to Katanga. All these conclusions necessarily apply, *mutatis mutandis*, as regards the provincial government in its relations with the Central Government.[46]

(2) Hammarskjöld's reasoning is based on two legal premises. The first is his understanding of the general constitutional limitation on all U.N. activities enshrined in article 2, paragraph 7 of the Charter which reads:

Nothing in the present Charter shall authorize the United Nations to inter-

46 Ibid.

vene in matters which are essentially within the domestic jurisdiction of any state or shall require the Members to submit such matters to settlement under the present Charter; but this principle shall not prejudice the application of enforcement measures under Chapter VII.

It seems that Hammarskjöld understood this limitation to apply to the activities of the U.N. in relation not only to States but also to subdivisions thereof.[47] If this was in fact his understanding, it would be rather peculiar. For the concept of domestic jurisdiction is a reformulation of the principle of sovereignty. As such, it can only be attributed to States or not at all.

In any case, Hammarskjöld considered that the U.N. could not intervene in an internal situation, even at the request of the government of the State concerned, except in case of collective measures.[48] This interpretation limits U.N. action to matters which fall objectively (i.e. according to general international law) outside the domestic jurisdiction of States, to the exclusion of those that are subjectively internationalized by the consent of the State (i.e. by assuming an international obligation over the matter). But on this interpretation, the U.N. would not have been able to assist the Congolese Government in the maintenance of law and order, a function which belongs to the hard core of internal sovereignty. Indeed it was on this basis that the U.S.S.R. contested from the beginning the legality for ONUC to assume this function in the Congo, insisting that its sole function was to repel external aggression.[49]

47 See his letter to Tshombe of 4 August: '... the entry of these [U.N.] military elements does not represent any interference in the internal affairs of the Republic of the Congo, *including its provinces*, or impede or modify in any way the free exercise of rights to act, in legal and democratic forms, in favour of one or another solution of constitutional problems as may in due time arise for the Congolese people' (S/4417, para. 6, emphasis added).

48 This comes out clearly from several statements of the Secretary-General, e.g. SCOR, 887 Mtg., 21 Aug. 1960, para 44: '... in the light of the domestic jurisdiction limitation of the Charter, it must be assumed that the Council would not authorize the Secretary-General to intervene with armed troops in an internal conflict, when the Council had not specifically adopted enforcement measures under Articles 41 and 42 of Chapter VII of the Charter'; S/4417, para 10. This limitative interpretation was refuted by several delegates, e.g. Sir Claude Corea (Ceylon): 'We are not dealing with the internal affairs of the Congo in this instance at all. We are dealing with certain matters connected with the internal administration of the Congo only because of the request made by the Republic of the Congo to the United Nations for its assistance' (SCOR, 878 Mtg., 21 July 1960, para. 70).

49 Thus Kuznetsov, after describing the 14 July resolution as 'a decision adopted under exceptional circumstances [which] should not, therefore, be considered as a precedent for the future', declared: 'We cannot regard that resolution, and the ensuing

It may be argued that assistance in the maintenance of law and order was non-controversial both internally and internationally, while assistance to the Central Government against Katanga was. But this is a political consideration extraneous to the legal nature of the matter at issue, unless by 'non-controversial' it is meant that the U.N. activity was accepted by all the internal parties. This brings us back, however, to the question whether the Charter protects the 'domestic jurisdiction' of entities and groups other than the State as represented by its recognized government; a question to which a positive answer is assumed if their consent in addition to that of the government is required to internationalize a situation or a dispute to which they are a party.

Hammarskjöld's interpretation thus attaches to the principle of non-intervention in internal affairs a more extensive meaning in the U.N. context than in inter-State relations. For it is questionable whether assistance to a recognized government at its own request, could be characterized as 'intervention' in the sense prohibited by general international law.[50]

For Hammarskjöld, however, the ultimate criterion of the propriety of action was political and not legal, though he endeavoured to articulate it in as objective and precise a legal formulation as possible. It was that the U.N. should not act as a Holy Alliance between the existing governments of member States against all revolutionary movements in these States. But it was precisely in relation to this fundamental consideration that another major argument came up against considering the controversy between the Central Government and Katanga as an internal issue, namely that the secessionist movement was not an authentic one, but a mere façade for foreign intervention, without which it could not have taken place nor consolidated

---

action for its implementation, as endowing the United Nations with the right to interfere in the domestic affairs of a State and to assume responsibility for a country's domestic laws and regulations. That is not, nor can it be, part of the functions of the United Nations as defined in its Charter. The fundamental purpose of the resolution is to be found in its demand for the withdrawal of the Belgian forces, which have no right to remain in the Republic of the Congo or be sent inside its frontiers without the consent, and *a fortiori* against the wishes, of the Republic's Government. It is precisely that demand which is the crux of the resolution of 14 July' (SCOR, 879 Mtg., 21 July 1960, paras. 118–20. Cf. S/5249 (2 Mar. 1963)).

50 Regardless of the attitude one adopts concerning the legality or illegality of 'intervention by invitation' in inter-State relations, the question is different and the possibilities of abuse are much reduced when the invitation is accepted by an international institution representing the organized international community.

its hold over the territory and the population in the area under its control.

It may be recalled that already on 9 July Tshombe had called for Belgian troops, that Belgian troops landed in Elisabethville on 10 July, and that on the evening of 11 July Tshombe declared Katanga independent.[51] Unlike other parts of the Congo, where they were instructed 'to intervene when Belgian lives were threatened', in Katanga Belgian troops were to occupy 'all centres of importance'. In other words, it was a complete military take-over. Moreover, 'the actions of the Belgian troops in Katanga went far beyond protecting Belgian nationals and they began systematically to round up and neutralize the units of the Force Publique', which were in large part loyal to the Central Government. This was done 'irrespective of whether the soldiers were really in a state of mutiny', as was clearly shown by the armed attack launched against the loyal troops of the *Force Publique* in the barracks of Kolwezi on 22 July. Once the *Force Publique* was neutralized, the Belgian officers who were detached to the Katanga government started to build up the Katanga *gendarmerie* from scratch.[52]

This is why several delegates in the Security Council debates of 8 and 9 August directly or indirectly challenged the assertion of the Secretary-General in his Second Report that the Katanga problem 'did not have its root in the Belgian attitude'. Basing themselves on the fact, described above, they emphasized that U.N. action in Katanga would not constitute intervention in an internal affair but a counter-intervention to bring to an end and eliminate the results of the initial Belgian intervention which already conferred on the situation an international character.[53]

51 Hoskyns, 95–9.
52 Ibid. 142–4.
53 See Slim (Tunisia) who spoke of the 'cause-and-effect relationship between the Belgian intervention in Katanga and ... developments [there]' (SCOR, 885 Mtg., 8 Aug. 1960, paras. 54–60). Similarly, Lewandowski (Poland) denied that U.N. action in Katanga—'in which authority rests completely with the Belgian troops, after the crushing of the opposition of the Congolese Army'—would constitute intervention in internal affairs. On the contrary, 'to refrain from sending troops into the province of Katanga would indicate indirect support of Belgian intervention and a direct acquaintance with [*sic*; read: recognition of] the occupation of that province, as well as with [read: of] the Belgian inspired opposition to the Government of the Congo. In turn, such a support would constitute an intervention in the internal affairs of the Republic of the Congo and would serve the Belgian and other colonial interests in that country' (SCOR, 886 Mtg, 8 Aug. 1960, para. 103). Cf. Kuznetsov (U.S.S.R): 'Inaction and procrastination in this matter will play into the hands of those who are flagrantly

But Hammarskjöld chose to set aside these arguments and the disturbing facts underlying them for reasons both of political opportunity and of legal principle. Tactically and at least in the short run, he preferred to direct his efforts at devising ways and means for eliminating these facts without having to take cognizance of them formally and hence to tackle them frontally. For this would have meant having to start by condemning those whose course of action he wanted to deflect, which would have been obviously self-defeating.[54] Moreover, as a matter of principle, Hammarskjöld was generally inclined to opt for the stricter interpretation.

(3) The second premiss of Hammarskjöld's interpretation was reasoning through precedents. The stock argument against such reasoning is that precedents are different from the case at hand; more particularly in the case of ONUC, that the mandates are not alike.[55]

Indeed, in Lebanon the observer group was created to establish whether or not there was foreign intervention, while in the Congo, the first resolution authorized the Secretary-General 'to provide the Government [of the Republic of the Congo] with such military assistance as may be necessary'. In the one case the purpose of the group was to act as a neutral observer, while in the other the purpose of the Force was to assist the Central Government. Moreover, the Security Council clearly favoured the unity and territorial integrity of the Republic of the Congo in its two resolutions of 22 July and 9 August, thus upholding the position of the Central Government against Katanga's claim to independence.

Here again the political role or aim of the Operation comes into play, and hence the political propriety of U.N. action in pursuit of this

---

intervening in the domestic affairs of the Congo and wish to legitimize their aggression' (ibid., para. 220); statement of the U.S.S.R. Government, S/4450 (21 Aug. 1960).

54 In this respect, he must have had in mind the lessons of the early episode concerning the U.S. airmen detained in China, when the General Assembly, in one and the same resolution (G.A. Res. 906 (IX) of 10 Dec. 1954) condemned the Government of the People's Republic of China for the continued detention of the airmen and directed the Secretary-General to negotiate their release with that very Government. It was in order to overcome the difficulties ensuing from this contradiction that Hammarskjöld developed what later became known as the 'Peking Formula'. It consisted of basing his mission, in his discussions with Chou En-lai, not on the General Assembly resolution, which was rejected by Peking, but on his constitutional responsibilities deriving directly from the Charter. On the Peking Formula, see Lash, loc. cit. 548; Urquhart, 105, 495.

55 This argument was in fact used by Lumumba in his exchange of correspondence with Hammarskjöld on 14 August (S/4417/Add. 7/II).

aim. Hammarskjöld had to balance two major considerations against one another: 'preserving the unity of the Congo people' on the one hand; 'protecting the democratic rights of everybody to let his influence bear ... on the final constitution of the Republic', on the other. 'I feel strongly that the United Nations would have failed in its mission if it maintained order while permitting democratic principles to be violated.'[56]

He tried to reconcile these two considerations by denying any intention of seceding on Tshombe's part, thus reducing the controversy between the Central and the Katanga provincial governments to one over the final constitutional form of a unified Congo. As such it was clearly a constitutional controversy and hence an internal one. By interpreting Tshombe's attitude—against clear evidence—in this manner, Hammarskjöld provided him with a diplomatic way out and a means of changing his position without apparently doing so, together with the guarantee of U.N. neutrality. He considered, on the other hand, that the deployment of the U.N. Force all over the Congo, including Katanga (together with the reciprocal withdrawal of Belgian troops) was a concrete manifestation of, and a sufficient contribution by the U.N. to, the unity and the territorial integrity of the Congo. Beyond that, the outcome had to be left to the democratic interplay of the contenders under the security and technical-assistance umbrella provided by the U.N.[57]

At this juncture Hammarskjöld's aim and design were to effect the peaceful deployment of the Force in Katanga and the withdrawal of the Belgian troops therefrom, while providing Tshombe with a diplomatic means out of secession, thus opening the way to a democratic search for a generally acceptable constitution. But in order to pursue this design it was not enough to adopt the resolution of 9 August; it was also necessary for Hammarskjöld in implementing it to combine his interpretation of paragraph 4 with the determination that the conflict between the Central Government and Tshombe was of a purely internal nature; a determination which was in turn based on two assumptions: (1) that the foreign element could be isolated and neutralized—i.e. that Belgian troops would withdraw, and that pending their withdrawal they would not affect the internal situation in any manner (leaving aside for the moment the other forms of foreign intervention which were progressively becoming more important

56 SCOR, 884 Mtg., 8 Aug. 1960, paras. 18, 27, 28.
57 SCOR, 887 Mtg., 21 Aug. 1960, para. 52.

than the Belgian military presence[58]); (2) that Tshombe did not intend to secede, but was simply seeking a more decentralized form of government for the Congo.

It was on these assumptions, it is true, that the resolution of 9 August (particularly its paragraph 4) was adopted. But it was justifiable to consider them as controlling the implementation of the resolution only to the extent to which they proved in practice to be true. For the correct implementation of the mandate depended not only on the correct interpretation of the texts but equally on the correct characterization of the factual situations.

Reaction of the Parties

In concluding the Memorandum, Hammarskjöld described its import to the Parties as he saw it:

The policy line stated here, in interpretation of operative paragraph 4, represents a unilateral declaration of interpretation by the Secretary-General. It can be contested before the Security Council. And it can be changed by the Security Council through an explanation of its intentions in the resolution of 9 August. The finding is not subject to agreement or negotiation.

He specified that were his interpretation to be challenged by either Party, he would immediately request the Security Council 'that it consider the interpretation and pronounce itself on its validity'. He further specified that were 'the Council ... to disapprove of the finding, this would obviously mean a change of assumptions for the actions of the provincial government which would justify a reconsideration of its stand, having been taken in good faith on the basis of the interpretation given by the Secretary-General'.[59]

(1) Tshombe

Though there was no direct reference in the Memorandum to

58 Hammarskjöld was not oblivious of the importance of these other forms of foreign intervention. A second layer of his strategy was to try to sever the remaining external roots of the Katanga secession (by putting pressure on Belgium and other countries to withdraw all their technicians and to channel all aid through the U.N.). This would compel Tshombe to turn to the U.N. for assistance; he would thus become more vulnerable, and hence amenable to a compromise with the Central Government. See Hammarskjöld's letter of 8 Oct. 1960 to Tshombe in this sense, S/4557/B 5; see also Tshombe's indignant cable answer of 27 October: '... as an integral part of the Republic of the Congo my honor and that of my people forbid to yield to such pressure'! (S/4557/B 6).

59 S/4417/Add. 6, paras. 9–11.

Tshombe's conditions, nor, most probably, were they brought up in the discussions between Hammarskjöld and Tshombe in Elisabethville,[60] the interpretation put forward by the Secretary-General satisfied most of these conditions. In Katanga it was widely held that eight out of the ten conditions were tacitly accepted by the U.N.[61]

On this basis, Tshombe accepted the deployment of the U.N. troops in Katanga and the Belgian troops were progressively withdrawn. This, however, did not include those officers who were detached to the provincial government of Katanga nor those who came to be directly employed by it, i.e. mercenaries.

Hammarskjöld considered the deployment of the U.N. Force in Katanga as a 'breakthrough'.[62] But the conditions under which this 'breakthrough' was achieved made it easy for Tshombe to accept it. For, by that time, the Belgian troops, having already neutralized and disbanded the *Force Publique* which was in large part loyal to the Central Government, were left largely inactive. At that point, what Katanga needed most was to build up its own forces and structures, a task for which those who counted most were the military and civilian advisers rather than Belgian troops. As long as the U.N. Force did not interfere with the accomplishment of this task, its deployment in Katanga and the withdrawal of the Belgian troops would not harm and could even contribute to this process of consolidation, by making the Katanga secession appear less directly dependent on Belgium.[63]

Tshombe had no difficulty in accepting the rules of the game proposed by Hammarskjöld because, at that juncture and on those terms, the deployment of U.N. troops in Katanga served his purposes. Beyond this, all he needed to do in order to give the impression of playing the role assigned to him in Hammarskjöld's design, was to reiterate his willingness to enter into hypothetical and undefined relations with the Central Government, while consolidating all the time the foundations of an independent Katanga.

But for these very reasons Lumumba had to reject Hammarskjöld's rules of the game. For he instinctively felt that they would inevitably lead to the consolidation of the Katanga secession into a *fait accompli*,

60 Urquhart, 427; Hoskyns, 172.

61 Ibid.; O'Brien, 90–2.

62 e.g. SCOR, 887 Mtg., 21 Aug. 1960, para. 28; 888 Mtg., 21 Aug. 1960, para. 9; GAOR (ES–IV), 859 Mtg., 18 Sept. 1960, para. 158.

63 Cf. Urquhart, 427–8; Hoskyns, 173.

by freezing the balance of power between the contenders on the basis of the *status quo* and proceeding from it.[64]

(2) *Lumumba*

When Hammarskjöld declared his intention to send Dr. Bunche to Katanga on 5 August, Vice-Prime Minister Gizenga had already requested that some Government members together with a detachment from the Ghana contingent should accompany Dr. Bunche. This request was vigorously resisted by the Secretary-General and was not followed through.[65]

On his way to Katanga for the meeting of 12 August, the Secretary-General stopped in Leopoldville but did not attempt to see the Prime Minister or other members of the Central Government. He probably did not want to discuss with them his interpretation of the resolution before achieving a measure of success in Katanga. But on 14 August, on his way back from Elisabethville, and after securing the 'breakthrough', he wrote to Foreign Minister Bomboko from Leopoldville, asking if he might report to the Government on the implementation of the resolution.[66] In response, he received a fiery letter from the Prime Minister, questioning his impartiality and proper implementation of the mandate and challenging his interpretation of the resolutions. To Lumumba, the resolution of 14 July made it abundantly 'clear that in its intervention in the Congo the United Nations is not to act as a neutral organization but rather that the Security Council is to place all its resources at the disposal of my Government'. It was equally clear that the resolution of 9 August (including paragraph 4) was 'a supplement to [and not a limitation on] the two preceding resolutions which remain intact', and that the precedents of Hungary and Lebanon were not relevant as the resolutions were not identical. Lumumba further protested against Hammarskjöld's discussions with Tshombe and the assurances given him without prior consultations with the Central Government, which, according to Lumumba, provided ample evidence that Hammarskjöld was intervening in the conflict between the provincial and the Central Governments and was using the U.N. Force 'to influence its outcome, which is formally prohibited by the very paragraph

64   In retrospect, this aspect of peace-keeping operations—i.e. their freezing of crises on the basis of the *status quo* obtaining at the moment of the U.N. intervention, but without commanding adequate means to resolve the disputes underlying them—proved to be the most serious shortcoming of these operations.

65   S/4417/Add. 2, 6 Aug. 1960.

66   S/4417/Add. 7/I.

which you invoked'. Finally Lumumba made five requests: (a) to send exclusively African and Congolese troops immediately to Katanga; (b) to withdraw all non-African troops therefrom; (c) to provide U.N. planes for the transport of Congolese civil and military personnel to Katanga; (d) to seize all arms and munitions distributed by the Belgians in Katanga and give them to the Central Government; and (e) to entrust the guarding of all airfields exclusively to Congolese army and police instead of U.N. troops.[67]

In his answer, the Secretary-General refused to respond to the substance but indicated that:

As the letter is an official communication I shall have it circulated today as a Security Council document. Should the Security Council consider it necessary to take a stand with regard to the action which I have taken or to my interpretation of its decision, I am prepared to submit my comments in person at a Council meeting. I hope that if such a meeting is convened you too will see fit to present your case to the Council in person. As far as the actions requested by you are concerned, I shall naturally follow the instructions which the Council may find it necessary or useful to give me.[68]

Following this exchange of correspondence, an atmosphere of hostility developed in the Congo against the U.N. Lumumba's threats were a source of great worries for the Secretary-General. The former's request that the A.N.C. should assume the exclusive control of all airports, had it been followed through, would have deprived the Force of its freedom of movement and communication;[69] not to mention the repeated threat to ask for the withdrawal of the Force in order to replace it by more friendly troops.[70] Moreover, several incidents of harassment of U.N. civilian and military personnel occurred, the most serious of which being the assault on fourteen Canadian soldiers in a U.N. plane at Njili airport (Leopoldville) on 18 August.[71]

The fourth round of discussion in the Security Council:

The Security Council convened on 21 and 22 August, at the request of the Secretary-General, to examine the controversy between him and Lumumba. In his opening statement, after rebutting the arguments used against his interpretation of the mandate, the Secretary-General specified that he did 'not see any reason for the Security

67 S/4417/Add. 7/II.
68 S/4417/Add. 7/III.
69 For this request see S/4417/Add. 7/II; S/4448. See also Urquhart, 432.
70 Urquhart, 405, 455; Alexander, op. cit., 44–6.
71 S/4417/Add. 8, 19 Aug. 1960.

Council to confirm his interpretation of the functions of the United Nations Force in the respect now challenged', his 'aim being solely . . . to arrive at a clarification of the attitude of the Council'. He added, however:

Should . . . any member of the Council be at variance with my interpretation on the basis indicated by the Prime Minister of the Republic of the Congo, or on any other basis, I am sure that they may wish to give expression, in a draft resolution, to what they consider to be the right interpretation.[72]

At the end of the debate, no resolution was adopted, a Russian draft resolution having been withdrawn for lack of support.[73] The President of the Council expressed the hope that despite the conflicting opinions expressed, 'the Secretary-General will have found in this debate the clarification which he desired, and that it will assist him in the pursuit of his mission'.[74]

4. THE PROCESS OF INTERPRETATION; ITS PLACE IN THE LEGAL STRATEGY OF THE SECRETARY-GENERAL

The decisions relating to the deployment of the U.N. Force in Katanga illustrate Dag Hammarskjöld's 'style', especially in casting collective action in pursuit of political aims in a clear legal framework, which in turn would be used to persuade the contenders to conform to the desired course of action, and in scrupulously following, especially when challenged, the process of interpretation described above.

His strategy in dealing with the contenders was to act on the assumption of their compliance with the law, as embodied in the resolutions of the Security Council and interpreted by him. On that basis he would proceed to distribute roles between the contenders according to a general design of action, which if accepted by all would point the way out of the crisis. One of his most potent means to persuade them to accept these roles and thus comply with the resolutions was his power of interpretation. Although he formally insisted that the resolutions and the mandate were not negotiable, he used this power to reach a substantive interpretation of the resolutions which, while consistent with the Charter and the mandate, would from a political point of view accommodate at least the minimal claims of all the contenders. At the same time he would bring the maximum legal

72 SCOR, 887 Mtg., 21 Aug. 1960, paras. 41, 53.
73 SCOR, 889 Mtg., 21 Aug. 1960, para. 142.
74 Ibid., para. 145.

and political pressure he could marshal to bear on each of them in order to make him comply.

The uses of interpretation

It is clear from this analysis that law played an important role in the strategy of the Secretary-General who made effective use of it both as a sword and as a shield. It provided him with an objective basis on which a solution to the crisis could be sought and protected him against claims based on pure political expediency. It made it possible for him to justify his claims on the contenders, both to those who considered them as going too far or not going far enough: to the former, because the claims were required for the implementation of the resolutions and the mandate; to the latter, because they could not go beyond the limits set by the resolutions and the mandate.

But obviously law here meant law as understood and interpreted by the Secretary-General; and the process of interpretation differed according to whether law was used by him as a sword or as a shield. The second and third resolutions of the Security Council of 22 July and 9 August clearly illustrate the former case. The Secretary-General would propose to the Council certain interpretations and elaborations of the mandate which, while not necessarily adding new elements to it, provided him with further means of pressure on the target State or entity. These consisted of a more specific articulation of the obligations of the target State or entity, of the powers of the Secretary-General in implementing the mandate, or of the legal implications of the principles governing the Operation. Such 'confirmation' of the Secretary-General's interpretation by the Council strengthened his status and relative bargaining power *vis-à-vis* the target State or entity.

This legal strategy was used in situations where Hammarskjöld wanted to obtain action or acquiescence to his and the Force's action from the other party. It is a preventive legal strategy, aiming at providing him with maximum legal protection and support and at putting the target entity in a clearly illegal posture for not acting or for not acquiescing to his action. The legal interpretation or elaboration is used as a preliminary to the desired action or attitude and as an element of persuasion in order to facilitate its realization.

The legal interpretation may also aim at reassuring the target State or entity, by clearly enunciating the limitations of the action and its effects in its regard. It is used in the case where what is sought is not action by the target entity, but its acquiescence to action by the executing organ. In other words, interpretation could be used not only to support, but also to circumscribe action by the executing organ.

This is the reason why such an interpretation is likely to be challenged by those who want the U.N. to act more vigorously, i.e. those who are partisans of a liberal interpretation of the mandate and a strict interpretation of its limitations. The legal strategy of the Secretary-General in the face of such a challenge is consequently different. Rather than seeking a confirmation of his interpretation from the Security Council, he challenges those who reject it to obtain a decision in favour of their own interpretation from the Council. In such cases he adopts a defensive posture, considering that, in the absence of a resolution infirming his interpretation, this interpretation continues to be accepted by the Council.[75] This attitude comes out clearly in his 'Memorandum on Implementation', and in the meetings of the Security Council which ensued from it, where he explained:

... the Security Council has asked me to implement the resolution. Implementation obviously means interpretation in the first instance. I gave an interpretation and that interpretation was challenged. I have referred the matter back to the Security Council. I have the right to expect guidance. That guidance can be given in any form. But it should be obvious that if the Security Council says nothing I have no other choice than to follow my conviction.[76]

---

75 The U.S.S.R. representative, Mr. Kuznetsov, tried to challenge this way of presenting the problem. But he knew the mechanisms of the Security Council too well to expect more from this challenge than a mere registration of disapproval: '... the Security Council gave the Secretary-General no mandate to interpret its resolution of 9 August. In this case, therefore, the interpretation of the Council's resolution, given by the Secretary-General in addendum 6, is his personal opinion and has no legal, binding significance.

There is only one possible procedure that could invest such an interpretation with some legal force. It is well known to the Secretary-General himself. All I mean, in fact, is that any member of the Council who thinks it appropriate may put forward for the Council's consideration a formal proposal to that effect' (SCOR, 888 Mtg., 21 Aug. 1960, paras. 56–9).

76 Ibid., para. 100. The last sentence, which may imply a criticism of the Council for not giving the Secretary-General sufficient direction, should be read in conjunction with his initial statement in that round of debates, where he repeated twice that he was not asking 'for confirmation by the Security Council of the obvious' (SCOR, 887 Mtg., 21 Aug. 1960, paras. 51, 41). In fact, at that juncture, the silence of the Council did serve his purposes, by giving the impression that his interpretation was backed by the Council, when it would not have obtained a positive confirmation had he sought one.

By thus throwing on the adversaries of his interpretation the burden of seeking a positive resolution from the Council, the Secretary-General put himself in a good defensive position. Because once there is a controversy within the Council on a mandate, the veto plays in favour of its continuation but against the adoption of authoritative interpretations; this leaves the Secretary-General with relatively free hands to use his power of interpretation as a means of persuasion and accommodation in pursuit of the political aims of the Operation.

Sharing the responsibility of interpretation

This is why the Secretary-General resisted the idea, first proposed by the Central Government and later adopted by the Soviet Union, of a Commission which would have shared his responsibilities in the day-to-day interpretation of the mandate in relation to concrete developments and situations.[77] The sharing of the power to interpret the mandate would have severely limited the margin of freedom of the Secretary-General in elaborating the diplomatic synthesis between legal powers and limitations on the one hand and the desired and attainable political ends on the other.

The proposal was not seriously pressed in the Security Council debates of 8 and 9 August. It was therefore easy for the Secretary-General to dismiss it in the discussions, as a proposal which had merit, but which he more or less followed informally in the composition of his staff dealing with the Operation.[78] But this argument was not completely true. For apart from the fact that Hammarskjöld's closest and most influential collaborators were not only Western but Americans, they were international civil servants, hierarchically dependent on the Secretary-General and consequently in a very different position from that of a commission composed of representatives of States.

It was after the controversy with Lumumba and during the fourth round of debates in the Security Council on 21 and 22 August that the question became a real issue. Hammarskjöld started by declaring his intention to create an Advisory Committee along the lines of the Advisory Committee for UNEF, composed of representatives of contributing members. He attributed the idea to the U.S.S.R.

77 S/4421, 7 Aug. 1960; SCOR, 886 Mtg., 8 Aug. 1960, paras. 115–17.

78 Ibid., paras., 131–2. The Secretary-General was referring to the senior staff of the Operation. However, his closest collaborators, those who came to be known as the 'Congo Club', were in large part Americans, including Bunche, Cordier, and Wieschoff. On the 'Congo Club', see O'Brien, 50–5; Urquhart, 473.

representative during the previous Congo debate.[79] But, as we have seen, the U.S.S.R. proposal was a reiteration of the Central Government's, which envisaged something radically different. This difference was brought to the fore by Gizenga[80] and once again taken over by the U.S.S.R. representative (who introduced a resolution to the same effect[81]). The difference was about the functions of the Committee. For Hammarskjöld it was to be a consultative body to which he could turn if he felt the need, but which would only give him advice that he could accept or reject; it would not legally share in, or assume any responsibility for, the decisions taken. For the Central Government and the U.S.S.R., the Committee was to share the responsibility of the Secretary-General in the day-to-day inter-pretation of the mandate and hence in the decisions taken according to this interpretation.

This difference in conception came out clearly in the Security Council debate when Kuznetzov said that: 'As we understood it, the Secretary-General now shares this idea of sending to the Congo a group of representatives from neutral countries';[82] the Secretary-General was quick to refute this understanding:

In various interventions, reference has been made to the question of some kind of group, and it was mentioned that I now seemed to favour a group of observers, or whatever they should be called, to be sent to the Congo. I want to make it clear that that is not what I proposed. I proposed a parallel to the Advisory Committee established in the case of the United Nations Emerg-ency Force; that is to say, an advisory committee meeting with the Secretary-General, it may be here or, in some cases, it may be in the Congo. But to station it in the Congo when I have to be here either for the Security Council or for the General Assembly would deprive me of the advantages of current consultation.[83]

The Security Council was thus informed, but did not approve or disapprove the proposal of the Secretary-General. Unlike the case of Suez—when the Advisory Committee was created by the General Assembly, though on a proposal of the Secretary-General[84]—in the Congo crisis the Committee was created exclusively by the

79 SCOR, 887 Mtg., 21 Aug. 1960, para. 36.

80 Ibid., paras. 78–9.

81 SCOR, 888 Mtg., 21 Aug. 1960. paras. 79–80; the draft resolution S/4453, 21 Aug. 1960. See *supra*, p. 48, n. 73.

82 SCOR, 888 Mtg., 21 Aug. 1960, para. 79.

83 Ibid., para. 108.

84 See *supra*, p. 4, n. 5.

Secretary-General. Constitutionally therefore, it was not a subsidiary organ of the Security Council, but a body attached to, and dependent on, the Secretary-General in the context of the implementation of the mandate.[85]

It is interesting to note that the Secretary-General started by considering that there was no need for a Committee at all. However, in the light of Lumumba's rising impatience and the Secretary-General's need to marshal support against the increasing pressure of the Central Government and the U.S.S.R., he decided to create an Advisory Committee. But this may have also been done to pre-empt the creation of a radically different responsibility-sharing body.

---

85 This aspect was to be used later by the U.S.S.R. to challenge the status of the Committee as a U.N. body and to deny it recognition. (See GAOR (ES–IV), 865 Mtg., 19 Sept. 1960, para. 133; SCOR, 942 Mtg., 20 Feb., 1961, para. 83.) However, the Committee was recognized by the General Assembly which directed it, in its Resolution 1474 (ES–IV) of 20 Sept. 1960, to appoint a Conciliation Commission for the Congo.

III

THE CONSTITUTIONAL CRISIS

1. THE A.N.C. CAMPAIGN IN KASAI

THE controversy between the Secretary-General and Prime Minister Lumumba over the interpretation of the mandate, culminating in the Security Council debate of 21–2 August, revealed the fundamental differences that existed between them both as to the ends and the means of the Operation, with attendant irritations and incidents.[1]

By that time Lumumba had realized that there was no hope of bringing Hammarskjöld to help him militarily against Katanga and that the only way left for him was to act on the basis of Hammarskjöld's thesis that Katanga was an internal problem and to mount his own military campaign against the secessionists.[2]

This campaign was at the basis of two developments which brought Lumumba into even sharper conflict with the Secretary-General. The first was that in order to secure means of transport for his troops, Lumumba accepted Russian assistance, consisting of 100 trucks (originally pledged by the Soviet Government to the U.N. but later delivered directly to the Central Government) and sixteen Ilyushin transport planes with their crews.[3] For Hammarskjöld, this meant the frustration of the very *raison d'être* of the Operation as he saw it, which was to forestall the extension of the cold—and perhaps hot—war to the Congo through the intervention and counter-intervention of the Super Powers in favour of one or the other of the local contenders. This is why he decided to bring all the influence he could marshal to bear, in order to stem Russian direct involvement before the cold-war pattern would set irremediably on the Congo.

The other development was the manner in which the campaign was conducted. Soldiers were transported to Luluabourg, from where they were supposed to move against the self-proclaimed State of South Kasai (under Kalonji) and then continue into Katanga. But they were not provided with adequate logistic support, especially

1 On these developments, see S/4417/Add. 8, 18 Aug. 1960; S/4531, 21 Sept. 1960, para. 18; *supra*, p. 47, n. 69–71. Cf. Urquhart, 435–6; Hoskyns, 191.

2 Ibid. 189–90.

3 Ibid.; Urquhart, 436.

food and mechanized means of land transport, and had to 'fend for themselves and live off the land'.[4] On 26 August, the A.N.C. occupied Bakwanga, the capital of the secessionist State of South Kasai. The troubles started soon thereafter when, in the process of requisitioning food and vehicles in order to move into Katanga, the soldiers turned against the local Balubas and the situation degenerated into tribal warfare. Atrocities ensued, including a massacre in a mission school where all the people who had taken refuge—more than seventy men, women, and children—were savagely killed.[5] Hammarskjöld considered that the U.N. could not remain passive in the face of such flagrant massive violations of the principles of the Charter.

The controversy over bilateral (Russian) aid

Concerning the first development, the Secretary-General considered that the provision of bilateral aid to the Congo outside the framework of the U.N. was in contradiction with the resolutions and constituted a means of intervention in the Congo affairs.

This was clearly true of the aid, especially military aid, furnished by Belgium to Katanga; for it ran counter to the Security Council resolution of 22 July 1960. But Hammarskjöld invoked substantially the same arguments against the military aid which was provided by the Soviet Union to the Central Government. Using rather guarded language, the Secretary-General described this aid as 'contrary to the spirit of the Security Council resolutions and tending to reintroduce elements of the very kind which the Security Council wished to eliminate when it requested the immediate withdrawal of Belgian troops'.[6]

The Soviet response to this criticism was both swift and predictable. In Zorin's words:

What really constitutes interference in the internal affairs of the Republic of the Congo is not the assistance accorded to the Congolese Government by friendly nations, but the support given by some States to forces opposing the lawful Government of the Congo and to all manner of separatists, both the open and the masked puppets of the colonial Powers.[7]

4 Hoskyns, 190.
5 SCOR, 896 Mtg., 9 Sept. 1960, para. 100 (Hammarskjöld's description); Urquhart, 435, 438.
6 Fourth Report, S/4482, 7 Sept. 1960, para. 11; S/4503/I (5 Sept. 1960). Cf. Mongi Slim (Tunisia), SCOR, 901 Mtg., 14 Sept. 1960, para. 115.
7 Ibid. para. 57.

The Soviet Government further implied that it was the Secretary-General's attempt 'which seeks to control the relations between the Republic of the Congo and other States' that constituted an impermissible intervention in the external relations of sovereign States. For neither has 'the Security Council ... given the Secretary-General any such mandate', nor does the Charter 'give any United Nations administrative officer, whoever he may be, the right to intervene in the relations between sovereign States unless they request his intervention'.[8] For his part, the representative of the Central Government considered that even 'the Security Council cannot take up this question of bilateral cooperation unless, and in so far as, it contemplates placing the Congo under trusteeship'.[9]

These were strong legal arguments indeed. For in spite of the primacy of the political objective the Secretary-General was defending, namely the international neutralization of the Congo, he did not have at his disposal adequate legal means to achieve this objective in this respect. This is why he had to base his request for the discontinuation of bilateral aid on a legal argument extrinsic to the question of the legality of the activity itself. This argument was that *the use to which the aid was put* was contrary to the Charter. Referring to the Bakwanga massacres, the Secretary-General declared in the Security Council:

... this is no longer a question of form and legal justification, but a question of very hard realities, where the use to which the assistance is put is more important than the heading in an export list under which it is registered, or the status of the one to whom it is addressed.[10]

This argument, though quite forceful, was not directly based on the resolutions nor on generally accepted legal prescriptions. This is why the Secretary-General tried to get this interpretation of the mandate adopted by the Security Council.

Group protection, non-intervention, and the limits of the use of force

While providing a strong argument for the discontinuation of bilateral military aid to the Central Government, the Bakwanga

8 S/4503/II (10 Sept. 1960).
9 S/4517, 14 Sept. 1960.
10 SCOR, 896 Mtg., 9 Sept. 1960, para. 108. (In para. 104 he had treated the problem in relation to Katanga.) It must have been quite surprising to hear Hammarskjöld, himself a master 'of form [i.e. formal propriety] and legal justification' arguing for transcending these considerations and assessing the situation on the basis of 'hard realities'.

massacres raised problems of a different order. According to Urquhart:

Hammarskjöld felt compelled to react to this new development, because the U.N. could not stand aside in what he called 'a case of incipient genocide' . . . 'Prohibition against intervention in internal conflicts', he cabled Cordier, 'cannot be considered to apply to senseless slaughter of civilians or fighting arising from tribal hostilities'. After a full discussion with the Congo Advisory Committee, he instructed Cordier, on September 2, to recommend strongly to Foreign Minister Bomboko that immediate steps be taken to control and discipline the army in Kasai. *He also authorized the interposing of UN troops, using force if necessary, to stop the massacre.*[11]

In other words, Hammarskjöld considered that tribal warfare involving the indiscriminate massacre of civilians was totally different from internal conflict to which the principle of non-intervention applied; that for ONUC, the stopping or prevention of large-scale violations of Human Rights and eventual genocide prevailed over the principles of non-intervention in internal affairs and the prohibition of the use of force except in self-defence.[12]

The controversy over disarming the A.N.C.

One of the measures contemplated by Hammarskjöld which involved the use of force, was the disarming of the A.N.C. units in South Kasai.[13] In his fourth report, released on 7 September 1960

11 Urquhart, 438, 441, 443 (emphasis added).
12 This line of reasoning was expressed by Hammarskjöld on several occasions, e.g. S/4482, paras. 11–12; SCOR, 896, 9 Sept. 1960, para. 101–2; S/4529, 18 Sept. 1960.
13 The question of disarming the A.N.C. was raised from the very beginning of the operation. It started when General Alexander, Ghana's (British expatriate) Chief of Defence Staff, who arrived in Leopoldville the day the first resolution was passed, proceeded to the voluntary disarmament of rebellious A.N.C. units, with the agreement of Gizenga, and the collaboration of Mpolo, the Minister of Youth and Sports (Alexander, *African Tightrope* (1965), 37–42). But as he described it: 'The object was not to disarm the soldiers completely, but to persuade them to place their weapons in their armouries, where they could be kept and issued to those who needed them for duty . . . [which] is the normal procedure adopted by all disciplined armies' (ibid.). This operation was stopped when Lumumba objected to it on his return to Leopoldville from his tour of the country with Kasavubu. General Alexander strongly pressed for a generalized scheme for disarming and retraining the A.N.C. with or without the consent of the Congolese authorities and criticized the hesitancy and lack of firmness of the U.N. in this regard (S/4445/Annex II, 19 Aug. 1960). Bunche's answer to this criticism was to emphasize the character of the U.N. Force as a 'peace force, not a fighting force [which was] in the Congo as a friend and partner, not as an army of occupation' (S/4451, 21 Aug. 1960).

(two days after the outbreak of the constitutional crisis) the Secretary-General recommended to the Security Council that:

... emphasis ... be put on the protection of the lives of the civilian population in the spirit of the Declaration of Human Rights and the Convention on the Prevention and Punishment of the Crime of Genocide. *This may necessitate a temporary disarming of military units* which, in view of present circumstances are an obstacle to the reestablishment of law and order in the interest of the people and the stability of the nation.[14]

However, in the face of very strong criticism from Lumumba and the U.S.S.R.[15] of what they considered as a declaration of intention on the part of the Secretary-General to commit a flagrant intervention against the Central Government, Hammarskjöld changed the ground on which he based his recommendation. Thus he declared before the Security Council:

... there is evidence that the soldiers have broken away from their command, which has been unable to control their action. Whatever, the motives for bringing the troops to the region, and whatever role they may have been intended to play in the domestic conflict, they have, of course, through such undisciplined actions, and once the authorities have lost control, ceased to be parts of a responsible army.[16]

This is a new and narrower line of legal justification than the one adopted in the fourth report—based on the primacy of prevention of flagrant violations of human rights and acts of genocide over the principles of non-intervention and the non-use of force. The new one was easier to defend as it presented the troops guilty of such acts as 'marauders', i.e. outlaws, even from the point of view of the Central Government from whose control they have broken away. This presentation had two major advantages: it permitted the Force to deal with these A.N.C. elements not as part of the National Army, i.e. of the Congolese Government, but as mere outlaws or criminals, within the general function of maintenance of law and order; it also provided the Central Government with a way out, permitting it to dissociate itself from the incriminating acts without loss of face. Whatever that may be, this new line represented a retreat from asking for a mandate to deal with A.N.C. troops in general to a legal justification of what took place in one instance.

14 S/4482, para. 12 (emphasis added).
15 S/4498 (10 Sept. 1960); SCOR, 901 Mtg., 14 Sept. 1960, para. 27.
16 SCOR, 896 Mtg., 9 Sept. 1960, para. 102.

2. THE OUTBREAK OF THE CONSTITUTIONAL CRISIS: ANDREW CORDIER'S DECISION TO CLOSE THE AIRFIELDS AND THE RADIO STATION

The Kasai campaign and the attendent developments brought about a radical change in Hammarskjöld's opinion of Lumumba. He no longer considered him as a sincere, if inexperienced and volatile, leader who 'both deserved and desperately needed help', but rather as a reckless and 'totally irresponsible' politician,[17] 'an incipient dictator who in his drive for power was prepared to wreck the Congo and the U.N.'[18] This practically meant, at that juncture, that Hammarskjöld considered Lumumba as the main threat to the success of the Operation as he conceived it, being both unco-operative and unpredictable.

In the last days of August 1960, Ralph Bunche left the Congo, having exhausted himself and his usefulness with the Central Government which was unwilling to deal with him any longer. He was relieved by Andrew Cordier who was to undertake 'a review of the whole administrative organization of ONUC and to hold the fort until the arrival' of the new Special Representative of the Secretary-General in the Congo, Ambassador Rajeshwar Dayal from India.[19] It was against this background of utter misunderstanding between Lumumba and the U.N. Secretariat, a widespread feeling of insecurity, apprehension for the fate of the Operation, and the explosiveness of the situation in U.N. circles on the one hand[20] and Cordier's arrival on the other, that the constitutional crisis broke out.

On the evening of 5 September President Kasavubu declared on the radio that, using his constitutional powers, he had dismissed Lumumba and six other ministers and had asked Mr. Ileo, the President of the Senate, to form the new Cabinet. Half an hour later Lumumba retorted, also on the radio, that Kasavubu had no power to

17 Urquhart, 435.

18 J. Lash, *Dag Hammarskjöld* (1961), 239; Hoskyns, 174–5. Both Hoskyns and Lash trace this change of opinion to an earlier date, namely to the lively exchange of letters which took place between the two in Leopoldville on 14 August.

19 Urquhart, 436.

20 This general feeling comes out clearly in Hammarskjöld's description of the precarious political atmosphere in the Advisory Committee: '... when I was in Leopoldville the first time I counted with the possibility of a very quick turn, via the radio, of opinion against the U.N., not specifically this or that movement, but a turn which, so to say, broke down the dams against xenophobia, excitement and hysteria' (Advisory Committee, 3 Mtg., 27 Aug. 1960, para. 32).

dismiss a Prime Minister who enjoyed the confidence of the Parliament and that by so doing he had defied the Parliament and the people; in consequence he was stripped of his office of President of the Republic and his functions were to be exercised by the Central Government. These measures, however, were to be approved by the Parliament. He concluded by stating that the dispute between himself and Kasavubu was an internal one in which neither the U.N. nor any outside power had any right to interfere.[21]

During the night of 5 to 6 September, in the exercise of the function of maintenance of law and order, Andrew Cordier ordered the closure of all major airports in the Congo to all but U.N. traffic; on the morning of 6 September he ordered the closure of the radio station at Leopoldville, which by that time was clearly in the hands of Lumumba supporters.[22]

This proved to be one of the most controversial decisions taken by the U.N. in the Congo crisis. It was officially defended on the basis of the maintenance of law and order. A civil war was going on in Kasai and on the Katanga border. The constitutional crisis threatened to create serious disorders and clashes between the supporters of the two leaders, especially the notorious youth formations attached to the different political parties. These excitable elements could be easily aroused through the radio.[23] The radio presented the danger of extending the conflict from the Leopoldville area to the rest of the country. The situation in Leopoldville also threatened to degenerate into civil war; rumours were circulating that the Russian planes based in Stanleyville were being prepared to transport A.N.C. troops loyal to Lumumba into Leopoldville.[24]

Thus it was not only to maintain law and order but also to prevent civil war that these measures were taken. The situation was explosive; the U.N. had to act rapidly, before it was too late, in order to face up to the emergency and to defuse its explosive potential. Both the seriousness of the threat and the choice and adequacy of the response depended on Cordier's evaluation of the situation.

21 For the text of the two broadcasts, see *Congo 1960*, 818–21.

22 Dayal's first progress report S/4531, 21 Sept. 1960, para. 20.

23 *Supra*, p. 59, n. 20.

24 Urquhart, 444–5. To some diplomatic circles the decision was confidentially justified on the basis of unconfirmed (U.S.?) intelligence reports to the effect that a Russian airfleet was stationed in an African country on the ready to undertake a massive airlift of material in support of Lumumba, which would have triggered a Spanish- or even Korean-type civil war. But this version was never confirmed.

The process of decision

One major justification of the decision was its emergency character. In this respect a preliminary question arises as to whether the U.N. Secretariat had prior knowledge of Kasavubu's intentions.

Urquhart confirms prior knowledge dating back to 3 September, when Cordier visited Kasavubu at the latter's request. Kasavubu started by telling Cordier that he intended to dismiss Lumumba and tried to give him a letter—stating that Lumumba was already dismissed—which Cordier refused to accept 'on the grounds that it attempted to make the U.N. a party to the dismissal of the Prime Minister'. Kasavubu then asked that ONUC should close the Parliament, a request which Cordier again declined. He then asked that ONUC should arrest twenty-five persons; Cordier again refused, and maintained his refusal when Kasavubu reduced the number to one, whom Cordier assumed to be Lumumba.[25]

Hammarskjöld's reaction to this probing by Kasavubu reflected his constant preoccupation with the respect of legal form and propriety in the process of U.N. action. It was twofold. First, as concerned the policy that should be followed in relations with Kasavubu, Hammarskjöld approved Cordier's attitude:

Prior to any change in political situation your line to Kasavubu is the only possible one: we maintain law and order under U.N. rules, not being a tool for anyone. Another U.N. stand taken prior to drastic action—even hypothetical discussion now of possible moves after such action—would make us parties to possible internal conflict.[26]

The other reaction of the Secretary-General was related to internal contingency planning by the U.N. to face up to the eventuality of a political showdown. Here the reaction of Hammarskjöld was not, on the face of it, very different from the policy line he adopted for dealing with external parties: 'even hypothetical discussion of later possibilities and our action in situation which may arise would place us in a most exposed situation'. But if he remained non-committal about the action to be taken in such an eventuality, his instructions pointed the direction which such action might take, by putting all the emphasis on the emergency character of both the action and the situation that would have called for it:

If you have to go ahead, time may be more important than our comments ... At any time you may face the situation of complete disintegration of authority

25 Ibid. 440.   26 Ibid. 441.

that would put you in a situation of emergency which in my view would entitle
you to greater freedom of action in protection of law and order. *The degree of
disintegration thus widening your rights is a question of judgement.*[27]

In other words, Hammarskjöld, while remaining non-committal as
to possible action, explicitly gave Cordier emergency powers to take
what he would consider the necessary decisions and actions; these
powers being contingent, however, on a prior determination—to be
made also by Cordier—that the situation (i.e. the disintegration of
authority) called for the exercise of these emergency powers. Then
there follows in the instructions a very revealing phrase which Hammarskjöld himself described as an 'irresponsible observation': 'In
such a situation, responsible people on the spot might commit themselves to what the Secretary-General could not justify doing himself—*taking the risk of being disowned when it no longer mattered.*'[28]

This sentence is too clear for comment. It stretches the powers of
the representative on the spot beyond the already widened limits of
'emergency interpretation', to actions which may be politically desir-
able but legally doubtful and hence which may be censured, but only
after they would have achieved their purpose, i.e. 'when it no longer
mattered'.

At the time of his broadcast of 5 September, Kasavubu officially
asked ONUC to take over forthwith the responsibility for the maintenance of law and order all over the Congo, to provide guards for the
Presidential Palace, the Parliament, and the radio station and
immediately to close all airports to all but ONUC aircraft.[29] This
time, both the timing and the manner in which the request was put
forward were in conformity with the formal requirements of legal
propriety.

However, Cordier's decision had to be based on his own deter-

27 Ibid. (emphasis added). On a subsequent occasion, referring to another immi-
nent danger, the outbreak of civil war with foreign intervention, Hammarskjöld
declared: '... in a situation of increased danger ... I believe that the mandate to protect
life and property and to act in self-defence may be given—let me call it—an "emergency interpretation", stretching the possibility of preventive action beyond what under
other circumstances would be reasonable and permissible. That is to say, the mandate,
unless changed or clarified, necessarily remains as determined from the beginning, but
its implementation should be adjusted to the seriousness of the threat that the United
Nations tries to stem' (GAOR, 957 Mtg., 19 Dec. 1960, para. 15).

28 Urquhart, 441 (emphasis added).

29 The requests were presented to Cordier first through Kasavubu's Belgian
adviser, van Bilsen, an hour before the broadcast; they were reiterated formally in two
letters sent by Kasavubu immediately after it (ibid. 442, 444).

mination as to the seriousness of the situation and as to the adequacy
of the measures requested by Kasavubu to diffuse its explosive potential.[30] In view of the circumstances, Cordier did accede to these
demands.

The controversy over 'intervention'

The measures ordered by Cordier were heavily attacked—by
Lumumba, the Soviet Union, and some Afro-Asians—as constituting
a blatant act of intervention in the internal affairs of the Congo,
whether considered in themselves or judged by their effect on the
internal political situation.

In the first place, the assistance which the Security Council authorized the Secretary-General to provide—including in the maintenance
of law and order—had to be provided *'in consultation with the Government
of the Republic of the Congo'*.[31] Any action taken without such consultation, the argument goes on, would thus fall beyond the mandate
and could not be legitimated by it. If such action consisted of acts of
sovereignty which are of the exclusive jurisdiction of the territorial
state, and *a fortiori* if it is directed against the Government of that
state, it constitutes a usurpation of sovereign functions, and as
such—by itself and regardless of its effects—an inadmissible intervention. This was exactly the case of Cordier's action in closing the
airports and the radio station. In the second place, this action clearly
and foreseeably favoured Kasavubu (who had asked for the measures
in question) and went against Lumumba.

The first ground raises the preliminary question of the real legal
import of 'prior consultations': was it a mere question of 'protocol', or
a requirement of a more substantive nature, i.e. a condition precedent
for U.N. action and a means of renewal of consent by the Congo
Government for concrete action envisaged by the U.N.? On the one
hand, the requirement of consultation was written into the initial
mandate and derived logically from the consensual basis of the Operation. Moreover the content of the mandate—providing aid to the
Congo Government, especially in the maintenance of law and order
and in keeping the state machinery and the public services running—covered activities that are of the very essence of internal
sovereignty; which seems logically to require prior consultations on a
continuous basis and not only in the initial stage of setting up the

30 Ibid.
31 Security Council Res. of 13 July 1960, reproduced *supra*, p. 13.

Operation. It cannot thus be reduced to a mere question of form, protocol, or procedure. On the other hand, interpreting the requirement of consultations as a condition precedent for any U.N. action would have reduced to *nil* the margin of freedom of the U.N. and imposed a pattern of joint decision-making between the U.N. and the Congo Government which would have completely negated the principle of the autonomy of the Force and the Operation.

One way of conciliating the requirement of consultations with the principle of the autonomous decision-making and implementation of the mandate by the U.N.—which was not articulated, but only hinted at in the Security Council debates—was to consider that consultations were to cover the broad outlines of U.N. action and the ways and means—i.e. type of action—by which it would provide assistance to the Republic of the Congo; but that concrete decisions and actions taken in pursuance of these general lines were to be left to the exclusive determination of the U.N.[32] But even on this basis, it would be difficult to contend that consultations had taken place on the type of action of which the controversial measures constituted an application.

In any case, Hammarskjöld's answer was that, in the circumstances, 'there was nobody with whom the U.N. representatives on the spot [i.e. Cordier], could consult without prejudging the constitutional issue'; and that, in consequence, 'they had to act on their own responsibility, within their general mandate, in order to meet the emergency which they were facing.'[33] This second argument goes beyond the question of consultations and deals with that of the effects of the action. It could be understood to mean that if the action was taken in the implementation of the mandate, then it does not constitute intervention even if it does affect the internal political situation.

This reasoning is acceptable, but with a caveat. It is acceptable because the maintenance of law and order is itself an act of sovereignty, 'one of the fundamental duties of any government'.[34] But the U.N. was invited by the territorial state to assist in it; an invitation

32 e.g. Amadeo (Argentina), SCOR, 902 Mtg., 15 Sept. 1960, para. 15.

33 SCOR, 896 Mtg., 9 Sept. 1960, para. 94. In the event, more than 'prior consultations' did take place. For as was mentioned above (*supra*, p. 62), Kasavubu had specifically asked for the measures which were taken by Cordier. But of course the Secretary-General could not reveal this information which would have consolidated the change of intervention in favour of one of the contestants against the other.

34 Amadeo (Argentina), SCOR, 902 Mtg., 15 Sept. 1960, para. 15.

whose acceptance, in the words of Dayal, 'automatically juxtaposed the international and the domestic spheres of action'.[35] Maintenance of law and order, especially in a situation of relative chaos and a power vacuum, inevitably had an impact on the internal political balance. The mere existence of a large U.N. Force in the Congo did affect the internal political situation, if only by radically changing the context within which the political struggle for power took place. In these circumstances every act of omission or commission by the Force had a potential effect on the internal situation.[36]

Facing this situation, the U.N. had to choose between two alternatives: either to abstain from any action, and indeed even to withdraw its Force from the Congo, in order to avoid affecting in any manner or degree the internal political situation—a solution which would have meant the abandonment of its mission in the Congo; or to reinterpret the principle of non-intervention in a manner which would enable the Force and the Secretary-General to implement the mandate. This was obviously the alternative to follow.

On the other hand—and this is the caveat—the realization that the mandate cannot be implemented without in some way affecting the internal political situation, does not release the U.N. from making every effort to avoid affecting the internal political balance. There exists here an obligation of *due diligence* whose fulfilment can be verified in each case, in the light of the general background of the measure or the decision in question.

A neutral decision?

Can it be said that such *due diligence* was observed in these controversial decisions? There is no way of answering this question with any certainty, but one can list the existing indices and interpret their significance.

(1) The relations between Lumumba and the U.N. were at their worst. He had humiliated Hammarskjöld in his correspondence; had refused to act according to the general plan proposed by the Secretary-General; had accepted Russian assistance, thus frustrating the very purpose of the Operation; had put in motion a military operation which led to massacres which Hammarskjöld considered as verging on genocide; and was considered as responsible for the harassment and hostility towards U.N. personnel in the Congo.

35 S/4531, para. 15.
36 Ibid., paras. 21, 29, 30; Dayal's second progress report S/4557, 2 Nov. 1960, para. 12.

Hammarskjöld had come to consider him an irresponsible leader and an incipient dictator who would wreck the Congo and the U.N. to satisfy his ambition and urge for power.

(2) Andrew Cordier was sent to the Congo as a stopgap between the departure of Bunche, who could no longer communicate with Lumumba, and the arrival of the new Special Representative Dayal. He came to examine and help redress the situation of the U.N. Operation in the Congo. His short interregnum and the determination revealed by his action predisposed him to take what he would consider as necessary but unpopular measures. Moreover, Cordier's close relations with the American Ambassador in the Congo, Clare Timberlake, were widely known in both diplomatic and U.N. circles in Leopoldville; and the U.S. considered that Lumumba was rapidly introducing Russian influence and perhaps communism into the Congo.

(3) That, objectively speaking, the measures taken by Cordier favoured Kasavubu and dealt a fatal blow to Lumumba from which he never recovered, is borne out by subsequent events. That this effect was known at the time the decision was taken should have been equally evident from the fact that they were requested by Kasavubu, though they were not even discussed with Lumumba. In fact, in Leopoldville Kasavubu was in his stronghold, the Bakongo area, where his political party, the Abako, was the strongest, while Lumumba was in consequence in hostile surroundings. The closure of the airports could only benefit Kasavubu by grounding any political or military support Lumumba might have received from other areas favourable to him, such as Stanleyville. The same applies to the closure of the radio station. Lumumba was much the more effective speaker and charismatic leader. Depriving both of the use of the radio (which was at that point in the hands of Lumumba's supporters) was in itself more harmful to Lumumba than to Kasavubu. Furthermore, in the event, Kasavubu had access to another radio, that of Congo Brazzaville, just across the river, controlled by his fellow Bakongo and ally Fulbert Youlou, while Lumumba had no such possibility.[37]

37 Urquhart (at 445) argues that Cordier did not know that Kasavubu would be given access to radio Brazzaville. However, given the clear political and ethnic affinities and the political configuration of the situation, such lack of knowledge, it is submitted, seems most unlikely; and if it were the case, it would have meant a gross oversight in the political calculations of persons who are supposed to be highly experienced in crisis management. In point of fact, even before 5 September, a 'secret' anti-Lumumba radio station was broadcasting from Brazzaville under the name of 'Radio Makala'. (See Hoskyns, 187, 202–4.)

(4) That both Cordier and Hammarskjöld were more inclined to favour Kasavubu emerges from the stand they took at the very beginning as to the constitutionality of the respective positions of the two. In reporting to Hammarskjöld on the closure of the radio and airports, Cordier cabled Hammarskjöld: 'We have not chosen sides, but *the constitutional party* has chosen to follow the U.N. line.'[38] In the first meeting of the Security Council on the Congo after Cordier's decisions, Hammarskjöld also declared:

... let me register as a fact, that, according to the Constitution, the President has the right to revoke the mandate of the Prime Minister and that his decisions are effective when countersigned by constitutionally responsible Ministers ... However, the Constitution does not entitle the Prime Minister under any circumstances to dismiss the Chief of State—least of all, of course, for an action to which the Chief of State is explicitly entitled by the Constitution.[39]

It was only natural that this stand would meet with Kasavubu's approval and gratitude[40] as well as with heavy criticism from Lumumba, who considered it a 'confirmation' of 'the flagrant interference of the United Nations in the internal affairs of the Congo', and of Hammarskjöld's taking sides in a genuinely internal constitutional controversy.[41] Lumumba's communication went on to point out that '[t]his position of the Secretary-General moreover runs counter to the sovereign decisions taken by the Congolese Parliament, which has annulled by two separate votes, each by a large majority, Mr. Kasavubu's illegal decree', before adding significantly that '[i]t is not for the Secretary-General of the United Nations to interpret the Fundamental Law; that is the responsibility of the Congolese Parliament.'[42]

38 Urquhart, 446 (emphasis added).
39 SCOR, 896 Mtg., 9 Sept. 1960, paras. 91–2.
40 S/4500, 10 Sept. 1960.
41 S/4498, 10 Sept. 1960.
42 Ibid.; see also S/4517, 14 Sept. 1960. The last sentence quoted in the text represents a more sophisticated formulation of the objection, namely that the interpretation of the Congolese constitution—and indeed of Congolese law in general—was a matter of Congolese exclusive domestic jurisdiction; and that none other than the Congolese themselves have the right to undertake it. This formula was used on different occasions by the representatives and the supporters of both Lumumba and Kasavubu, as well as by other delegates, and became generally accepted as the proper interpretation of the Charter and the mandate in this respect.

Hammarskjöld did not respond directly to this attack.[43] But it is clear that he realized that he might have overstepped the legal bounds. He became very cautious thereafter not to pronounce on the internal constitutional question.

The critical analysis of Cordier's decision has then to be directed in the first place to the circumstances surrounding his invocation of his emergency powers, i.e. to his *determination* of the existence of an emergency based on his evaluation of the seriousness and needs of the situation. It has to be directed in the second place to the *decision* properly speaking, i.e. the measures taken to face up to the situation: were they taken exclusively to prevent the breakdown of law and order or were they also intended to help bring about a new situation more congenial to the fruitful continuation of the U.N. Operation in the Congo? To what extent were they taken in a non-partisan and neutral spirit? And to what extent were their effects on the relative position of the parties taken into consideration or discounted as lying beyond the factors which have to be taken into account when planning U.N. action, provided it could be justified in terms of maintenance of law and order?

These are subjective questions to which it is impossible to provide a definite answer. All that can be said about the role of law in such situations is that in public law it is the distribution and limitations of jurisdiction and power that can be effectively controlled. In the present case, Hammarskjöld was scrupulous in very clearly defining Cordier's powers. Beyond that, the effective exercise of jurisdiction is very difficult to scrutinize, because of the importance of motives and intentions. For as long as the actions are formally motivated, and as long as the justification invoked is one of the grounds for which jurisdiction is granted and its invocation in relation to these actions is

43 On 10 September Hammarskjöld tried to justify indirectly the stand he took the previous evening. Quoting a letter he had just received from Lumumba in which the latter described the constitutional situation after the parliamentary debate in the following terms: 'In their interpretation the Congolese legislative Chambers further state that the Government headed by Prime Minister Patrice Lumumba and the Head of State, Mr. Kasavubu, having been separately invested with office by Parliament, the latter alone has the power to dismiss one or the other' (S/4498), he added: 'This letter is signed by Mr. Lumumba, and I think that the quotation I have given shows that Mr. Lumumba himself acknowledges that his decision that Mr. Kasavubu is no longer President is not valid' (SCOR, 897 Mtg., 10 Sept. 1960, para. 65). He did not, however, draw the other conclusion which necessarily flows if the legal reasoning is accepted, namely that the destitution of Lumumba by Kasavubu was equally invalid.

not implausible, it becomes extremely difficult to disprove it.[44] It is difficult to judge by the results of the decisions which may be unforeseen at the time they are taken and thus constitute an extraneous element in relation to them.[45]

Cordier followed the formal rule of law, by exercising his powers within the ambit set for them and by justifying his actions by the proper legal categories (maintenance of law and order). Beyond that it is a question of real intentions and one can reach only tentative conclusions based on the coalescence of indices in rendering one interpretation more plausible than another.

One can thus confidently say that law as a formal system of distribution of competence and powers, as a formal process, played an important role and was followed. Whether as a substantive standard of behaviour it has also been effective or was simply used as a justification for action which had another purpose, perhaps even contrary to the spirit and purpose of the pertinent legal regulations, remains an open question.

3. THE GENERAL ASSEMBLY RESOLUTION

Hammarskjöld may have been 'taken aback' and even 'dismayed' by Cordier's decisions.[46] But his attitude was that it was necessary to go on with the job. Indeed, as with previous developments, the Secretary-General had in mind a plan for action which he intended to propose to the Security Council for approval and adoption. This plan was devised before the outbreak of the constitutional crisis and in response to Lumumba's military campaign against Kasai and

44 This is the great difference between the concepts of *dépassement de pouvoir* and *détournement de pouvoir* in French public law.

45 This is the abstract type of reasoning which explains whether in general certain elements should be considered legally relevant or not. For in the case at hand, the results were clearly foreseeable and could not have been ignored by Cordier and his staff (see *supra*, p. 66).

46 Urquhart writes: 'Hammarskjöld, dismayed though he was by Cordier's decisions, gave full public support to a subordinate who was in difficulty. He informed Cordier of the arguments he would use to defend the closing of the radio station "which, according to agencies, is now a—basically regrettable—fact". The words "basically regrettable" written into the typed draft of the cable in his own hand-writing, give an indication of his true feelings'. He provides another indication of Hammarskjöld's true feelings: 'A year later, when the question of taking over Radio Katanga arose, Hammarskjöld commented that taking over Radio Katanga under paragraph A–1 of the 21 February 1961 resolution, which had been adopted in the interim, had justification and validity which did not exist in case of similar action of 5 September 1960, in Leo-[poldville]; this action was justified in Secco [the Security Council] solely on "emergency rights" basis' (Urquhart, 445–6).

Katanga. The proposed action was included in the Fourth Report, issued on 7 September[47] and discussed in the fifth round of debate in the Security Council which started on 9 September 1960.[48]

The action proposed by the Secretary-General was once again based on a further elaboration of the mandate to meet the new developments on the one hand, and to introduce new means of persuasion with a view to making the protagonists more amenable to the interpretation proposed by Hammarskjöld, on the other. The thrust of the plan, now that the U.N. Force was deployed all over the Congo, was to de-emphasize the military aspect of the Operation and to try to convert it into 'a large scale program of civilian assistance'.[49]

Thus, in the Report and in his introductory statement, the Secretary-General proposed the creation of a 'United Nations Fund for the Congo ... to help in the restoration of economic life and to carry on ... public services'.[50] But for this assistance to be forthcoming and to have any useful effect, order had to be re-established, which in turn meant that political leaders had to co-operate with the U.N. and to agree to resolve their internal problems by peaceful means and on the basis of the unity and integrity of the country. This would be easier to obtain if they were cut off from their respective external sources of support which in turn could be achieved if all aid were to be channelled through the U.N. Such a solution would resolve the double problem of 'military assistance to Katanga' and of 'the abuse of technical assistance in other parts of the Congo'.[51] Moreover, it would provide the Secretary-General with powerful leverage vis-à-vis the different political leaders in his efforts to bring them to accept the rules of the game proposed by him, especially as to the process and framework for settling their internal disputes and evolving a viable political system for a unified Congo.

Hammarskjöld could not, however, completely avoid discussing in his statement in the Security Council the decisions taken by Cordier. In fact, on 8 September Lumumba had already asked for the convening of the Security Council in Leopoldville (according to Article 28, Paragraph 3, of the Charter) in order 'to give the members of the

47 S/4482.
48 SCOR, 896 Mtg., 9 Sept. 1960–906 Mtg., 17 Sept. 1960.
49 Urquhart, 438.
50 S/4482, paras. 6–7.
51 SCOR, 896 Mtg., 9–10 Sept. 1960, para. 110; in the fourth report this aspect was not put in such frank terms, but rather in the bland ones of a 'request to all States to refrain from any action which might tend to impede the restoration of law and order or to aggravate differences' (S/4482, para. 12).

Security Council the opportunity to see for themselves the situation existing in the Republic of the Congo as a result of the United Nations authorities interference in the Congo's domestic problems ...'[52] On the same day, the Soviet Union issued a statement condemning the measures taken by Cordier as a 'flagrant interference in the internal affairs of the Republic of the Congo', the U.N. Command for having 'actually become the lackey of the colonialists', and finally Hammarskjöld for his 'unseemly role', for having 'failed to display the minimum of impartiality required from him in the situation ...' and for 'functioning most unashamedly on the side of the colonialists, thus compromising the United Nations in the eyes of the world.'[53]

The Secretary-General did not centre his oral statement on Cordier's decisions but on his proposed plan. He discussed them in the process of describing the practical difficulties the U.N. were facing in the Congo, presenting them as measures ordered by his representatives in the field, on their own responsibility, to prevent a breakdown of law and order and the outbreak of civil war. He added that he was not consulted but that he fully endorsed the decisions and assumed full responsibility for them; he had hoped after the votes in the two Chambers of Parliament that the situation would stabilize, which would have allowed him to cancel the emergency measures. 'However, the situation remains such that I feel I have to submit the question of the closing of the airports and the closing of the national radio to the Security Council for its consideration and instructions.'[54]

The Secretary-General probably hoped that as on previous occasions, in spite of the controversy over Cordier's measures, he would be able to marshal consensus on a concrete plan of action. His proposed plan consisted of:

(a) an appeal by the Council to Member States to contribute to a U.N. Fund for the Congo;

(b) an appeal to Member States 'to refrain from all action which

---

52 S/4486.

53 S/4497, para. 13; these attacks were repeated at greater length and with more violence by Zorin, who succeeded Kuznetsov as permanent representative of the U.S.S.R. in the U.N. (SCOR, 901 Mtg., 14–15 Sept. 1960, paras. 2–70). Other countries had also shown their intention to centre the discussions on Cordier's decisions (e.g. Yugoslavia, S/4485, 8 Sept. 1960); without counting the informal *démarches* which must have been made to the Secretary-General by other Members, especially the Africans and some of the Asians.

54 SCOR, 896 Mtg., 9–10 Sept. 1960, para. 98; see also paras. 94, 96. The Chambers had met on 7 September; they voted to annul the respective decisions of Kasavubu and Lumumba and declared their intent to conciliate them (see *infra*, p. 75).

might tend to impede the restoration of law and order or to aggravate differences'; and to that effect to channel all aid to the Republic of the Congo through the U.N.;

(c) an appeal to all parties within the Congo to seek a peaceful solution of the conflicts aiming at overcoming 'present threats to the unity and integrity of the country without further disruption and threats to civil lives';

(d) a clarification in appropriate terms of the mandate of the U.N. Force, especially as to 'the protection of the lives of the civilian population in the spirit of the Declaration of Human Rights and the Convention on the Prevention and Punishment of the Crime of Genocide'.[55]

This proposed plan of action, with the exception of the last point, was included in a draft resolution, significantly presented this time by the U.S.[56] But the U.S.S.R. was not willing to go along, especially since the paragraph concerning the channelling of all aid through the U.N. was clearly directed against it. Instead, the U.S.S.R. representative Zorin submitted a draft resolution amounting to a motion of censure against the Secretary-General.[57] As a result, both these draft resolutions failed to be adopted. Finally, the U.S.S.R. vetoed a compromise draft resolution, also based on Hammarskjöld's proposals—but limiting the channelling of aid through the U.N. to military aid—submitted by Tunisia and Ceylon.[58] Thus, for the first time since the beginning of the Congo crisis, the Security Council reached a deadlock. As a result, the U.S. delegate submitted a draft resolution to convene an emergency session of the General Assembly, under the procedure of the Uniting for Peace Resolution.[59] The draft was adopted, in spite of the negative vote of the U.S.S.R., this being considered as a procedural matter.[60]

The Fourth Emergency Session of the General Assembly met on 17 September, just before the beginning of the fifteenth regular session. The arguments were essentially the same as in the Security Council. The Russians and their allies continued their attack against the Secretary-General; the Western Powers defended him; the Afro-Asians, while showing their over-all support for him, made clear their

55 S/4482, para. 12.

56 S/4516, in SCOR, 902 Mtg., 15 Sept. 1960, para. 45.

57 S/4519, in SCOR, 903 Mtg., 15 Sept. 1960, para. 93.

58 S/4523, 16 Sept. 1960.

59 G.A.Res. 377 A(V), 3 Nov. 1950.

60 Draft resolution S/4525, SCOR, 906 Mtg., 17 Sept. 1960, para. 173; voting, ibid., para. 198.

anxiety and reservations as to the recent developments in the Congo.[61] As a result, a draft resolution, based on the Tunisia–Ceylon draft in the Security Council, but more elaborate and stronger in tone, was agreed upon by the nine African members of the U.N., which were joined by eight Asian co-sponsors. The Afro-Asian draft was adopted by the General Assembly on 20 September 1960. It reads:

The General Assembly,
Having considered the situation in the Republic of the Congo,
Taking note of the resolutions of 14 July, 22 July and 9 August 1960 of the Security Council,
Taking into account the unsatisfactory economic and political conditions that continue in the Republic of the Congo,
Considering that, with a view to preserving the unity, territorial integrity and political independence of the Congo, to protecting and advancing the welfare of its people, and to safeguarding international peace, it is essential for the United Nations to continue to assist the Central Government of the Congo,
1. *Fully supports* the resolutions of 14 July, 22 July and 9 August of the Security Council;
2. *Requests* the Secretary-General to continue to take vigorous action in accordance with the terms of the aforesaid resolutions and to assist the Central Government of the Congo in the restoration and maintenance of law and order throughout the territory of the Republic of the Congo and to safeguard its unity, territorial integrity, and political independence in the interests of international peace and security;
3. *Appeals* to all Congolese within the Republic of the Congo to seek a speedy solution by peaceful means of all their internal conflicts for the unity and integrity of the Congo, with the assistance, as appropriate, of Asian and African representatives appointed by the Advisory Committee on the Congo, in consultation with the Secretary-General, for the purpose of conciliation;
4. *Appeals* to all Member Governments for urgent voluntary contributions to a United Nations Fund for the Congo to be used under United Nations control and in consultation with the Central Government for the purpose of rendering the fullest possible assistance to achieve the objective mentioned in the preamble;
5. *Requests:*
(a) All States to refrain from any action which might tend to impede the restoration of law and order and the exercise by the Government of the Republic of the Congo of its authority and also to refrain from any action which might undermine the unity, territorial integrity and the political independence of the Republic of the Congo;
(b) All Member States, in accordance with Articles 25 and 49 of the Charter of the United Nations, to accept and carry out the decisions of the Security

61 Hoskyns, 233.

Council and to afford mutual assistance in carrying out measures decided upon by the Security Council;

6. Without prejudice to the sovereign rights of the Republic of the Congo, *calls upon* all States to refrain from the direct and indirect provision of arms or other materials of war and military personnel and other assistance for military purposes in the Congo during the temporary period of military assistance through the United Nations, except upon the request of the United Nations through the Secretary-General for carrying out the purposes of this resolution and of the resolutions of 14 July, 22 July and 9 August of the Security Council.[62]

The resolution was adopted by 70 votes to none with 11 abstentions: the Eastern-bloc countries, France, and South Africa. Hammarskjöld considered it as an overwhelming vote of confidence in the face of the Soviet challenge, especially on the part of the Afro-Asians. In his remarks after the vote he noted 'the correspondence between the attitude reflected in the resolution and that of the Secretariat as presented most recently in the fourth report', and found 'in this fact evidence of a fundamental agreement with and within the African world regarding the aims and the very philosophy of this major United Nations operation'.[63]

In fact the view of Hammarskjöld and the Afro-Asian members were not completely identical. It is true that the resolution was based on the draft submitted by Tunisia and Ceylon in the Security Council, which in turn—like the previous draft resolutions which were adopted—was based on the Secretary-General's proposals. But the Afro-Asian endorsement was at a price. This appears partly from the resolution itself and partly from the debates: emphasis was put on the 'vigorous' character of the action to be taken by the Secretary-General; the terms of the resolution were more detailed, thus leaving a narrower margin of interpretation to the executive organ, and the Afro-Asian members were to play a more direct role in the conduct of the operation under operative paragraph 3. Finally, though only obliquely mentioned in the resolution itself, it was clear from the debates that the Afro-Asians insisted as part of the price for their support that what took place would not be considered as a *fait accompli*, i.e. that Lumumba's elimination would not be sealed, that no other solution would be recognized in the interim, and that he would be considered as a legitimate party in the conciliation effort. In Hoskyns's words, 'they saw the resolution as giving the United

62 G.A.Res. 1474 (ES–IV), 20 Sept. 1960.
63 GAOR (ES–IV) 863 Mtg., 19–20 Sept. 1960, para. 276.

Nations a chance to adopt a new and dynamic policy and to get away from the hesitations and inconsistencies of the past weeks'.[64]

On the other hand, the Western Powers went along with the Afro-Asians in the Council and in the Assembly, primarily to bring about a Russian defeat. They saw the General Assembly resolution 'more as an endorsement of past policy than a guideline for the future'.[65] And it was from these quarters that 'a new and active United Nations policy of reconciliation and reconstruction in the Congo, as suggested by Hammarskjöld, would now be hampered ...'[66]

4. THE POLICY OF NON-RECOGNITION OF UNCONSTITUTIONAL AUTHORITIES AND SITUATIONS

Internal developments

Though seriously hampered in his efforts to marshal support by the measures taken by Cordier, Lumumba quickly regained the initiative, by basing himself on the Parliament. Thus, on 7 September the Chamber voted a motion declaring invalid both Kasavubu's and Lumumba's mutual dismissal. The following day the Senate voted a similar motion, but only against Kasavubu's decision. During the same day, 8 September, the Chamber created a Commission of seven members to reconcile the differences between the two leaders. At the same time, Kasavubu returned to his immobilism, ignoring the appeals and decisions of the Parliament and insisting that Lumumba's Government no longer existed. Meanwhile, Ileo was trying to form a new cabinet and on 10 September issued a list of ministers (several of whom protested that they were not informed in advance), but at no time did he attempt to have it approved by Parliament.

On 13 September the Chamber and the Senate met in a joint session to discuss the crisis. They voted under doubtful circumstances (lack of quorum and presence of pro-Lumumba soldiers in the building) to grant Lumumba full powers, but appointed a parliamentary committee to supervise their exercise. The following day Kasavubu adjourned both houses of Parliament for a period of one month, according to articles 31 and 70 of the *Loi Fondamentale*.[67]

Noting that Lumumba was regaining the initiative in the week after his dismissal by Kasavubu, the anti-Lumumba forces moved this

64 Hoskyns, 235–6.
65 Ibid. 236.
66 Urquhart, 446.
67 Hoskyns, 204–5; *Congo 1960*, 861–2.

time through a more potent vehicle, the army. Thus, on the evening of 14 September Colonel Mobutu, Chief of Staff of the A.N.C. and a protégé of Lumumba, declared on the radio that the army was 'neutralizing' the politicians, including the President, the two rival governments of Lumumba and Ileo, and the Parliament until 31 December 1960. He specified that this was not a *coup d'état*, but a peaceful revolution, and that in the meantime he was calling in technicians to run the government. He later on designated them as a *Collège d'universitaires* and finally as a *Collège de Commissaires-Généraux*.[68]

These developments, together with the expulsion on the spur of the moment by Mobutu of the Russian and Czech diplomats, may have been at the basis of the toughening of the Russian attitude in the Security Council. They were also clearly on the minds of the Afro-Asians during the Fourth Emergency Session of the General Assembly; the non-acquiescence of the U.N. to the resulting situation was part of the price they required for their support of the Secretary-General. Hence the request to the Secretary-General in the resolution 'to assist the Central Government of the Congo', the current terms of reference to Lumumba's Government, thus excluding Mobutu's Commissioners.

Efforts at conciliation between Kasavubu and Lumumba by the parliamentary Commission and by the African Ambassadors in Leopoldville started before Mobutu's action and continued in spite of it. The African Ambassadors' effort almost succeeded in bringing the two to agree, but Kasavubu recoiled at the last moment. This was probably the result of external pressures from sources which did not want to see Lumumba back in power and of Kasavubu's conviction that Lumumbas's return would render a reconciliation with Tshombe impossible.[69]

The Commissioners, who were supposed to act as technicians and not to take sides in the political conflict, clearly sided with Kasavubu. On 20 September Kasavubu signed an ordinance appointing the Commissioners, and on 29 September, far from being 'neutralized', he swore them in and declared that he ratified Mobutu's decision to

68 For the text of Mobutu's broadcast and subsequent impromptu press conference, see ibid. 869.

69 Hoskyns, 219–22. It seems that Kasavubu had given his consent to the text of a reconciliation agreement, then refused to sign it in the last minute. This document was communicated by Lumumba to Hammarskjöld in an unpublished letter on 20 September, in which he stated that the agreement 'virtually puts an end to the Congo crisis' (Urquhart, 455).

install the *Collège*. He also declared that he was pursuing the project (favoured by Mobutu) of calling a round-table Conference.

On 11 October the Chief of State signed a 'constitutional decree-law' creating the Council of Commissioners-General, conferring on himself the authority to name and revoke the Commissioners-General and their deputies, adjourning the Parliament, transferring to that Council the legislative power granted to Parliament by the Fundamental Law (this new authority to be exercised by decree-law) and devolving the executive authority of the Prime-minister upon the President of the Council and that of ministers upon the respective Commissioners-General.[70]

Kasavubu was thus asserting his powers by trying to give legal cover to the *Collège de Commissaires*. He did not, however, repudiate Ileo's government. As a result, there were at the same time three competing and mutually exclusive 'governments'. The *Collège* was the one that had a measure of effectiveness, under the protection of the army. But this measure was rather limited; in any case limited to the capital. Disintegration and feuding were spreading to all levels and all over the Congo.[71]

ONUC's policy line

ONUC's reaction to Mobutu's move on 14 September was very different from its reaction to the events of 5 September. This was no doubt due to the differences between the two situations and to the controversy aroused by the first measures. But it was also, and in no small part, due to the change in the leadership of the Operation in the field.

Dayal arrived in Leopoldville on 5 September. He was not consulted by Cordier on the measures the latter was about to take. He was also 'taken aback', according to Urquhart, 'by Cordier's decisions'; so much so 'that for a moment he considered resigning'.[72] Dayal took over from Cordier on 8 September; and although in his first Progress Report he cogently defended the U.N. measures he did not approve of,[73] he did 'his best to rescind them as soon as possible'.[74] After

70 S/4557, paras. 18, 25; Hoskyns, 238, remarks that the 'constitutional decree law' though published in the official journal *Le Moniteur Congolais* on 10 (and not 11) October, was back-dated 29 September.

71 See in general S/4557.

72 Urquhart, 446.

73 S/4531, 21 Sept. 1960, para. 20.

74 Urquhart, 447.

negotiations with Kasavubu, Lumumba, and parliamentary leaders, he succeeded in getting them all to agree, on 12 September, to the reopening of the radio station and the airports, on condition that they should be used exclusively for peaceful purposes and on an equal footing by all political parties.[75]

It was at this juncture that Mobutu's *coup* took place. Dayal's reaction to it was directly related to his reaction to Cordier's decisions. For if he felt that something fundamentally wrong had occurred on 5 September, he knew that in order to repair the harm done it was not sufficient to rescind the decisions; it was also necessary to eliminate or at least to attenuate their continuing effects. It was much beyond the mandate of ONUC to re-establish the *status quo ante*. But at least ONUC could to some extent neutralize the effects of the decisions by withholding recognition from illegal situations which materialized in the meantime. Of course this test of legality was difficult to apply and could be considered as an intervention in internal affairs. However, the manner in which it was developed and applied aimed at reducing this risk. Thus it was used only when the act or situation was prima facie illegal, i.e. when, at the face of it, it could have no possible basis in law.

Preventing Lumumba's arrest

This policy line was first followed in relation to the successive attempts to arrest Lumumba, whose residence was guarded by a U.N. detachment. The first was on 15 September, when both Kasavubu and Ileo requested the U.N. to arrest Lumumba, a request which Dayal 'firmly declined, explaining that this was entirely outside the functions of ONUC.'[76] But this was a mere refusal by ONUC to act on behalf of one of the factions.

The situation was different when on 10 October A.N.C. elements tried to arrest Lumumba on the basis of a warrant citing articles of the Penal Code, and requested that the ONUC guard 'be instructed to facilitate the arrest', i.e. not to resist its execution. Dayal rejected this request, considering that the warrant was patently illegal. Lumumba was undisputedly a member of Parliament; he thus enjoyed parliamentary immunity, and as long as Parliament was not in session, the immunity—which according to general principles and the *Loi Fon-*

---

75 According to Urquhart, 450, this was done under instructions from Hammarskjöld.

76 S/4531, para. 27.

damentale could be waived only by Parliament itself—had to be respected; hence the prima facie illegality of the warrant.[77]

Kasavubu raised a 'final, solemn protest against the unacceptable, not to say ludicrous interference of the United Nations in the purely internal and largely judicial affairs of the Congo . . . by discussing the interpretation of our domestic laws in order to hamper in an out-rageous manner the regular functioning of justice'.[78] Dayal's answer to this protest was that '[a]lthough ONUC had not the competence to interpret domestic law, neither could it withdraw from its functions in order to facilitate an arbitrary military arrest which amounted to an act of political violence'.[79] His argument was that far from being an attitude of non-interference in the working of the due process of law, the acquiescence of ONUC in the execution of such a patently illegal act would constitute collusion on its part with one of the internal parties in what amounted to mere political violence committed against another; and this would have constituted not only a failure in carrying out the mandate of maintenance of law and order but also an act of intervention in internal affairs.

The non-recognition of the Collège de Commissaires

The same criterion of legality, when applied to the competing governments, led to the conclusion that if both Lumumba's and Ileo's governments based their claims on different interpretations of the *Loi Fondamentale*, and consequently the U.N. had to take a position of neutrality between them, the *Collège de Commissaires* was based solely on military power and was thus prima facie unconstitutional and could not be recognized as a government by the U.N. At the same time, since the *Collège* was the only competing 'government' with a measure of effectiveness, ONUC had to deal with it if it was to avoid complete paralysis. Dayal described the way he coped with this dilemma in his Second Progress Report in the following terms:

Committed to the principle of neutrality, it [ONUC] could not have chosen between rival governments, nor could it respond to the continuing appeals that it install one or another government or 'reinstate the legal Government'. Equally committed to the principle of legality, it was now unable to give recognition to a regime founded in fact only on military force. On the other

77 S/4557, para. 22.
78 A/4560/Annex (13 Oct. 1960).
79 S/4557, para. 22.

hand, its mission could not be accomplished without many routine day-to-day contacts with ministries, for urgent arrangements in specific fields of work must be undertaken if the grave situation of the country is not to deteriorate further.

ONUC accordingly, while taking no position on the legality of the constitutional decree-law of 11 October 1960 creating the Council of Commissioners-General, has continued to follow its policy of dealing, in routine matters, with whatever authority it finds in the ministerial chairs. It has thus maintained useful contacts of an informal character on all matters of practical value in the fields of administration and technical assistance, without admitting any element of political recognition.[80]

Dayal's Second Progress Report

Dayal may have sought by following such a policy 'to keep scrupulously aloof from the political merry-go-round while doing his best to promote reconciliation, to keep the country going, and to protect all parties from actual physical harm'.[81] But the policy of non-recognition and the resistance to attempts to arrest Lumumba brought on him in particular and on the U.N. in general the wrath of Mobutu, Kasavubu, the Commissioners-General, and the Western Powers which were backing them, especially the U.S. and Belgium.[82]

Dayal was not deterred by these attacks and answered them in his Second Progress Report, issued on 2 November 1960, in which he very frankly described the deterioration of the situation in the Congo and discussed its causes.[83] Prominent among these were the eruption of the army into the political scene and its increasing indiscipline and arbitrariness; the continued Belgian support to Katanga; and the disruptive anti-U.N. role of the Belgian advisers who were invited back in large numbers by the Commissioners-General. Most significant were Dayal's proposals for a solution of the crisis through conciliation on the basis of a return to legality:

In the confused political situation which prevails, the only two institutions whose foundations still stand are the office of the Chief of State and the Parliament. If the minimum conditions of non-interference and security mentioned earlier could be established, it would open the way to the leaders of

80 Ibid., paras. 28–30, 123.
81 Urquhart, 473.
82 Ibid. 475; Hoskyns, 253.
83 Urquhart, 475, confirms that this was done 'with Hammarkjöld's full backing'.

the country to seek peaceful political solutions through the medium of these two institutions.[84]

The report drew very sharp reactions from Mobutu and his entourage, from Mr. Wigny, the Belgian Foreign Minister, and, significantly, from the State Department.[85] What worried the anti-Lumumba forces most was not so much Dayal's criticism of the Mobutu regime and of Belgium as the emphasis on reconciliation around the Parliament (which was Lumumba's strong-hold)—coming in the wake of ONUC's resistance to attempts to arrest Lumumba and of the policy of non-recognition of the Mobutu regime—which threatened, from their point of view, to open the way to Lumumba's return to power.

Even before the publication of Dayal's Second Report, but especially after it, the U.S. was accompanying its criticisms of ONUC's policies with hints of the withdrawal of its support for the Congo Operation if Hammarskjöld persisted in these policies and facilitated Lumumba's come-back. It is an indication of the U.S. evaluation of both the importance and the imminence of this threat that it immediately embarked on a vast diplomatic campaign to stem such an eventuality by seeking to obtain recognition by the U.N. of the *status quo* in the Congo; and this at the risk of an open clash with the Afro-Asians and a less open one with the Secretariat.[86]

5. THE DECISION TO SEAT KASAVUBU'S DELEGATION IN THE GENERAL ASSEMBLY

The Security Council unanimously recommended the Republic of the Congo for admission to membership in the U.N. on 7 July 1960.[87]

84 S/4557, para. 127.

85 Wigny declared in New York on 14 November that Belgium might have to consider withdrawing from the U.N. The spokesman of the State Department refuted the criticism against Belgium and the Belgian advisers. He added that the U.S. would accept a return to parliamentary Government only under 'the nominee of President Kasavubu for Premier', i.e. under Ileo and not Lumumba (Hoskyns, 254).

86 See Urquhart, 476, for the U.S. threats and the Secretary-General's reaction. Hoskyns, 254, quotes an article by W. R. Frye, in the *Christian Science Monitor*, of 7 November 1960, commenting on the unprecedented declaration of the State Department on Dayal's report, in which he wrote: 'Never before on the Congo issue, and rarely if ever before in Mr. Hammarskjöld's term of office has the United States publicly disagreed with the Secretary-General or disputed his judgement on a major issue. ... The United States must have felt that a restoration of Mr. Lumumba was so at hand and so impossible to contemplate that much should be risked to stave it off.'

87 S/4377.

The Congo Cabinet included a Minister-Delegate to the U.N., Mr. Thomas Kanza. The Congo Government was not represented in the first round of debates in the Security Council on 13–14 July. In the following three rounds, delegates were designated by the Government.[88]

It was only after the outbreak of the constitutional crisis that competing delegations were designated to represent the Republic of the Congo in the fifth round of debates in the Security Council which started on 9 September.[89]

The General Assembly, by its resolution 1480 (XV) admitted the Republic of the Congo to membership on 20 September 1960 during the first meeting of its fifteenth regular session. Immediately after declaring the admission of the Republic of the Congo, the President of the Assembly, Frederick Boland from Ireland, added that as 'the constitutional and political position in that country still remains, unhappily, far from clear', the implementation of the decision just adopted posed some problems which had to be solved by the Assembly itself. He therefore proposed to refer the question to the Credentials Committee, a proposal which was adopted.[90]

The President did not specifically mention the problem of competing delegations. But the import of his proposal was to keep the seat of the Congo empty pending a decision on the report of the Credentials Committee. As the Committee usually submits its report around the end of the session, and as the General Assembly had just adopted—on the same day, at the close of the Fourth Emergency Session—resolution 1474 (ES–IV) which put much emphasis on conciliation, it was hoped that by the time the Committee submitted its report the problem would have disappeared.

However, on 10 October, in his speech in the General debate, the Guinean President Sekou Touré submitted a draft resolution with a view to seating provisionally the representative of the Central Government of the Congo (i.e. the Lumumba Government) according to rule 29 of the Rules of Procedure, pending the decision of the Assembly on the report of the Credentials Committee.[91] On 28 October a revised draft resolution sponsored by Ceylon, Ghana,

88 S/4403, 20 July 1960; S/4423, 8 Aug. 1960.
89 S/4504 and S/4504/Add. 1, 11 Sept. 1960; S/4512, 14 Sept. 1960.
90 GAOR(XV), 864 Mtg., 20 Sept. 1960, paras. 62–3.
91 A/L 319 in GAOR(XV), 896 Mtg., 10 Oct. 1960, para. 62. Rule 29 provides: 'Any representative to whose admission a Member has made objection shall be seated provisionally with the same rights as other representatives until the Credentials Committee has reported and the General Assembly has given its decision.'

Guinea, India, Indonesia, Mali, Morocco, and the U.A.R. was submitted; it included in addition a request to the Secretary-General 'to
take all necessary steps to promote, and to ensure the security of, a
meeting of the Parliament of the Republic of the Congo as soon as
possible'.[92] This draft, followed four days later by Dayal's Second
Progress Report, was interpreted by the anti-Lumumba forces as the
first step in a movement to return Lumumba to power; and their
reaction was swift and massive.

In the first place, Kasavubu hurriedly arrived in New York and
addressed the Assembly on 8 November. He declared from the ros-
trum the composition of his delegation, with himself as its head, and
requested that it be seated without delay.[93] He also let it be known
that he would stay in New York until his delegation was seated.

In the meantime, the Advisory Committee, after long discussions,
agreed, in its ninth session on 5 November, upon the manner of giving
effect to operative paragraph 3 of General Assembly resolution 1474
(ES–IV). This was by establishing a Conciliation Commission composed of the representatives of its fifteen Afro-Asian members.[94]
When informed by Dayal of its establishment, composition, and
terms of reference, Kasavubu objected to its dispatch to the Congo
without his prior agreement; he withheld his consent in spite of
Dayal's and Hammarskjöld's assurances that the purpose of the
Commission was not to impose a solution but to conciliate. He
privately explained that eight out of the fifteen members were favourable to Lumumba and said that he would accept the Commission only
once his delegation was seated.[95]

In the General Assembly, after Kasavubu had delivered his speech
on 8 November, the debate started on item 85 of the Agenda, entitled
'The situation in the Republic of the Congo', mainly on the basis of
the Afro-Asian draft resolution and Dayal's Second Progress
Report.[96] In other words, although the debate was on the situation in

92 A/L. 319/Rev. 2.

93 GAOR(XV). 912 Mtg., 8 Nov. 1960, paras. 2–26.

94 A/4592, 24 Nov. 1960.

95 These two considerations were alluded to in Kasavubu's letter of 15 Nov. 1960 to
Dayal (ibid., Annex II). On 23 November, the day after his delegation was seated in the
General Assembly, he met with the Advisory Committee. Though he did not reject the
Conciliation Commission in principle, and even said that he considered it as part of the
assistance rendered by the U.N. to the Congo, he remained non-committal as to the
date at which he would be willing to receive it in the Congo (ibid., para. 5). In its final
report, the Commission describes Kasavubu's unsuccessful demands to alter its composition (A/4711, 20 Mar. 1961, para. 12).

96 GAOR(XV). 912 Mtg., 8 Nov. 1960, paras. 27–9.

the Congo in general, it was centred on the question of representation, as was shown by the documents cited by the President and referred to in the title of the item, and the statements of the first four speakers in this debate.[97] But at this point, the representative of Ghana moved to adjourn the debate on the item, on the basis of article 76 of the Rules of Procedure. He argued that the debate in the Assembly would prejudice the chances of success of the Conciliation Commission which was to leave shortly for the Congo; in consequence it should be adjourned until the Commission reported to the Assembly.[98] In spite of American resistance, the motion was carried, on 9 December, by 48 votes to 30 with 18 abstentions.[99]

This radical change of tactics on the part of Ghana and other pro-Lumumba Afro-Asian members is easy to explain. At that point, American pressures to seat the Kasavubu delegation were beginning to make themselves felt. These, combined with the stronger legal grounds on which Kasavubu stood, gave him a greater chance of winning if a choice were to be made between the two delegations. Another new factor which bore on the situation was the role played by the newly independent French African territories which were admitted to membership at the same time as the Congo, on 20 September 1960, and which had not taken part in the debates in the Security Council or in the Fourth Emergency Session of the General Assembly. These countries were closely toeing the French line and with the exception of Mali and Togo, were wholeheartedly behind Kasavubu (especially President Fulbert Youlou of Congo Brazzaville, who was a fellow Bakongo). As a result they diluted the unity of the Afro-Asian front.[100]

One of the U.S. moves in its campaign to seat the Kasavubu delegation which precipitated the Afro-Asian motion was its pressure, on 8 November—the day Kasavubu addressed the Assembly—together with its allies on the Credentials Committee, for an

97 The representatives of Guinea and the U.S.S.R. during the 912th meeting and those of Poland and Argentina at the beginning of the 913th meeting of the Assembly, on 9 Nov. 1960.

98 GAOR(XV). 913 Mtg., 9 Nov. 1960, paras. 75–8.

99 Ibid., para. 162. All members of the Advisory Committee voted for the motion with the exception of Canada, which abstained.

100 On Afro-Asian attitudes and alignments in the U.N. during the Congo crisis, see Hoskyns, 256–9; R. C. Good, 'The Congo Crisis: a Study of Postcolonial Politics', in L. W. Martin (ed.), *Neutralism and Nonalignment, The New States in World Affairs* (1962), 34–63; S. B. Farajallah, *Le Groupe afro-asiatique dans le cadre des Nations Unies* (1963), 283–339.

immediate meeting of this Committee.[101] As these constituted the majority, a meeting was held the following day. The Committee then decided—against the objections of the U.S.S.R. and the two African members, Morocco and the U.A.R., which sought to adjourn *sine die*—to go on with the work. On 10 November it adopted by 5 votes to 3 with 1 abstention, a proposal of the U.S. that it should consider in priority the credentials of the representatives of the Republic of the Congo.[102]

The U.S. submitted a draft resolution recommending to the General Assembly the acceptance of the credentials issued by Kasavubu. The representatives of the U.S.S.R., Morocco, and the U.A.R. opposed the consideration of the U.S. draft resolution on the following grounds:

They pointed out that the Credentials Committee normally met towards the end of the session of the General Assembly. Moreover, they pointed out, the decision taken by the General Assembly on its 913th plenary meeting to adjourn discussion of item 85 (The situation in the Republic of the Congo) precluded consideration of the credentials of the representatives of the Republic of the Congo (Leopoldville) by the Credentials Committee at this time. No decision, they considered, should be taken which could affect the work of the Conciliation Commission that was about to depart for the Republic of the Congo ... They pointed out that the question involved political decisions which could not be hastily made and that the Committee must avoid taking sides on questions involving the internal political affairs of the Congo. They contended that the documentation was incomplete, since there was another delegation from the Republic of the Congo whose credentials the Committee should examine.[103]

The last argument refers to an intricate procedural point which played an important role in determining the decision of the Committee. The Central Government had on occasion issued credentials for its representatives to attend different Security Council debates, including the fifth round which took place after the outbreak of the constitutional crisis.[104] But it did not issue credentials for attending the fifteenth session of the General Assembly. Kasavubu, on the other hand, had issued such credentials which he communicated to the President of the General assembly in a letter of 8 November 1960.[105]

101 The Credentials Committee was composed of Costa-Rica, Haiti, Morocco, New Zealand, the Philippines, Spain, the U.S.S.R., the U.A.R., and the U.S.A.

102 A/4578, 17 Nov. 1960, paras. 1–3.

103 Ibid., para. 9.

104 See *supra*, p. 82, n. 88.

105 A/4578, para. 6.

At the beginning of the examination of the credentials of the representatives of the Congo Republic, the Chairman of the Committee, Mr. Shanahan from New Zealand, 'ruled that the only documents before the Committee were those which were relevant to the Credentials Committee of the General Assembly and that documents concerned with credentials for any other body, including, for example, the Security Council, were not before the Committee and would not be in order at its meeting'.[106]

This meant that through this formal oversight of the Lumumba Government, the Committee, rather than having to weigh and choose between the two sets of credentials, had simply to verify and pronounce itself on the validity of the credentials issued by Kasavubu. From a legal point of view, this oversight greatly facilitated the task of Kasavubu's supporters. Their arguments were simple enough: the Credentials Committee had a 'limited function', namely, 'to pass only on the legal questions concerning the validity of the credentials before it ... while political or other considerations should be left to the General Assembly'; rule 27 of the Rules of Procedure provides that 'credentials shall be issued either by the Head of the State or Government or by the Minister for Foreign Affairs'; President Kasavubu 'was undeniably the Chief of State of the Republic of the Congo', he 'had been heard as Chief of State by the General Assembly without objection'; hence the credentials he had issued are in conformity with rule 27.[107]

As a result, the U.S. draft resolution was adopted by the Credentials Committee on 10 November by 6 votes to 1 (the U.S.S.R.), the representatives of Morocco and the U.A.R. having stated that they were unable to participate in the vote.[108]

Once the Committee had reached its decision, another obstacle had to be removed before Kasavubu's delegation could be seated. This was to get the General Assembly to adopt the recommendation of the Credentials Committee, in spite of its decision to adjourn *sine die* the debate on the situation in the Congo. The American effort was thus directed first towards bringing the President of the General Assembly to call a meeting of the Assembly in order to examine the report of the Credentials Committee, and second, towards exercising sufficient diplomatic pressure to obtain the desired result. In consequence, a

106 Ibid.
107 Ibid., para. 8.
108 Ibid., para. 12.

vast diplomatic campaign was launched by the U.S., using maximum diplomatic pressure and 'arm-twisting' to achieve these goals.[109]

On the other hand, both the Secretary-General and the Advisory Committee were most anxious to maximize the chances of success of the Conciliation Commission and were keenly aware of the obvious fact that the formal recognition of the delegation of one of the factions would destroy the basis on which conciliation between them could take place. According to Urquhart, 'Hammarskjöld made no secret of his strong disapproval of the campaign to seat Kasavubu's representatives.'[110] And when it was announced that the President of the General Assembly had called a meeting of the Assembly for 18 November, to discuss the report of the Credentials Committee, the members of the Advisory Committee, without exception, as well as the Secretary-General, let it be known that they strongly disagreed with this move.[111]

When the General Assembly met on 18 November, the representative of Ghana opposed the resumption of the debate on Congolese representation, on the grounds that when the Assembly decided on 9 November to adjourn the debate, it had before it a draft resolution concerning the seating of a Congolese delegation; hence a decision taken by a two-thirds majority was needed to rescind the previous decision.[112] The President interpreted this objection—against its clear intent—as constituting a motion to adjourn under rule 76 of the Rules of Procedure.[113] When put to vote, the motion was rejected by 51 to 36, with 11 abstentions.[114] As soon as the vote was taken, the representative of India raised a point of order. To him the rejection of the motion to adjourn did 'not amount to an automatic resumption of the debate on the report of the Credentials Committee'. For this, a specific motion for the resumption of the debate was necessary; and this motion, given the decision of the Assembly on 9 November, required a two-thirds majority. He pointed

---

109 Hoskyns, 262–4; Urquhart, 477.

110 Ibid.

111 This disapproval, though only unofficially voiced, was explicitly referred to by Mr. Touré (Guinea): 'What is the use of the Advisory Committee for the Congo, if, despite its unanimous opinion, one delegation—that of the United States—can stand in the way of postponing the debate on the situation in the Congo?' (GAOR(XV), 920 Mtg., 21 Nov. 1960, para. 34). See also *supra*, p. 84, n. 99.

112 GAOR(XV). 917 Mtg., 18 Nov. 1960, paras. 29–31.

113 Ibid., para. 32.

114 Ibid., para. 113; from the members of the Advisory Committee, only Senegal voted against, while Canada, Liberia, and Pakistan abstained.

out that agenda item 85 included in its very title a reference to the
Afro-Asian draft resolution on the provisional seating of the representatives of the Central Government. It was the debate on this
draft resolution, and hence on this very issue of representation, which
was adjourned, and it could not be resumed unless the Assembly
decided by a two-thirds majority to change its previous decision.[115]

The President ruled, however, that there were two separate though
closely related items of the agenda. One was item 85 'The situation in
the Republic of the Congo', the other item 3 'Credentials of Representatives to the fifteenth session of the General Assembly ... (b)
Report of the Credentials Committee'. The adjournment of the debate on one could not prevent the debate on the other. He added that
when the Assembly took its decision on 9 November, it did not have
before it the report of the Credentials Committee, which thus represented a new fact; and that it was not possible to interpret this
decision as meaning 'that the Assembly wished at that time to post-
pone its debate on a report which it had not yet even seen'. On these
grounds, he ruled that a two-thirds majority was not necessary to
enable the Assembly to proceed with its debate on the report of the
Credentials Committee.[116]

This ruling by the President on the grounds of the existence of two
agenda items, was attacked in the subsequent debate as based on 'an
extremely artificial and formalistic approach'[117] and as being 'inconsistent with the substance and spirit of agreements reached'.[118] After a
stormy debate, the General Assembly adopted, on 24 November, the
recommendation of the Credentials Committee to seat Kasavubu's
delegation, by 53 votes to 24, with 19 abstentions.[119]

6. LUMUMBA'S ESCAPE AND CAPTURE: THE CONTROVERSY
   OVER WIDENING THE MANDATE

Urquhart ably sums up the general feelings of the Secretariat and
the older Afro-Asian States as regards the General Assembly resol-

115 Ibid., paras. 119–26.
116 GAOR(XV), 918 Mtg., 18 Nov. 1960, paras. 1–6.
117 Mr. Vidic (Yugoslavia), GAOR(XV), 920 Mtg., 21 Nov. 1960, para. 108.
118 Mr. Bisbe (Cuba), GAOR(XV), 922 Mtg., 21 Nov. 1960, para. 9.
119 GAOR(XV). 924 Mtg., 22 Nov. 1960, para. 200. From the members of the
Advisory Committee, only Senegal voted for; Ceylon, Ghana, Guinea, India,
Indonesia, Mali, Morocco, U.A.R., Yugoslavia voted against; Canada, Ethiopia,
Ireland, Liberia, Pakistan, Sweden, Tunisia abstained. Nigeria did not participated in
the vote, its representative explaining that in his capacity as president of the Conciliation Commission he could not take a stand on the question.

ution to seat Kasavubu's delegation when he describes it as a 'partisan decision, which as a result of Western pressure formally put the Assembly on the side of one of the factions in the political conflict in the Congo' and which, '[f]ar from promoting reconciliation and reducing partisanship ... intensified both the political crisis in the Congo and the division between the members within the U.N. itself over the Congo question'.[120]

Up to that point, though neutralized, Lumumba remained an active political force to be contended with in Leopoldville. But the decision of the General Assembly destroyed whatever remained of his formal claim to power and left the U.N. with no leverage over Kasavubu, Mobutu, and their backers. Moreover, Lumumba feared that the General Assembly's decision would lead to a change in the Force's attitude as regards his protection in that it would no longer oppose his arrest.[121]

Both these considerations led him to the conclusion that he could no longer expect anything from the U.N., and to his decision to move quickly to try to make for his stronghold in the Oriental province. On the evening of 27 November—the day Kasavubu returned to Leopoldville—Lumumba clandestinely left his house and the protection of the U.N. on his way to Stanleyville.

It goes beyond the scope of this essay to describe in detail the escape of Lumumba, his capture by the A.N.C., his imprisonment and maltreatment in captivity, his transfer to Katanga, and his tragic end. What interests us here is to trace the impact of these events, which were triggered by the General Assembly's decision to seat Kasavubu's delegation, upon the evolution of the internal political situation in the Congo and more particularly upon the U.N. responses to these developments.

Lumumba was captured on 1 December;[122] on 12 December Gizenga declared that the Capital of the Republic was transferred to Stanleyville and that the Central Government would continue its work from there.[123] The A.N.C. was also divided into those loyal to Mobutu and the Leopoldville regime and those loyal to Lumumba and the Stanleyville regime. The country was thus torn between three antagonistic regimes, those of Leopoldville, Stanleyville, and Elisabethville. The threat of civil war between them was looming

120 Urquhart, 478.
121 Ibid. 479.
122 Hoskyns, 267.
123 Ibid. 290.

large over the Congo,[124] with an even greater threat from the point of view of international peace and security, namely that of massive intervention by their respective backers, leading to a Spanish- or even Korean-type civil war.

The controversy over the limits of U.N. protection

Even before the outbreak of the constitutional crisis the U.N. had developed a practice of protecting the residences of political leaders and embassies who requested it as part of its function of maintenance of law and order. At the outbreak of the constitutional crisis Lumumba, Kasavubu, and Mobutu all requested and obtained such protection. It was understood that the protection would be limited to the residence but would not cover the person in question if he chose to move outside it. U.N. troops would use force to defend their positions around the residence of the protected persons. But this was within the meaning of self-defence which included the defence of positions held under orders.

The protection provided by the U.N. to Lumumba around the official residence of the Prime Minister had been an obstacle to the attempts made by the A.N.C. to arrest him. After Lumumba's escape and capture, both in the Security Council and later in the General Assembly, the Secretary-General and the Force were criticized for not protecting him against arrest, and for not delivering him once arrested. Hammarskjöld's answer was invariably that this would have required the taking of military initiative by the U.N. troops, an initiative which lay beyond their mandate and was in violation of the principle of the non-use of force.[125] This argument was true of the situation arising after the arrest of Lumumba, but not before it. Referring to the latter, Hammarskjöld declared in the Security Council on 15 February 1961 that:

Mr. Lumumba escaped from his residence in a way unknown to the United Nations and travelled east, without any possibility for the United Nations to know where he was and thus without possibility for the Organization to give him protection. He was arrested out in the country without any possibility for the United Nations to stop this action, as it was not in control of the situation.[126]

Hammarskjöld here invokes the material impossibility of pro-

124 For a description of the situation of each of these three regimes, see ibid. 274–92.
125 e.g. SCOR, 913 Mtg., 7 Dec. 1960, para. 30; SCOR, 917 Mtg., 10 Dec. 1960, para. 62; SCOR, 935 Mtg., 15 Feb. 1961, para. 10.
126 Ibid., para. 9.

tecting Lumumba before his arrest. This statement, however, needs qualification. For as revealed now by Urquhart, when the Ghanaian Brigade stationed in Kasai (the province in which Lumumba's pursuit took place, and where he was finally arrested) asked ONUC headquarters on 3 November 'to confirm its assumption' that Lumumba could be taken into 'protective custody' if he seemed 'in danger of arrest', it was ordered not to get involved in any way.[127]

Here the controlling consideration was not the principle of the non-use of force. For had Lumumba been taken into protective custody before actual arrest, there would have been no need for the Force to take any military initiative; and if it were attacked by Lumumba's pursuers, it would have been within its mandate to defend itself. The controlling consideration was the principle of non-intervention which was at the basis of the limitation of U.N. protection to the residence of the protected persons. It was considered that protecting a political leader on the move in pursuit of political aims or *en route* to his stronghold would constitute an impermissible intervention in the internal political situation in his favour.[128]

But of course in the case at hand, the protection of Lumumba, even in his residence, did have a very important political effect, by keeping him out of the clutches of his foes and in the political arena as a leader to be contended with. The drawing of the line as to the extent of protection which was compatible with the mandate, hence not constituting intervention, reflected a subjective determination. When the first concrete situations were faced, the import of the general principles of non-intervention and the non-use of force to the problem of protection was vague and unsettled. It was through the interpretation given to these principles by the U.N. personnel that the practice of protection started to take shape. That protection was provided at all was one step; that it was provided against arbitrary arrest was another; but that it was limited to the residence of the protected person was yet another. At each of these steps there was a certain margin of discretion exercised not only on the basis of legal considerations, but also—and perhaps more important—on the basis of political propriety. But once the line was drawn, it established a precedent and hardened through repetition and justification into principle.

127 Urquhart, 480.
128 Ibid. 479. On the whole episode of Lumumba's escape and capture, see S/4571, 5 Dec. 1960 and Add. 1. For the argument of principle, see S/4757, 2 Mar. 1961.

Security Council and General Assembly meetings

On 6 December the U.S.S.R. issued a statement heavily criticizing the Secretary-General for failing to protect Lumumba against arrest, and denouncing him as a 'lackey of the colonialists'.[129] It also requested the convening of the Security Council. The Council met on 7 December. Its debates, which continued until 14 December—apart from the criticisms of Hammarskjöld's conduct of the Operation and his reply to them—turned around two draft resolutions placed before it. The first was a U.S.S.R. draft submitted on 7 December, calling upon the Secretary-General 'to secure the immediate release of Patrice Lumumba' and other political personalities, requesting ONUC's Command 'immediately to disarm the terrorist bands of Mobutu' and calling upon Belgium 'immediately to withdraw Belgian military, paramilitary and civil personnel from the Congo'.[130] The other draft resolution was also submitted on 7 December, by Argentina, Italy, the U.K., and the U.S.A. It declared that any violation of human rights in the Congo was inconsistent with the purposes of the U.N.; expressed the expectation that 'no measures contrary to recognized rules of law and order' would be taken against prisoners or arrested persons, and the hope 'that the International Committee of the Red Cross would be allowed to examine detained persons throughout the Republic ...'[131] Both these draft resolutions failed to be adopted.[132]

A last-minute draft resolution submitted by Poland, requesting 'the Secretary-General to undertake the necessary measures to obtain the immediate release of Mr. Patrice Lumumba and of all persons who are now under arrest or detention despite their parliamentary immunity' also failed to be adopted.[133] Towards the end of the debate, both the representatives of Ceylon and of Tunisia declared that they were working on an Afro-Asian draft resolution, but that the reactions of the members of the Council did not encourage them to submit it.[134]

129 S/4573.

130 S/4579 in SCOR, 914 Mtg., 8 Dec. 1960, para. 62.

131 S/4578/Rev. 1, 13 Dec. 1960.

132 The vote on the U.S.S.R. draft resolution was 2 to 8, with 1 abstention (Ceylon) (SCOR, 920 Mtg., 12 Dec. 1960, para. 159); the four-power draft resolution obtained 7 votes to 3 (U.S.S.R., Poland, and Ceylon) with Tunisia abstaining. It was thus vetoed by the U.S.S.R., after its amendments to the draft resolution were rejected (ibid., para. 156).

133 Ibid., paras. 169, 177. The votes were 3 for (U.S.S.R., Poland, Ceylon), 6 against and 2 abstentions (Tunisia and Argentina).

134 SCOR, 919 Mtg., 12 Dec. 1960, para. 183–8; SCOR, 920 Mtg., 12 Dec. 1960, para. 144.

The debate on the Congo was thus closed in the Security Council without reaching any concrete result, and it was resumed in the General Assembly on 16 December. It revolved around the same themes and also focused on two draft resolutions. The first was an Afro-Asian draft submitted by Ceylon, Ghana, India, Indonesia, Iraq, Morocco, the U.A.R., and Yugoslavia. Its purpose was to spur the U.N. into following a more energetic policy in the Congo: it declared that 'the United Nations *must henceforth* implement its mandate fully'; it urged 'the immediate release of all political prisoners', particularly those enjoying parliamentary immunity, the immediate convening of the Parliament, the prevention of armed units and personnel from interfering in the political life and from receiving any material or other support from abroad; it demanded that 'all Belgian military and quasi-military personnel, advisers and technicians be immediately withdrawn'.[135]

The other draft resolution was submitted by the U.K. and the U.S.A. Though more detailed, it was very similar to the four-Power draft submitted in the Security Council.[136]

Those who defended the Afro-Asian draft tended to criticize, in varying degrees, the timidity and inconsistency of ONUC's policy and actions. Those who attacked it, i.e. the Western and some Latin American countries, and the newly independent French African territories, considered that the measures it envisaged went beyond the powers of the U.N. and amounted to imposing a trusteeship over a member State. Among this group, the Western and Latin American countries favoured the U.S.–U.K. draft, while the former French African territories considered even this as an intervention in the internal affairs of the Congo.

Hammarskjöld also opposed the Afro-Asian draft resolution. It implied that up to that point he had not 'implemented fully the mandate', and the measures it required ONUC to undertake were precisely those he was criticized for not having taken. He repeatedly pointed out both in the Security Council and in the General Assembly that these measures amounted to 'overriding by force the authority of the Chief of State in his own country',[137] either by substituting for him (enforcing the Constitution, convening the Parliament,[138]), or by

---

135 A/L 331 (emphasis added). On the internal controversy which divided the Afro-Asians at that juncture, see Hoskyns, 270; Urquhart, 488.

136 A/L 332.

137 SCOR, 917 Mtg., 10 Dec. 1960, para. 63.

138 As concerns the convening of Parliament, that was not the exact constitutional

acting against those whom he covered by his authority such as
Mobutu and his A.N.C. In other words, they would have constituted
'enforcement action'.[139] To Hammarskjöld this went far beyond the
mandate as it stood and against the principles of non-intervention and
the non-use of force (as well as that of sovereign equality). He further
considered that even a widening of the mandate to include such
measures would go beyond the legal limitations imposed by the
Charter on the powers of the Security Council[140] (and *a fortiori* of the
General Assembly) as well as the proper political role the U.N. could
usefully perform in such a crisis. This role was not 'to create a stable
government within the framework of the constitution' but rather to
create conditions which would enable the people of the Congo to bring
about such a result.[141]

---

situation. For as was pointed out by Omar Loutfi (U.A.R.), article 69 of the *Loi
Fondamentale* provided for the meeting of the Chambers '*as of right* every year on the first
Monday of March and November, unless they have been convoked earlier by the Chief
of State' (SCOR, 928 Mtg., 1 Feb. 1961, para. 117; 938 Mtg., 17 Feb. 1961, paras.
28–30). This meant that if the U.N. could guarantee the transport and safety of the
parliamentarians they could have met by virtue of the *Loi Fondamentale* itself, without
the U.N. usurping any constitutional powers. As to the transport and protection of the
parliamentarians during the session (which could have met in one of the bases for
example), it would have fallen within the normal function of maintenance of law and
order which would not have required any military initiative. However, this proposal
was never seriously considered. And it is possible that Hammarskjöld could not see
clearly the legalities of the argument; or that he considered that helping the Parliament
to convene through measures falling within the mandate, though by itself it would not
constitute intervention, it would by its 'effects', to the extent that the Lumumbists were
the strongest party in Parliament, but no longer outside it. Indeed, there are even
indications that Hammarskjöld and his associates considered Parliament as such as
one of the internal 'competitive power groups', among which they had to observe strict
neutrality (Cf. Dayal's first progress report, S/4531, 21 Sept. 1960, para. 16).
Moreover, he may have feared that such measures may set the U.N. on the slippery
path of taking more drastic action, ultimately amounting to the 'enforcement of the
Constitution'.

139 SCOR, 920 Mtg., 13 Dec. 1960, para. 73.

140 For a sample of the frequent reminders by the Secretary-General of the limitations imposed by the Charter on the powers of the Council and the Assembly, see
ibid., para. 10; SCOR, 913 Mtg., 7 Dec. 1960, para. 29; 917 Mtg., 10 Dec. 1960, para.
66; 920 Mtg., 13 Dec. 1960, paras. 85, 97.

141 SCOR, 913 Mtg., 7 Dec. 1960, paras. 50–1. Later on, in the General Assembly,
he gave two reasons for the rejection of the proposed measures: 'First, I reject everything that would have a touch of control or direction of the Congo's internal affairs . . .
second, I do not believe that the use of military initiative or pressure is the way to bring
about the political structure, in terms of persons and institutions, which at present is the
first need of the Congo.' He then added: 'The United Nations can help in such a

At the end of the debate, the two draft resolutions failed to obtain the required majority.[142] Immediately after the vote, the Secretary-General remarked that the failure to reach a decision in the Security Council and in the General Assembly revealed 'the present split' among the member states over the policy to be followed by the U.N. in the Congo. He concluded:

Naturally, the operation will be continued under the previous decisions with all energy, within the limits of the law, with an adjustment—to the best of our understanding—of the implementation of our mandate to the needs, and with aims which, in spite of all, I believe remain common, at least, to the vast majority of Member States. However, the outcome here, as it now stands, has not given us the moral or political support of which the operation is in need.[143]

The threat of civil war

Hammarskjöld did however envisage the withdrawal of the U.N. in one contingency, namely that of civil war. Examining the courses of action open to the Force in such an eventuality, he considered that:

a taking of sides would be impermissible under the general rules applied, and a standing aside ... would ... place the United Nations and its Force in an untenable position ... of a passive witness to developments diametrically opposed to those which the Organization wished to further ... [Nor could] the United Nations try to interpose itself [for][p]ractically every act of inter-position in such a situation might lend itself to the interpretation that it was taken in order to help one side or the other.

He therefore concluded that if such a situation materialized, he 'would have to put up to the Security Council the question whether the United Nations Force should not withdraw'. Hammarskjöld considered that such a drastic measure 'would mean the failure of a great effort to keep the cold war in its sharper forms out of Africa, and the failure also to stabilize the situation of the Congo through such means as the Charter makes available to the Organization'.[144] In other

---

direction, but that is by the normal political and diplomatic means of persuasion and advice, not by the use of force or intimidation' (GAOR(XV), 953 Mtg., 17 Dec. 1960, para. 182).

142 The Afro-Asian draft was rejected by 42 votes to 28 with 27 abstentions; the two-power resolution failed to obtain the required two-thirds majority, though receiving 43 favourable votes to 22, with 32 abstentions (GAOR(XV), 958 Mtg., 20 Dec. 1960, paras. 129, 130).

143 Ibid., paras. 132–3.

144 GAOR(XV), 957 Mtg., 19 Dec. 1960, paras. 16–17, 20.

words, it would mean the failure of the preventive-diplomacy effort in the Congo.

This was no mere speculation. By the end of the year, the threat of civil war was looming large over the Congo. Lumumbist forces, having regrouped around the Stanleyville regime, put themselves in a position from which they could extend their control over the areas where they enjoyed wide popular support. Thus, on Christmas day, they took control, without fighting, over Bukavu, the capital of the Kivu province. A counter-attack to recapture Kivu via the Belgian trust territory of Ruanda-Urundi was attempted by Mobutu on New Year's day, but was a complete failure. Then, on 9 January 1961, Stanleyville forces penetrated through Kivu into Northern Katanga and captured Manono, and there were widespread rumours of an offensive to take Coquihatville, the capital of Equateur.

On the international, and more particularly the African, level, a similar process of polarization was also taking place. On 15 December the former French African territories held a meeting in Brazzaville to which several Congolese leaders (but not Lumumba) were invited, in an attempt at mediation. But the 'Brazzaville group' as it came to be known, was basically interested in mediating between 'moderate' Congolese leaders, i.e. Kasavubu and Tshombe, to strengthen them in their effort to eliminate the Lumumbists from the political scene. It requested the U.N. 'to continue to provide the Congo with technical assistance' but cautioned it against seeking 'to supplant the Congolese authorities' (i.e. Kasavubu).[145]

On the other hand, Ceylon, Ghana, Guinea, Libya, Mali, the U.A.R., and the representatives of the G.P.R.A. (the Algerian Provisional Government) meeting in Casablanca from 3 to 7 January 1961, urged the U.N. to adopt a more energetic policy along the lines of the Afro-Asian draft resolution which was submitted in the General Assembly, in order to bring about a return to legality in the Congo. They declared that they would withdraw their contingents from the U.N. Force, and that failing the adoption of their proposed line of action by the U.N., they would feel free to take 'appropriate action', i.e. to offer direct help to the Stanleyville Government.[146]

---

145 Hoskyns, 275–6.
146 For the text of the Conference 'Declaration Concerning the Situation in the Congo', see S/4626, 13 Jan. 1960.

The assassination of Lumumba

The Leopoldville regime was thus subjected to mounting pressures both internally and externally. Moreover, persistent rumours were circulating to the effect that the incoming Kennedy administration would adopt a new Congo policy, closer to the Afro-Asian line and favouring national reconciliation. There were also increasing manifestations of the pro-Lumumba opposition within the areas controlled by the Leopoldville regime. This wave reached even the army. On 13 January a mutiny broke out in the Thysville camp where Lumumba was detained and he was almost liberated by the mutineers.[147]

All these factors determined Kasavubu and Mobutu to take radical measures in order to bar the way to any possibility of setting Lumumba free and his re-entry into the political scene. Thus, on 17 January, he was flown to Katanga together with Okito, the acting President of the Senate, and Mpolo, a Minister in the first Cabinet. On 9 February, a provisional Government headed by Ileo was proclaimed by Kasavubu, to replace the *Collège de Commissaires*. This move was taken, *inter alia*, to bar the way to the U.N. playing a role in the formation of a new Government of national conciliation. On 10 February Munungo, the Minister of Interior of Katanga, declared that Lumumba escaped and, on the 13th, that he had been killed, together with his two companions, by the inhabitants of an unidentified village.[148]

7. THE SECURITY COUNCIL RESOLUTION OF 21 FEBRUARY 1961

As soon as Lumumba's transfer to Katanga became known, both the Casablanca group and Yugoslavia on the one hand, and the Soviet Union on the other, requested the convening of the Security Council.[149] The debate started on 1 February, the Secretary-General being subjected to increasing attacks from the U.S.S.R. and mounting pressures for more vigorous action on the part of Afro-Asian members with the exception of the Brazzaville group. It was during this protracted round of discussions and while the Afro-Asians were negotiating among themselves and with the others—with a view to elaborating a draft resolution which would reflect a generally acceptable new

147 Hoskyns, 303.
148 For the text of Munungo's declaration, see S/4688/Add. 1.
149 S/4641, 26 Jan. 1961 and S/4644, 29 Jan. 1961, respectively. Kasavubu also asked for a meeting to examine the question of an unauthorized landing of a U.A.R. plane in the Congo (S/4639, 24 Jan. 1961).

line of action for the U.N. in the Congo—that the assassination of Lumumba became known on 13 February. This crime aroused world-wide indignation. The Government of the U.S.S.R. issued a statement attributing to the Secretary-General direct responsibility for Lumumba's murder and declaring that it would no longer recognize him as a U.N. official.[150] The reaction of the Afro-Asians, though severely critical of the U.N., did not go so far.

On 15 February the Secretary-General defended his position against the Russian attacks and accusations. He outlined what he considered as the 'essential elements of a constructive policy for the Congo', in the following five points:

First, I have already suggested an international investigation of the circumstances surrounding the assassination of Mr. Lumumba and his colleagues ... Secondly, instructions have already been given to the Force to protect the civilian population against attacks from armed units, whatever the authority under which they are acting ...

Thirdly, instructions have already been given that in case a clash between armed units is threatening, the United Nations should use all means, short of force, to forestall such clashes through negotiations, through the establishment of neutralized zones, through cease-fire arrangements and through similar measures ... But the use of force in support of cease-fire arrangements should not therefore be excluded. Fourthly, on February 1 I proposed (928 Mtg) that the United Nations reactivate its basic attitude on the Armée Nationale Congolaise and take appropriate steps for its reorganization for its normal purposes in the service of the national Government, thus withdrawing all its various factions from their present engagement in the political strife. Fifthly, and lastly, already on 8 October of last year, ... I addressed myself to the Government of Belgium and to Mr. Tshombe, pointing out the necessity to eliminate the Belgian political element in the Congo (S/4557, Part B, sects 1 and 5).[151]

He added that on these five points he had 'already taken action' and that all of them were 'such that no new legal mandate [was] required', but that there was 'definitely ... a need for moral and political support for the Secretary-General'.[152] He was opposed, however, to the other measures proposed by the Afro-Asians—e.g. the control of arms imports and transfer of funds, the convening of Parliament—which he considered as an infringement of the sovereignty of the Congo.

---

150 S/4704, 14 Feb. 1961.

151 SCOR, 935 Mtg., 15 Feb. 1961, paras. 30, 31.

152 Ibid., para. 35. Earlier in the statement, the Secretary-General had requested more bluntly 'an endorsement' for his plan 'that only in part has been forthcoming in the past' (ibid., para. 31).

They were 'of a different nature' from the measures envisaged in his plan.

> They are points on which it is for this Council and only for this Council *to decide what it feels entitled to do* and what it wants to do ... it is for the Security Council to determine the end and to decide on the means, in full awareness of its responsibility for the maintenance of peace and security but also its duty to respect the sovereignty of a Member nation. It cannot shirk its responsibilities by expecting from the Secretariat action on which it is not prepared to take decisions itself.[153]

Also on 15 February, Stevenson, the new U.S. representative, made a declaration indicating the willingness of the new Kennedy administration to adopt a more flexible policy on the Congo. He spoke before Hammarskjöld, but his proposals were quite similar to the former's five-point programme. Thus, both made an important move toward the Afro-Asian position.[154]

On 17 February, after intense negotiations, Ceylon, Liberia, and the U.A.R. (the latter two having become members of the Council from 1 January 1961) submitted a draft resolution which they considered mild enough to be acceptable to the U.S. and strong enough for the U.S.S.R. not to veto it.[155] Until 20 February, however, 'it seemed likely ... that the Americans would press for amendments which if accepted would entail a Russian veto'.[156] But on that date the murder of six prominent Lumumbists in Bakwanga was announced. This led Stevenson to declare his acceptance of the Afro-Asian draft, while presenting the substance of his proposed amendments in the form of interpretations of certain parts of the draft resolution.

The way was thus open for the adoption of the resolution. It was backed by a common front of Afro-Asian states—with the exception of the Brazzaville group—and the Kennedy administration; in the face of which the U.S.S.R. did not exercise its veto, though it abstained, considering the resolution not strong enough and leaving much room for interpretation.[157] The resolution, was adopted in the early hours of 21 February, by 9 votes with 2 abstentions (U.S.S.R. and France); it reads:

153 Ibid., para. 35. In para. 32 he significantly declared: 'The legal advice I have sought and obtained indicates that we have no such right to search for arms imports.'
154 For Stevenson's statement, see SCOR, 934 Mtg., 15 Feb. 1961, paras. 23–64.
155 S/4722.
156 Hoskyns, 332.
157 SCOR, 942 Mtg., 20–1 Feb. 1961, paras. 187–8.

A. *The Security Council,*

Having considered the situation in the Congo,

Having learnt with deep regret the announcement of the killing of the Congolese leaders, Mr. Patrice Lumumba, Mr. Maurice Mpolo and Mr. Joseph Okito,

Deeply concerned at the grave repercussions of these crimes and the danger of wide-spread civil war and bloodshed in the Congo and the threat to international peace and security,

Noting the report of the Secretary-General's Special Representative (S/4691) dated 12 February 1961 bringing to light the development of a serious civil war situation and preparations therefor,

1. *Urges* that the United Nations take immediately all appropriate measures to prevent the occurrence of civil war in the Congo, including arrangements for cease-fires, the halting of all military operations, the prevention of clashes and the use of force, if necessary, in the last resort;

2. *Urges* that measures be taken for the immediate withdrawal and evacuation from the Congo of all Belgian and other foreign military and para military personnel and political advisers not under the United Nations Command, and mercenaries;

3. *Calls* upon all States to take immediate and energetic measures to prevent the departure of such personnel for the Congo from their territories, and for the denial of transit and other facilities to them;

4. *Decides* that an immediate and impartial investigation be held in order to ascertain the circumstances of the death of Mr. Lumumba and his colleagues and that the perpetrators of these crimes be punished;

5. *Reaffirms* the Security Council resolutions of 14 July, 22 July and 9 August 1960 and the General Assembly resolution 1474 (ES–IV) of 20 September 1960 and reminds all States of their obligation under these resolutions.

B. *The Security Council,*

Gravely concerned at the continuing deterioration in the Congo, and the prevalence of conditions which seriously imperil peace and order, and the unity and territorial integrity of the Congo, and threaten international peace and security,

Noting with deep regret and concern the systematic violations of human rights and fundamental freedoms and the general absence of rule of law in the Congo,

Recognizing the imperative necessity of the restoration of parliamentary institutions in the Congo in accordance with the fundamental law of the country, so that the will of the people should be reflected through the freely elected Parliament,

Convinced that the solution of the problem of the Congo lies in the hands of the Congolese people themselves without any interference from outside and that there can be no solution without conciliation,

Convinced further that the imposition of any solution, including the formation of any government not based on genuine conciliation would, far from settling any issues, greatly enhance the dangers of conflict within the Congo and threat to international peace and security,

1. *Urges* the convening of the Parliament and the taking of necessary protective measures in that connexion;

2. *Urges* that Congolese armed units and personnel should be reorganized and brought under discipline and control, and arrangements be made on impartial and equitable bases to that end and with a view to the elimination of any possibility of interference by such units and personnel in the political life of the Congo;

3. *Calls* upon all States to extend their full co-operation and assistance and take such measures as may be necessary on their part, for the implementation of this resolution.[158]

Several important points have to be underlined in relation to this resolution:

(1) Though the resolution did not go as far as the Afro-Asians would have liked, it still went beyond anything that had been adopted by the Council or the Assembly up to that point. Thus, for the first time the Council explicitly characterized the situation in the Congo as a 'threat to international peace and security' and authorized the use of force beyond self-defence in the carrying out of one of the functions of the Force under the mandate, namely the prevention of civil war, though only 'if necessary, in the last resort'.

(2) Another function under the mandate was mentioned for the first time, namely the withdrawal and evacuation of Belgian and other 'foreign military and paramilitary personnel, mercenaries as well as political advisers'. The modalities of carrying out this function were left open and were to cause great difficulties later on.[159]

(3) Other measures that the U.S.S.R. and the Afro-Asians wanted the U.N. to take by authority—the reconvening of Parliament and the reorganization of the A.N.C. with a view to neutralizing its interference in politics—were included in the second part of the resolution. This part, in spite of its language (referring to 'the threat to international peace and security' and using the word 'urges' in its operative paragraphs, as in the first part which was considered peremptory) was generally regarded as referring to desired measures to be sought by the U.N. exclusively by diplomatic (and not forcible) means.

158 S/4741.
159 See *infra*, Chapter IV. In this respect, one of Stevenson's interpretations was that the call to all States, in paragraph 3 of Part A, covered both military personnel and military material. (SCOR, 941 Mtg., 20 Feb. 1961, paras. 91–4).

(4) Finally, and perhaps most significantly, though the resolution confirmed the previous ones, it did not mention the Secretary-General, either to commend his past action or to entrust him with the implementation of the resolution. This was a concession to the U.S.S.R. to induce it not to vote against the resolution. Though several delegations, especially the U.S. and the U.K., expressed their understanding that the only interpretation of the resolution consistent with the Charter required that the Secretary-General should be in charge of its implementation, Hammarskjöld strongly resented the omission. After the vote, he made the following declaration:

I strongly welcome the ... three-Power resolution adopted by the Council (S/4722) as giving a stronger and more clear framework for United Nations action although, as so often before, it does not provide a wider legal basis or new means for implementation.

I note the reaffirmation of previous resolutions which entrusted the Secretary-General with execution of the decisions of the Security Council in the Congo affairs. On that basis I shall urgently avail myself of the valuable assistance of the Advisory Committee. It is from its members, fifteen of whom are from African and Asian countries, that I will seek guidance in the implementation.[160]

The second paragraph clearly asserts, by reference to previous resolutions, the executive functions of the Secretary-General under the resolution just adopted, while putting much more emphasis than before on the role of the Advisory Committee in this respect.

The first paragraph indicates the adoption of a restrictive inter-pretation of the resolution as not providing 'a wider legal basis or new means of implementation'.[161] As already mentioned, although the Secretary-General had moved a long way towards the Afro-Asian position, he was not favourable to a widening of the mandate. His five-point plan was a clear indication of this stand. He had acquiesced in the three-Power resolution and even welcomed it as strengthening his position *vis-à-vis* Congolese authorities and Belgium. But given the ambiguities of the language of the resolution, he hastened to interpret it restrictively, in the sense of his plan. It should be kept in mind that this was the first resolution adopted on the Congo which was not

160 SCOR, 942 Mtg., 20–1 Feb. 1961, paras. 216–17.
161 The restrictive interpretation was reiterated in his appeal for additional troops: 'I do not believe that such additions to troops—or at least their maintenance—will require renegotiations since I understand the reaffirmation of the earlier resolutions as clearly indicating that those additions to troops would be on the same legal basis as previous contributions' (ibid., para. 218).

of his direct inspiration; and he had to integrate it into his own scheme.

The Charter basis of the resolution

At the beginning of the Operation, Hammarskjöld did not provide an explicit analysis of its Charter basis. But his invocation of article 99 implied, in his understanding of this article, a finding by him that the crisis constituted at least 'a threat to peace and security', and as such fell within the ambit of article 39, i.e. of Chapter VII of the Charter.[162] On the other hand, since the Operation was undertaken at the request and with the consent of the territorial State, it was not of the nature of enforcement action; the only alternative left open under Chapter VII was to consider it of the nature of provisional measures under article 40, an interpretation which was explicitly put forward later on by the Secretary-General.[163]

This interpretation was not challenged as such. But the demands of the Socialist and Afro-Asian members (whether made directly to him or presented in form of draft resolutions) after Lumumba's arrest for measures falling within the category of 'enforcement action', and hence under articles 41 and 42, constituted an indirect challenge. Hammarskjöld refuted these demands as going beyond the mandate as it stood and even beyond the Charter limitations on the jurisdiction of the Security Council. However, he did not specifically explain the reason why he considered that the possibility of a resolution based on article 42 should be completely excluded. There is only a hint at a possible reason in one of his statements in the General Assembly:

Under the Charter, such an [military] initiative requires a decision on enforcement measures, when it is a question of international affairs, the minimum, in the case of a national affair, is of course the same, *if you regard the Charter as authorizing such military initiative in the national field at all.*[164]

---

162 See *supra*, p. 11, n. 26.

163 e.g. SCOR, 920 Mtg., 13 Dec. 1960, para. 75. See also the revealing article of Oscar Schachter, Hammarskjöld's principal legal adviser during the Congo crisis (first published under the pseudonym of Miller), 'Legal Aspects of the United Nations Action in the Congo', 55 *AJIL* (1961), especially at 4. It is to be noted, however, that even in a situation falling within the ambit of article 39, the Security Council is free to choose between using its powers under Chapter VI or Chapter VII. But the articles of Chapter VI (unlike article 14 in relation to the General Assembly) do not provide an explicit and readily usable basis for operational activities, albeit of a non-coercive nature, whence the superiority of article 40 in this regard.

164 GAOR(XV), 950 Mtg., 16 Dec. 1960, para. 104 (emphasis added).

In other words, it is probable that in Hammarskjöld's understanding of the Charter, article 42 is not applicable at all in an internal
conflict—i.e. that enforcement measures can be taken only 'against a
state'. This understanding may have been based in turn on the
difficulty, if not the impossibility, of the prior designation in an
internal conflict of an aggressor—in the accepted meaning of the term
in international law—against whom the enforcement measures could
be ordered.[165]

Be that as it may, with the adoption of the Security Council
resolution of 21 February 1961, which explicitly empowered the U.N.
Force to take 'all appropriate measures to prevent the occurrence of
civil war in the Congo, including ... the use of force, if necessary, in
the last resort', the question arose whether this did not alter the
Charter basis of the Operation by bringing article 42 into it. As we
have seen earlier, Hammarskjöld hastened to declare that the new
resolution did 'not provide a wider legal basis'. In this he was supported by several Western delegates, especially by Adlaï Stevenson of
the U.S., who based his argument partly on the qualifying phrase 'in
the last resort'.[166]

This restrictive interpretation, though not formally challenged in
the Council, was not unanimously accepted. For if it were not on the
basis of article 42, on what basis would U.N. troops be authorized to

---

165 Such an inference may be drawn from the formulation of article 50 of the
Charter which starts as follows: 'If preventive or enforcement measures *against any state*
are taken by the Security Council ...' (emphasis added). An indication that this was
Hammarskjöld's understanding can be found in Schachter's article (loc. cit. at 8):
'Certainly, the expectation at San Francisco was that article 42 would be resorted to for
military action of an international character—that is to say, directed against the troops of a
state or another governmental authority which bore responsibility for a breach of peace
or act of aggression' (emphasis added). The same understanding is reflected in the
Advisory Opinion of the I.C.J. on *Certain Expenses of the United Nations (I.C.J.Rep. 1962,
151 at 177)*: '... the operations of ONUC did not include a use of armed force against a
State which the Security Council, under Article 39, determined to have committed an
act of aggression or to have breached the peace'. This understanding of article 42, it is
submitted, is unduly restrictive. First, nowhere in either articles 39, 41, or 42 is it
required that enforcement measures be taken 'against a state'. Second, these measures
can be ordered in any of the cases provided for in article 39, including that of a 'threat to
peace', a case whose existence can be determined by the Security Council without
designation of a guilty party. The measures can also be ordered in a situation (in the
meaning of article 34) with no clearly identified parties, provided the Council considers
it as presenting a 'threat to peace'. Such a situation can be an internal conflict. (Cf. H.
Kelsen, *The Law of the United Nations* (1950), 728–31).

166 SCOR, 941 Mtg., 20 Feb. 1961, para. 83; see also U.K. representative, SCOR,
942 Mtg., 20 Feb. 1961, para. 20.

use force beyond self-defence—albeit in the last resort—to prevent civil war? It is true that the authorization to use force was limited to a specific purpose and subjected to certain conditions. But there is nothing in article 42 that makes it necessary that an authorization to use force under it should be all-embracing, or which prohibits the Security Council from circumscribing such an authorization: *in plus stat minus*. On the other hand, it would be difficult to justify satisfactorily this authorization to use force on another basis in the Charter.

In fact, the general tenor of the resolution indicates the direction of a plausible legal explanation: paragraph 1 *urges* the U.N. to 'take immediately all appropriate measures to prevent the occurrence of civil war in the Congo, including arrangements of cease-fires, the halting of all military operations, the prevention of clashes' before it adds 'and the use of force, if necessary, in the last resort'. The first category of measures are of the nature of provisional measures in the meaning of article 40. Article 40 provides in its last sentence: 'The Security Council shall duly take account of failure to comply with such provisional measures.' In other words, although provisional measures are 'without prejudice to the rights, claims or position of the parties concerned', non-compliance with them may entail the ordering by the Security Council of enforcement measures against the non-complying party, orders which in turn can be limited to the enforcement of the provisional measures. The 'use of force, if necessary, in the last resort' in the resolution of 21 February accords perfectly with this hypothesis.

Hammarskjöld, however, understood the resolution as extending the scope of activities of ONUC to the prevention of civil war, but not its powers in the fulfilment of this function. He thus envisaged a more active role for ONUC in the promotion and supervision of agreed arrangements to that end, such as cease-fires and neutralized zones, as well as in the peaceful (i.e. unopposed) occupation of strategic points, thus extending the scope of its interposition.

But, as he argued in a letter to a number of Heads of African States contributing to the Force, he considered that the resolution did not 'derogate from the position that U.N. troops should not become parties to armed conflict in the Congo' (i.e. from article 2/7 of the Charter):

If United Nations troops engaged in defensive action, when attacked while holding positions occupied to prevent a civil war risk, this would not in my opinion mean that they become a party to a conflict; while the possibility of becoming such a party would be open, were troops to take the initiative in an armed attack on an organized army group in the Congo.[167]

In other words, he limited the possibility of the use of force to situations in which the Force was already interposed, in defence of positions it held under orders—a hypothesis already covered by self-defence—excluding the possibility of interposition once fighting had started, to stop the operations and separate the combatants.

Such an interpretation—which was necessary if the Operation was to remain within the ambit of article 40 (and outside article 42)—does not seem to accord with the language of the resolution, the intention of its drafters, or the gist of the debates in the Security Council which led to it.[168] However, in the final analysis, Hammarskjold's understanding was determinant, as he was in charge of the conduct of the Operation. And to him—one gets the impression—the only contribution of the resolution in this respect was to overcome the objection to interposition in case of civil war—to which he referred in the General Assembly in December 1960, and which led him to envisage the withdrawal of the Force in such an eventuality—namely that such an interposition would inevitably be interpreted as helping one side against the other (and would in fact produce that effect, if only by providing a shield to the weaker party and an obstacle to the progress of the stronger party of the moment). To Hammarskjöld, the resolution merely neutralized the objection to the act of interposition as constituting intervention by its effects.

Paradoxical as it may seem, this very understanding of the resolution (which integrates it in Hammarskjöld's general scheme for the Operation) militates in favour of the thesis that paragraph A1 of the resolution was based on article 42. For how can the principle of non-intervention be neutralized, though only partly and in relation to a specific function, if not on the basis of article 42 which provides, together with article 41 (which is irrelevant to the case at hand), the only exceptions in the Charter to article 2, paragraph 7?

8. THE IMPLEMENTATION OF THE RESOLUTION AND THE SETTLEMENT OF THE CONSTITUTIONAL CRISIS

The manner in which Hammarskjöld sought to bring the different parties to accept the resolution and to co-operate in its implementa-

167 S/4752/Annex VII (24 Feb. 1961). Cf. *supra*, p. 102, n. 161.

168 Much emphasis was put by Western delegates on the 'last resort' character of the authorization to use force, but this does not imply (nor does anything else in the resolution) limiting it to the defence of positions already held.

tion is revelatory of his concept of the role of the U.N. in the crisis, both as to its scope and its limitations.

In Leopoldville the resolution was very badly received. It was misunderstood as allowing ONUC to use force in order to disarm the A.N.C. and to reconvene Parliament. This misunderstanding was due to the ambiguous language of the resolution and the confusion in the minds of the Congolese leaders between the initial demands of the Casablanca group and the resolution itself, confusion which was deliberately fostered by some of their European advisers.[169] Meanwhile, Dayal was in no position to dissipate this misunderstanding owing to the total breakdown of communication between him and Kasavubu, who had formally and repeatedly asked for his recall.[170] The resolution was thus vehemently attacked by Kasavubu, Ileo, and other leaders as infringing Congolese sovereignty and seeking to impose a trusteeship on the Congo; and they declared their determination to resist its implementation by all the means available to them.[171]

Military reactions

On the military level, A.N.C. soldiers were incited against the U.N. which was attributed with the intention of disarming them. Acts of hostility and harassment against U.N. civilian and military personnel multiplied, culminating, on 3 March, in military attacks against U.N. units in the Bakongo area, especially in Banana, Kitona, and the port of Matadi. Most serious was the situation in Matadi, which is the Congo's only outlet to the sea, thus a vital point for the U.N. lines of supply and communications. The U.N. Sudanese detachment there,

169 Though Hammarskjöld did try to explain the import of the resolution, perhaps not sufficiently clearly, in a letter to Kasavubu (S/4752/Annex IV, 27 Feb. 1961). See in general Urquhart, 511; Hoskyns, 338.

170 Hammarskjöld rejected this demand not only by refuting the substance of Kasavubu's allegations against Dayal (of *insouciance et partialité*), but also on the basis of the principle of the non-negotiability of the mandate which covers in addition to its content the organs charged with its implementation (for the correspondence between Kasavubu and Hammarskjöld on this subject, see S/4629, 16 Jan. 1961). However, though the point of principle was formally safeguarded, Hammarskjöld ended up by recalling Dayal to New York for consultations in early March; and he did not go back to the Congo, as a result of Kasavubu's threat of withdrawal of collaboration (see Urquhart, 516–18).

171 For a sample of these reactions see S/4743 (22 Feb. 1961); S/4758 (3 Mar. 1961); S/4761/Annex I (8 Mar. 1961).

under heavy attack and largely outnumbered by the A.N.C., had to agree to evacuate Matadi.[172]

As the Leopoldville authorities refused to let U.N. troops reoccupy their positions in Matadi, the U.N. was faced with the unenviable choice of either acquiescing and thus losing freedom of movement and communication and hence the autonomy of the Operation, or trying to reoccupy the positions by force if necessary. The first alternative was totally unacceptable: not only did it negate one of the basic principles of the Operation, and prevent ONUC from fulfilling its functions properly; but by putting ONUC under the control of one of the internal parties it would have inevitably compromised its neutrality. In such a situation the withdrawal of the Force had to be contemplated in view of the fact that conditions under which it could work no longer obtained. But withdrawal was not a politically acceptable solution either.

The second alternative raised problems of a different order. For as the U.N. troops were already out of Matadi, reoccupying their positions there by force could not, strictly speaking, be considered as an exercise of the right of self-defence. It was argued in the Advisory Committee, however, that the right to reoccupy the U.N. positions in Matadi was a necessary corollary of the right of the troops to defend by force positions they occupy under orders, especially if the positions in question were essential for the freedom of movement and communication of the Force.[173] Indeed, this last ground could be considered in its own right as another exception to the principle of the non-use of force. But here again the Secretary-General opted for the restrictive interpretation, considering that a more liberal one should be formally authorized by the Security Council; which left him only with the possibility of negotiations.

In the protracted exchanges with Kasavubu, Hammarskjöld tried

172 On these incidents, see S/4758 (3 Mar. 1961) and Add. 1–6.

173 This line of reasoning is reminiscent of the one put forward in the debate over the possibility of deploying the United Nations troops in Katanga against the objection and resistance of Tshombe (*supra*, p. 33, n. 37). But there the question was whether the right to use force to defend positions occupied under orders implied the right to use force in order to occupy these positions in the first place. In other words, it involved more drastic action than in the case at hand, which involved the 'reoccupying' of positions previously held and abandoned under military pressure; a reoccupation which could be more easily defended as a kind of 'delayed' self-defence. The new ground for use of force introduced by the resolution of 21 Feb. 1961, i.e. the prevention of civil war, was not helpful in this case, because the Lower Congo region was solidly under the control of Kasavubu and Mobutu and there were no possibilities of clashes between factions in or around Matadi.

to impress on him the legal reasons which made it imperative for U.N. troops to be allowed back in Matadi (and in so doing, he expounded his understanding of the legal basis of the Operation):

The considerations ruling the relationship between the Republic of the Congo and the United Nations . . . should not be seen solely in the light of the request of the Government and what flows from that request. The status, rights and functions of the United Nations are basically determined by the fact that *the action was taken in order to counteract an international threat to peace* . . . [It] is *not merely a contractual relationship* in which the Republic can impose its conditions as host State and thereby determine the circumstances under which the United Nations operates. It is rather *a relationship governed by mandatory decisions of the Security Council.* The consequence of this is that no Government, including the host Government, can by unilateral action determine how measures taken by the Security Council in this context should be carried out.[174]

In other words, since the action was taken in response to a situation provided for in article 39 (the resolution of 21 February explicitly classified the situation in the Congo as a threat to international peace and security), it fell within the scope of Chapter VII; whence its 'mandatory' character which went beyond the subjective and contractual element of the consent of the territorial state. This in turn brought into operation the obligations of member states, including the territorial state, under articles 25 and 49 (specifically mentioned in the Security Council resolution of August 9) 'to accept and carry out decisions of the Security Council and, in particular, to afford mutual assistance in carrying out measures decided by the Council'.[175]

The Secretary-General also hinted at another argument of a more political nature. It was based on the close link between the military and the civilian components of the Operation; if the former had to be withdrawn as a result of continued denial of freedom of movement and communications, the latter would have also to follow suit. The formal reason was that the U.N. civilian personnel could not be left unprotected in the precarious conditions prevailing in the Congo; but the real one was that the Congolese authorities would not be able to cope with the technical responsibilities of government without the U.N. assistance. Thus the continuation of the civilian operation would be used as a lever for the continuation of the military one.[176] The Secretary-General did not push this argument too far, however, lest the leaders of the Leopoldville regime, in their shortsightedness,

174 S/4775/I (8 Mar. 1961).
175 Ibid.
176 Ibid. Cf. SCOR, 887 Mtg., 21 Aug. 1960, para. 6.

should challenge the U.N. to withdraw and invite the Belgians back to fill the vacuum.

In spite of the forcefulness of these arguments and of the frequency of Hammarskjöld's representations, it became clear by the middle of March that this approach was leading nowhere.

Political reactions

On the political front, the reaction to the resolution was even swifter. On 28 February, Ileo, as Prime Minister of the Provisional Government, signed a military pact in Elisabethville with Tshombe and Kalonji, to 'pool their military resources'. On 5 March, a Congolese summit conference was opened in Tananarive, the capital of Madagascar, which consecrated the Katangese thesis by reaching agreement a week later on the creation of a loose 'confederation', headed by Kasavubu, between the 'States' of the former Belgian Congo. The Conference condemned the resolution as a violation both of the principles of the Charter and of the sovereignty of the 'confederation' and reiterated its rejection by 'the president of the confederation and the other authorities of the former Belgian Congo'. In the final communiqué it was stated that cables were addressed to the President of the General Assembly and to the Secretary-General requesting 'the annulment of the Security Council resolution of 21 February, this resolution no longer having any *raison d'être*, since reunion has been achieved between the authorities of the former Belgian Congo'.[177]

After this initial period of high tension, there came a turn to a more co-operative attitude both in New York and in Leopoldville. In the face of the determined resistance of the Congolese and the Belgians to the implementation of the resolution, Hammarskjöld's strongly worded letters and representations did not yield any concrete results.[178] This led him to try a new and more flexible approach by proposing to Kasavubu, in a letter of 16 March, to send a delegation of three African members of the Secretariat (two of whom were recruited especially for that purpose) to discuss with him the best means of giving effect to the resolution. He took as a starting-point a proposal of Kasavubu, made in a letter dating back to 5 March (before the aggravation of the Matadi situation), concerning the reorganization

---

177 Resolution No. 5 concerning relations with the United Nations, in *Congo 1961*, 39, 42.

178 e.g. his letter to Kasavubu (S/4752/Annex IV (27 Feb. 1961)) and his *note verbale* to the Belgian representative (ibid., Annex 1 (22 Feb. 1961)).

of the A.N.C. Hammarskjöld also declared in this letter that he intended to send another emissary, Ambassador Sahbani of Tunisia, to Brussels to discuss the same questions with the Belgian authorities.[179]

Hammarskjöld's proposal was well received in Leopoldville. Several factors contributed to this change of attitude. Dayal had been called to New York for consultations on 10 March and replaced in the interim by Mekki Abbas, the Sudanese Executive Secretary of the Economic Commission for Africa. This eased the relations between ONUC and Kasavubu and made it possible to dissipate the misunderstanding as to the import of the resolution. Moreover, the Leopoldville leaders were having second thoughts about the Tananarive agreement, as it became clear to them that all the concessions were made to Tshombe but none by him. Finally, Kasavubu must have taken into consideration the strengthening of his political position which would result from co-operating with the U.N., as he would be the only official instance with which the Organization had to consult and through which it had to clear and channel all its activities in the Congo.

Agreement with Kasavubu

On 21 March, Robert Gardiner from Ghana and Francis Nwodeki from Nigeria went to Leopoldville as the special emissaries of the Secretary-General and were joined by Mahmoud Khiary from Tunisia who was already with ONUC. Through skilful and patient negotiations—in an atmosphere less hostile to the U.N., but not devoid of suspicion in its regard—they managed to reach an agreement on 17 April with Kasavubu, by which the latter recognized the obligation of the Republic of the Congo 'to carry out the resolution of the Security Council', and the U.N. reaffirmed 'its respect for the sovereignty of the Republic of the Congo in the implementation of the resolution'. As regards the repatriation of foreign personnel, whether civilian or military, a distinction was made: if they were not recruited or recalled under the authority of the President, the U.N. was 'to assist the President ... so that [they] ... be repatriated from the Congo within the shortest possible period of time', i.e. the U.N. was authorized to proceed automatically in their regard. But it was left to the President 'to reexamine the appointments which were made under his authority'. This was coupled with a promise of assistance by the U.N. in recruiting and training technicians to fill the ensuing

179 S/4775/V (16 Mar. 1961).

gaps. As regards the reorganization of the A.N.C., it was simply stated that it was to be carried out 'under the authority of the President ... with United Nations assistance', on the basis of Kasavubu's proposal in his letter of 5 March to the Secretary-General.[180]

In discussing the agreement in the Advisory Committee, an objection was made to the effect that it might be at variance with the compulsory character of the resolution, given the wide measure of discretion left to Kasavubu in determining those foreign personnel to whom the resolution applied. In his letter to Kasavubu of 26 April, signifying his final approval of the agreement, Hammarskjöld tried to eliminate the basis of this objection:

It is worth noting that in striking the balance between your obligations and the intention of the United Nations, nothing has been included in the agreement that could be construed as being at variance with the terms and meaning of the Security Council resolution.[181]

This strong reaffirmation of the principle of non-negotiability of the mandate exemplifies once again Hammarskjöld's style of action, combining a strong formal stand on principle with great flexibility in negotiating modalities of implementation acceptable to the interested parties. And once again this flexibility was made possible through the power of the Secretary-General to interpret the mandate, at least in the first instance.

The settlement of the constitutional crisis

One of the fundamental reasons given by Hammarskjöld in defence of the agreement in the Advisory Committee was that it would help to detach Kasavubu from Tshombe; which proved to be in effect the case. The breach between the two became clear in the second round-table Conference which opened in Coquihatville, the capital of the province of Equateur, on 24 April. There, Tshombe threatened to withdraw unless Kasavubu and the other leaders denounced the agreement with the U.N. and returned to the Tananarive decisions; he ended up by being arrested.[182] At the same time a *rapprochement* was taking place between Leopoldville and Stanleyville, leading to an agreement between their respective representatives on 19 June on the reconvening of Parliament. This was in large part due to the patient

180 S/4807/Annex I.
181 S/4807/Annex II.
182 See Hoskyns, 359.

diplomacy and good offices of Gardiner, Nwodeki, and Khiary. The U.N. undertook to provide the transport facilities and security guarantees to the parliamentarians.[183]

This cleared the way to the Lovanium session of the Parliament which opened on 22 July for the Senate and on 23 July for the Chamber and from which, on 2 August, the new Adoula Government emerged. In a resolution adopted unanimously on that day by the Chamber and the Senate it was declared as 'the legal successor of the first Central Government of the Republic of the Congo'.[184]

Thus, in August 1961, almost a year after it broke out, the Congolese constitutional crisis found its solution. However, both the Central Government and the U.N. found themselves in the same position as in August 1960 in relation to Katanga, except that during that year, the Katanga secession had hardened and the foreign roots on which it fed had grown in a much more diffuse manner, thus becoming more difficult to identify, control, and sever.

9. THE PROCESS OF INTERPRETATION: CONSTITUTIONAL POWER AND RESPONSIBILITY OF THE SECRETARY-GENERAL

Challenging the doctrine of 'tacit approval' by the Security Council

The measures taken by Cordier brought dramatically into the limelight the large margin of discretionary power left to the Secretary-General and his subordinates in the interpretation of the mandate.

Even before the outbreak of the constitutional crisis—during the Security Council debate on the controversy between Hammarskjöld and Lumumba—the delegate of the U.S.S.R. challenged the Secretary-General's submission that his interpretation of the mandate, once discussed in the Council, was deemed to have been approved by it, unless overruled by a new resolution.[185] In the

183 S/4841(20 Jun. 1961). The text of the agreement is reproduced in Annex III; a parallel Protocol of agreement was passed between Tshombe (while still under arrest) and representatives of Leopoldville, for the participation of the Katanga parliamentarians in the Lovanium session (S/4841/Add. 2 (29 Jun. 1961)), but was not honoured by Tshombe once he was released; and this despite the last minute efforts of Khiary (O'Brien, 186).

184 S/4913/Annex III (2 Aug. 1961); Annex II contains the text of a resolution adopted unanimously by the Chamber, thanking the U.N. for the security arrangements. See on the role of the U.N. in general, S/4914 (3 Aug. 1961); S/4923 (13 Aug. 1961).

185 See *supra*, p. 50, n. 75.

meetings of the Security Council following the outbreak of the constitutional crisis, this challenge was reiterated with more vigour; it
was most cogently formulated by the Polish representative:

We express our grave concern over the Secretary-General's contention that
his interpretation, which was used as a basis for action of far-reaching
consequences, was approved by the majority of the Council when in fact there
was no decision of the Council in that respect. Were this practice to be
followed in the future, it could bring us to abrogation of the Council's rights
and therefore to complete departure from the Charter. And this would be a
dangerous path to take, indeed.[186]

Hammarskjöld had come to the Security Council formally 'to
submit the question of the closing of the airports and the closing of the
national radio to the Security Council for its consideration and
instructions'; but in fact he had a plan of action in mind, which if
adopted, would have constituted an indirect ratification of his past
interpretation and implementation of the mandate. However, the
draft resolution based on his plan and submitted by the U.S. was not
adopted by the Council; nor was the draft resolution submitted by the
U.S.S.R. which amounted to a motion of censure of the Secretary-
General.

For Hammarskjöld, the significance of the lack of decision in this
instance was not the same as in the previous round of discussions in
the Council on 21 and 22 August over the controversy between him
and Lumumba. He had then explicitly stated that he was not seeking
a confirmation of his interpretation by the Security Council, while in
the case at hand he did seek such a confirmation, in the wake of highly
controversial acts taken under his authority. There is here a slight
shift from a process of interpretation and elaboration of the mandate
to one approximating the vote of confidence in constitutional law.

This is why, though legally covered, it was politically necessary for
Hammarskjöld to get his proposed plan of action adopted by the other
competent organ, i.e. the General Assembly. This he managed to do,
but with the understanding on the part of the Afro-Asians who
supported him, that the situation resulting from past action—i.e. the
political elimination of Lumumba and the military take-over by
Mobutu—would not be considered by the U.N. as a *fait accompli*;
moreover, the role of the Afro-Asians in reconciling the contenders
was emphasized.[187]

    186 SCOR, 904, 16 Sept. 1960, para. 47. Cf. Kuznetsov (U.S.S.R.), SCOR, 897
Mtg., 10 Sept. 1960, paras. 35–9.
    187 See *supra*, pp. 69–75.

The withdrawal of Russian confidence and the controversy over the office of the Secretary-General

Russian criticism of Hammarskjöld's action escalated with the arrival of Krushchev to attend the fifteenth regular session of the General Assembly, culminating in his speech on 23 September, in which he said:

It is deplorable that the colonialists have been doing their dirty work in the Congo through the Secretary-General of the United nations and his staff...

The Assembly should administer a rebuff to the colonialists and their followers, it should call Mr. Hammarskjöld to order and ensure that he does not misuse the position of the Secretary-General but carries out his functions in strict accordance with the provisions of the United Nations Charter and the decisions of the Security Council.

He then attacked the office of the Secretary-General as such:

Conditions have clearly matured to the point where the post of Secretary-General, who alone directs the staff and alone interprets and executes the decisions of the Security Council and the decisions of the General Assembly, should be abolished.[188]

He suggested instead a 'collective executive organ', composed of a triumvirate, a 'troika', representing the Western, Socialist, and Neutralist countries. In other words, as it became apparent to the U.S.S.R. that once the Security Council adopts a resolution conferring a mandate on the Secretary-General, the veto could not be used to overrule his interpretation and implementation of this mandate, the Soviet Union tried to extend the veto to the level of the Secretariat itself—i.e. from the authorizing to the executing organ—an extension which would have destroyed the independent character of the Secretariat.

For Hammarskjöld this was a question of principle on which depended the future of the Organization and its capacity to play an effective role in world affairs. He was determined to fight the troika proposal with all his power. This is why he was deeply disturbed by certain compromise formulae suggested by some Afro-Asian leaders to meet the troika proposal half-way, such as Nkruma's suggestion for appointing three deputy Secretaries-General and Nehru's idea of a consultative council to advise the Secretary-General.[189]

188 GAOR(XV), 869 Mtg., 23 Sept. 1960, paras. 142–53, 288.
189 Urquhart, 461–2. Nkrumah's suggestion was made in a speech to the U.N. Correspondents Association on 30 Sept. 1960, but was never officially proposed; Nehru's was not made public, as he was persuaded not to follow it up. Cf. Lash, loc. cit. 563.

On 3 October Krushchev resumed his attack on Hammarskjöld, significantly threatening that '[i]f he himself cannot muster the courage to resign in, let us say, a chivalrous way, we shall draw the inevitable conclusions from the situation'.[190] Hammarskjöld's answer came that afternoon; it turned on the question of principle:

I said the other day that I would not wish to continue to serve as Secretary-General one day longer than such continued service was considered to be in the best interests of the Organization. The statement this morning seems to indicate that the Soviet Union finds it impossible to work with the present Secretary-General. This may seem to provide a strong reason why I should resign. However, the Soviet Union has also made it clear that if the present Secretary-General were to resign now, it would not wish to elect a new incumbent but insist on an arrangement which—and this is my firm conviction based on broad experience—would make it impossible to maintain an effective executive. By resigning I would, therefore, at the present difficult and dangerous juncture throw the Organization to the winds. I have no right to do so because I have a responsibility to all those Member States for which the Organization is of decisive importance—a responsibility which over-rides all other considerations.

It is not the Soviet Union or indeed any other big Powers which need the United Nations for their protection. It is all the others. In this sense, the Organization is first of all their Organization and I deeply believe in the wisdom with which they will be able to use it and guide it. I shall remain in my post during the term of office as a servant of the Organization in the interest of all those other nations as long as they wish me to do so.[191]

Since the Suez crisis Hammarskjöld had made it clear that he would resign if the permanent members of the Security Council no longer accepted his understanding of his responsibilities.[192] But in view of the considerations elaborated in his statement, he revised the conditions of his 'standing offer of resignation' to bring the 'General Assembly ... into the picture, too'. Its new formulation, as given by him on a subsequent occasion, was the following:

... if the Secretary-General has lost the support of one of the permanent members of the Security Council, which presumably is one of the conditions for his functioning, and if, moreover, he does not have the support of at least

190 GAOR(XV), 882 Mtg., 3 Oct. 1960, para. 30.
191 GAOR(XV), 883 Mtg., 3 Oct. 1960, paras. 10–11. Cf. SCOR, 955 Mtg., 15 Feb. 1961, paras. 3–14; GAOR(XV), 977 Mtg., 5 Apr. 1961, paras. 39–41; Lash, loc. cit. 565–6.
192 SCOR, 751 Mtg., 31 Oct. 1956, paras. 4–5 (Suez); SCOR, 754 Mtg., 4 Nov. 1956, para. 76 (Hungary). Cf. Lash, loc cit. 565.

two-thirds of the General Assembly, he is no longer in a position to function.[193]

The controversy was not then simply a legal or a procedural one, but as with all constitutional controversies, it was eminently political. It did not turn on a mere question of interpretation of the mandate. It called to mind the institution of 'vote of confidence' and of the 'political responsibility' of executive organs in a parliamentary system of government.[194] But within the U.N. context, it had to be anchored to questions of interpretation of powers, on the basis of controversial acts of omission or commission.

Proposals for 'sharing of responsibilities'

The great weight given by Hammarskjöld to the small Powers, especially the Afro-Asians, as his constituency in the Assembly, made it important to associate them more closely in the decision-making process. This brought about a change in Hammarskjöld's attitude to the problem of sharing of responsibilities. Thus, in response to mounting criticism, and in the face of the inability of the Security Council and the General Assembly to adopt any resolution—after that of 20 September 1960—Hammarskjöld started in his turn to criticize the major organs for not facing up to their responsibility in giving him clearer and more detailed instructions and for failing to assume their fair share in the day-to-day conduct of the Operation.[195] During the Security Council debate after Lumumba's arrest, Hammarskjöld himself asked for a sharing of responsibilities:

I would further invite the Council to consider such arrangements as would mean that Member nations would assume formally their part of the responsibility for the policy pursued from day to day in the Congo ... there are daily decisions, involving interpretations in detail of the extent of our power, which I and my collaborators now have had to take alone for five months. Representatives of the Council or the General Assembly might well shoulder on behalf of the General Assembly or the Council the fair share of

193 Press Conference on the Oxford Lecture, 12 June 1961, reproduced in Foote, op. cit., 349, at 353.

194 In answering a question on 'the standing offer of resignation', he said: 'That represents a *de facto* development ... There is nothing in the Charter indicating that form. You may perhaps say that it is built on a kind of parliamentary theory in the interpretation of the Charter, a parliamentary theory which, however, I have never, so to say, spelled out' (ibid. 352, followed by the quotation in the text).

195 e.g. SCOR, 920 Mtg., 13 Dec. 1960, para. 61; SCOR, 935 Mtg., 15 Feb. 1961, para. 7.

the responsibility of those organs for current interpretations of the mandate.[196]

When the fifteenth session of the General Assembly resumed its work in March 1961, a group of Afro-Asian States submitted a draft resolution on the Congo, which they subsequently revised to include a paragraph 7, along the lines suggested by the Secretary-General, which provided:

The General Assembly
...
7. *Decides* that a standing delegation, appointed by the General Assembly and representing it, which should function in full cooperation with the Special representative of the Secretary-General, be located in the Congo. The delegation should be composed of the representatives of such Member States as have been considered by the General Assembly itself as specially qualified to advise on the United Nations operations in the Congo.[197]

The draft resolution failed, however, to be adopted; and though the question of creating a permanent body was occasionally mentioned in subsequent debates, it was not seriously taken up beyond that point.

It is important before leaving this subject to clarify the Secretary-General's concept of 'sharing of responsibilities'. Before the Security Council he specified that it did not 'mean that the operations of the Secretary-General or his Special Representative should be put under some kind of stultifying control of a parliamentary body', but that it went beyond the formula of the Advisory Committee whose members 'do not carry any formal responsibility for the policy pursued.' However, he did not positively specify the modalities of participation on the part of the proposed representative body in the day-to-day decision-making process; only that it should assume a 'fair share of the responsibility' for the ensuing decisions or interpretations.[198]

What Hammarskjöld really meant by 'sharing of responsibilities' was revealed some time later. Commenting on the concept of neutrality, he remarked that: 'Caesar's wife must not even be suspected. ... any international civil service should be willing to submit itself to all checks and controls which are found constitutionally advisable ...' He then significantly added:

You may remember that I have at various stages during the Congo operation ... invited decisions to the effect that there would be what I called a *sharing of*

196 SCOR, 920 Mtg., 13 Dec. 1960, para. 97. Cf. GAOR(XV), 957 Mtg., 19 Dec. 1960, paras. 21–2.
197 Doc. A/L 331/Rev. 1.
198 SCOR, 920 Mtg., 13 Dec. 1960, para. 97.

responsibilities. You can also say that such a sharing of responsibilities means that people will have the chance to look at the spirit, the way in which decisions are carried out so as to ascertain that there is this neutrality of action to which I referred.[199]

What he envisaged was not an actual sharing in the decision-making process itself, but a closer or continuous system of scrutiny by a parliamentary body of his decisions, actions, or interpretations, which would afford him protection against unjustified criticism.

The 'omission' in the resolution of 21 February

The Afro-Asian draft resolution adopted on 21 February 1961, though widening the mandate, did not refer to the conduct of the Operation by the Secretary-General until then, or to his responsibility in implementing the new resolution. This omission was a necessary concession to the U.S.S.R. in order to avoid its veto. In explaining his abstention, in spite of what he considered as serious defects in the resolution, the U.S.S.R. representative Zorin singled out the fact that 'the resolution gives no concrete instructions to the Secretary-General ... no mandate'; he added: 'This is a positive factor, because it means that confidence in the Secretary-General—at least on the part of those countries which submitted the resolution—is not so great as to warrant the issue of fresh instructions to him.'[200]

But Stevenson expounded a very different understanding:

It is obvious that any Security Council resolution calling for United Nations action must be carried out by the Secretary-General. Under Article 97 of the Charter, he is the Chief administrative officer of the Organization. To the extent that this resolution creates further authority for the United Nations in the Congo or calls for implementation of previous decisions, the Organization's executive officer must be responsible.[201]

In his declaration after the vote, Hammarskjöld reiterated the same interpretation.[202]

Three points stand out in this declaration. The first is that it already constituted an interpretation of the resolution by the Secretary-General, i.e. an exercise of the very power which was contested. The second is that this interpretation was restrictive as to the substance of the resolution, which was considered by the

199 Press Conference of 12 June 1961, in Foote, op. cit. 349 at 352 (emphasis added).
200 SCOR, 942 Mtg., 20 Feb. 1961, para. 196.
201 SCOR, 941 Mtg., 20 Feb. 1961, paras. 79–80. Cf. U.K. representative, SCOR, 942 Mtg., 20 Feb. 1960, para. 23.
202 Ibid., paras. 216–17, quoted *supra*, p. 102.

Secretary-General as not providing 'a wider legal basis or new means of implementation'. And though what he meant by 'new means of implementation' is not very clear on the face of it, it appears from the general context that what he had in mind was not so much the scope of the powers and functions entrusted to the executive organ, as the clear confirmation of the mandate and the expression of confidence in his implementation.[203]

The third point is that although Hammarskjöld's interpretation of the substance of the resolution was restrictive, it was rather liberal as concerns his responsibility for its implementation. But finding himself in a more exposed position as a result of the absence of reference to him in the text, he tried to make up for this weakness by an explicit reference to the Advisory Committee. In other words, he felt he had to associate the Committee *more visibly* in his day-to-day interpretation of the mandate, more particularly of the new resolution.

This does not mean that he had not made real use of the Advisory Committee until then, as some writers deduced from the statement in the Council and other frequent references to the Advisory Committee thereafter.[204] It is true that the Secretary-General had to marshal the widest possible support, and in the first place the unreserved backing of the members of the Advisory Committee, for his interpretation of the resolution as to his responsibility for its implementation. It is also true that he may have consulted the Committee more closely on the draft letters to the different contenders and on his instructions to his subordinates in the field as well as on general questions of policy and strategy. However, all these types of consultation did take place before the adoption of the resolution, though perhaps somewhat less frequently. But what caught the attention of outside observers was the emphasis put by Hammarskjöld from that moment on in his reports and statements on the close association of the Advisory Committee with the implementation of the mandate.[205]

It was also in the meeting of the Advisory Committee held just after the adoption of the resolution of 21 February that Hammarskjöld revealed that in late July and early August he had intended to propose

203 Urquhart, 509, who reproduces a phrase from a letter by Hammarskjöld to Dayal in which he described the resolution as 'noble aims and no new means or legal rights'.

204 e.g. Lash, loc. cit. 564; Lefever, *Uncertain Mandate* (1967), 32.

205 See e.g. the opening paragraphs of the first two reports of the Secretary-General on the implementation of the February resolution, S/4752 (27 Feb. 1961) paras. 1–2, 5, 9; S/4807 (17 May 1961) paras. 1, 3, 4, 7. Cf. GAOR(XV), 980 Mtg., 7 Apr. 1961, para. 84.

to the General Assembly the creation of a separate UNRWA-like body to take over the executive responsibility for the Congo Operation. But subsequent difficulties made it impractical. For 'one does not switch responsibility for administration when every minute is needed for practical work'. He added significantly: 'But the idea has never died in my mind, and I would like to see it put into effect as soon as we get the situation under control.'[206]

This idea, which amounted to a divestment of the Secretary-General of all responsibility in the implementation of the mandate, never materialized, and could not have materialized after attitudes had polarized. But he did bring in a new task force, composed of several new members of the Secretariat, mainly African, such as Gardiner, Nwodeki, and Sahbani, to negotiate the application of the resolution by different Congolese factions and by Belgium. It was yet another step to associate the Afro-Asians *more visibly* with the conduct of the operation, this time not merely on the consultative side but within the executive machinery itself.

The 'vote of confidence'

What dismayed Hammarskjöld most in the absence of any reference to him in the resolution—more than the constitutional question of the responsibility of the Secretary-General for the implementation of the resolution, a question to which there was in fact only one workable answer—was the lack of support, the lack of a vote of confidence in him, i.e. the absence of new means of implementation in the sense explained above. Disappointment, even bitterness, was reflected in his private reactions after the adoption of the resolution. In a letter to Mahmoud Fawzi, the Foreign Minister of the U.A.R., he wrote:

206 Advisory Committee, 23 Mtg., 21 Feb. 1961, paras. 38–41: 'That has proved, in another very delicate field operation, an excellent arrangement. It has the advantage of current advice by people who live with the problem, with an administrative responsibility. It has the further advantage of not putting within the Secretariat tasks which, through their sheer mass, and also due to their quality, tend to swell like a kind of cancer and eat out all other necessary functions. The Congo operation has been and remains such a big burden on the Secretariat, one which encroaches very heavily on other tasks.

Another reason for that kind of arrangement is obviously that decisions of the type which have to be taken should as far as possible be detached from the specific responsibilities which fall on the Secretary-General under the Charter ... A certain division of the formal functions in the political field is wise.'

[I]t is not the beatings which matter now. I feel much more strongly the absence of support from quarters who, of course, know the full story ... Naturally I understand why it was considered wise not to mention the Secretary-General in the U.A.R. sponsored resolution—although I think that it was a great mistake—and, naturally, I understand that Loutfi (and the other sponsors) found it difficult to say anything when Zorin in the debate interpreted this omission as an expression of no confidence. But, it must be sad to have to bow in this way, with fresh memory of your own experiences. For me, your doing so is still something I have to get over.[207]

In another letter to Östen Undén, Sweden's Foreign Minister, he wrote:

Of course, the Soviet line can claim only a weak minority in the General Assembly, but how many abstentions may they squeeze out and how should these abstentions be evaluated? In the case of a quasi 'vote of confidence', I personally regard abstentions as negative votes. And with the special weight I have to give to the votes of the Afro-Asians, I can see the possibility of an outcome in the General Assembly which, under the very terms I explained in the Security Council, should in principle lead me to resign ... Here I have on the one side the howling from the East and on the other side the Western attitude regarding my staying on as the absolutely obvious thing, while the Afro-Asians express their strong hopes that I stay, when they talk in private, prepared, no doubt, in many cases later not to give expression to that attitude in a vote.[208]

The supreme importance of this question in Hammarskjöld's mind is revealed in an episode which took place during the second part of the fifteenth session of the General Assembly which reconvened on 7 March 1961. A draft resolution submitted by a group of Afro-Asian countries requested, *inter alia*, that necessary and effective measures should be taken by the Secretary-General to prevent the introduction into the Congo of military material.[209] On 14 April the Guinean delegate introduced an amendment to this draft resolution, replacing the words 'by the Secretary-General' with 'by all interested authorities'.[210] This move publicly to censure the conduct of the operation by the Secretary-General provided the occasion for 'what was generally regarded as an overwhelming vote of confidence'.[211] For although the Guinean amendment was with-

207 Urquhart, 510.
208 Ibid. 511.
209 A/L 340, 5 Apr. 1961.
210 A/L 348 in GAOR (XV) 982 Mtg., 14 Apr. 1961, para. 48.
211 Hoskyns, 353.
212 GAOR(XV) 985 Mtg., 15 Apr. 1961, para. 78.

drawn before the draft resolution was put to vote, on 15 April,[212] a request was made for a separate vote on the words 'by the Secretary-General' in the draft resolution as it originally stood.[213] The vote was overwhelmingly in favour of their retention: 85 for, 11 against (the Soviet bloc, Guinea, and Cuba) with 5 abstentions (France, Mali, Morocco, Portugal, and Yugoslavia).[214] For Hammarskjöld, this 'vote of confidence' was essential after the omission in the Security Council resolution.

213 Ibid., paras. 176, 204. These were two declarations by the President to the effect that such a request was made, but in neither did he specify the country or countries which made it. It is most probable that the request was made at the instigation of the Secretary-General, who may have considered, as he did on a prior occasion, that once the question of confidence had been raised, 'he could not possibly accept a resolution from which it had been dropped' (Urquhart, 434).

214 GAOR(XV) 985 Mtg., 15 Apr. 1961, paras. 204–5. The whole draft resolution was adopted (as G.A.Res. 1600(XV)) by 60 to 16 with 23 abstentions (ibid., para. 210).

IV

THE ENDING OF THE
KATANGA SECESSION

I. THE PROBLEM OF MILITARY PERSONNEL, POLITICAL ADVISERS, AND MERCENARIES IN KATANGA: DIPLOMATIC EFFORTS

THOUGH the Katanga secession in July 1960 was soon to be overshadowed by the constitutional crisis, the problem of foreign personnel in the Congo in general and in Katanga in particular remained a critical issue throughout the phase of the constitutional crisis. It had replaced Belgian military presence as the major form of foreign intervention in the Congo, and was generally considered as the main cause of the continued Katanga secession.

Several attempts were made in the Security Council and the General Assembly, to put an end to this type of intervention (or 'aid').[1] Finally, part A of the resolution of 21 February provided:

The Security Council
. . .
2. *Urges* that measures be taken for the immediate withdrawal and evacuation from the Congo of all Belgian and other foreign military and para-military personnel and political advisers not under the United Nations Command and mercenaries.
3. *Calls* upon all States to take immediate and energetic measures to prevent the departure of such personnel for the Congo from their territories, and for the denial of transit and other facilities to them.[2]

To obtain compliance the Secretary-General followed his typically two-pronged strategy combining a firm stand on principle—by invoking the mandatory and non-negotiable character of the resolution—with a flexible approach to implementation—by sending special emissaries to negotiate the modalities with Kasavubu and Belgium. This approach led to the agreement of 17 April 1961 with President Kasavubu.[3]

---

1 *Supra*, pp. 71–4, 92–3.
2 For the full text of the resolution, see *supra*, p. 100.
3 *Supra*, p. 111.

Belgian reaction

The attitude of the Belgian Government was evasive: (a) they agreed to recall the few regular Belgian army officers seconded to Katanga; (b) as to the officers of the former *Force Publique*, they considered them as 'contributing to the purposes of the resolution' through 'the reorganization and officering of forces responsible for order and security', but promised to ask the 'Congolese authorities' (meaning Katanga) to relieve them as soon as they could be replaced 'with equal effectiveness, and in agreement with those authorities, by the U.N. Forces'; (c) as to the mercenaries, they were taking measures to stop recruitment and prevent departures, but had no control over those already in the Congo, unless they still had military obligations in Belgium; in which case they would be called up; (d) finally as to political advisers, having been appointed exclusively by the Congolese authorities, it was not in the power of the Belgian Government to withdraw them, nor to intervene in the contractual arrangements between them and Congolese authorities.[4]

Although Spaak, who became Foreign Minister in the new Belgian Government formed on 25 April (and who was severely critical of the former Government's Congo policy) proved more co-operative on the question of political advisers, he still insisted on the prior replacement of any officers recalled. This led to the preparation of the 'Egge Plan' (named after its author, a Norwegian Colonel with ONUC), which consisted of making a survey of all foreign personnel working with the Katanga *gendarmerie* and assessing the necessary replacements and the possibilities of securing them through the U.N. It proposed the withdrawal of 208 Belgian officers and 304 mercenaries of different nationalities, and their replacement by 460 U.N.-recruited officers, over a period of three months.[5]

Katangese reaction

The Katanga leaders reacted violently to the Security Council resolution, by launching a military campaign against the Baluba in North Katanga. On 30 March, the foreign-officered *gendarmerie* overran Manono. When they tried to take over Kabolo a week later, however, the Ethiopian U.N. contingent there succeeded in pushing them back, in the process sinking a barge carrying mercenaries and *gendarmes*, and capturing thirty English-speaking mercenaries whose

4 S/4752/Annex II (27 Feb. 1961).
5 Hoskyns, 394–6.

plane had landed in Kabolo during the attack.[6] The successful defence of Kabolo by U.N. Forces and the expulsion of the captured mercenaries were considered by the Secretary-General as constituting the first full-scale application of paragraphs 1 and 2 of Part A of the Security Council resolution.[7]

A few days later, on 17 April, agreement was reached with President Kasavubu on the implementation of the resolution. This led in turn to the rift between Tshombe and Kasavubu during the Coquihatville Conference convened on 24 April, and to Tshombe's arrest as he was trying to leave town. During Tshombe's detention in May and June, Munongo, the Minister of the Interior (the strongest political personality in Katanga and an extreme secessionist), made some conciliatory statements concerning the application of the resolution. But it soon became apparent that he was playing for time.[8]

The U.N. line of action

It was clear then that the implementation of the resolution 'required a new and firm hand in Katanga'. The choice fell on Conor Cruise O'Brien, an Irish scholar–diplomat, who arrived in Elisabethville on 14 June. During the month of June negotiations, persuasion, and combined pressure from the U.N. and Belgium—an attitude which earned Spaak the criticism of the Belgian press and the open hostility of the Belgian population in Katanga—led to the departure of a handful of advisers.[9] But once Tshombe was back on 24 June (after signing an agreement renouncing secession which he repudiated on his arrival), the Katanga position hardened both as to political reconciliation with Leopoldville and participation in the coming session of Parliament and as to further withdrawals of foreign personnel.

In early July [Urquhart writes], ONUC Headquarters asked the Secretary-General whether, since peaceful and civilized methods seemed to be getting nowhere, it was not time to consider a swift take-over of Katanga by force as being the only means of avoiding another disastrous deterioration throughout the Congo. Hammarskjöld immediately replied that such an extreme departure from approved policy was inconceivable. Instead, he told Linner, ONUC must build up a position of strength to back up its demands for the

6 S/4791, 15 Apr. 1961.
7 Advisory Committee, 43 Mtg., 15 Apr. 1961, 7–12.
8 Urquhart, 551–2; O'Brien, 104–6.
9 Ibid. 126–7; Urquhart, 548, 552.

expulsion of the foreign officers, although this position of strength should not be used in action.[10]

The toughening of the U.N. policy was reflected in the forcible expulsion on 7 July of Georges Thyssens, an obnoxious adviser of Tshombe who was widely considered responsible for the repudiation of Tshombe's agreement with the Central Government; and 'O'Brien announced that such forceful actions would be repeated unless real progress was made in reducing foreign influences.'[11]

Though causing an incident with the Katangese, the Thyssens episode had a salutary effect; it led Tshombe to co-operate with the U.N. in the preparation of a list of European advisers, which included eleven names and was declared to be exhaustive for this category. He also sent some Katanga parliamentarians on 7 August to Leopoldville to participate in the work of the Parliament; stating, however, 'that this was merely "a gesture towards reconciliation" and did not mean that Katanga was altering its position or giving up her rights'.[12]

These developments seemed encouraging. But on the major problem of foreign military personnel with the *gendarmerie* nothing had yet been achieved. It is true that Belgium had accepted the Egge plan. But apart from the fundamental political objection to this plan, i.e. its assumption that the U.N. should help to officer a force whose main purpose was to resist the realization of the U.N. objectives in Katanga, its implementation encountered two major practical obstacles. The first was that Belgium could only promise to withdraw the 208 ex-*Force Publique* officers. As for the 304 mercenaries (according to the very conservative Katangese official estimates)—including the fanatical ex-French officers who had joined the *gendarmerie* after the failure of the Algiers April *putsch*—their respective countries claimed to have no control over them.[13] The second obstacle was that if the U.N. were to act as it should on the assumption of the unity of the Congo, the Central Government had to consent to the plan, a consent which was hardly likely to be given to a scheme which left Katanga's military strength intact.[14]

10 Ibid. Linner was the Swedish former head of the Civilian Operation who became Officer-in-Charge of the whole ONUC after the resignation of Dayal, the post of Special Representative of the Secretary-General having been abolished then.

11 Ibid.

12 Hoskyns, 398–400.

13 Urquhart, 554.

14 O'Brien, 203.

In the meantime, criticism of the conduct of the Operation was mounting among the Afro-Asian representatives in New York. They considered that five months after the adoption of their resolution urging the *immediate* withdrawal and evacuation of *all* foreign military personnel and mercenaries, the scanty results obtained until then fell far short of satisfactory implementation; and it was rumoured that they were planning, together with the Socialist bloc countries, to censure the Secretary-General publicly for this failure during the sixteenth session of the General Assembly which was due to start late in September.[15].

However, the main reason for the Secretary-General to envisage taking more radical action was the preservation of the hard-found unity of the Central Government. Indeed, Gizenga, while accepting the Deputy Premiership, remained in Stanleyville to leave open the possibility of a breakaway if nothing was done in Katanga. Within the Cabinet, Adoula was subjected to increasing pressure from the Lumumbists for action by the A.N.C., an army which 'was in no condition to engage in a military expedition of any kind anywhere'.[16]

It was in these circumstances that Adoula turned to the Secretary-General to ask 'urgently what assistance he could expect from the U.N.' Hammarskjöld asked the Central Government, as a prelude to possible U.N. action against foreign personnel in Katanga, to issue an ordinance for their expulsion and formally to request U.N. assistance in its execution.[17] Ordinance 70/1961 was adopted and transmitted to the U.N. with a formal request for assistance on 24 August 1961.[18]

The day before, two events indicated a hardening in Katanga's position. The first was the recall of the leader of the Katanga parliamentarians in Leopoldville back to Elisabethville. The other was the arrest of Mr. Bintou (the leader of the large community of Kasai Baluba resident in Katanga) in an obvious act of retaliation against Kalonji's renunciation of secession and his joining the Central Government; an indication that the Kasai Baluba would be treated from there on as enemies in Katanga.[19]

---

15 Hoskyns, 401.

16 Urquhart, 554.

17 Ibid. 553–4.

18 S/4940/Annex I (24 Aug. 1961). There are indications that the first drafts of the ordinance and the letter were prepared by the Secretariat.

19 O'Brien, 208–14.

2. OPERATION RUMPUNCH

All the strands were converging to point to the need for urgent and vigorous U.N. action. O'Brien was asked 'to inform Tshombe that under a formal directive from the Secretary-General he was going to proceed to the expulsion of all non Congolese officers and mercenaries ... and ask him to take the necessary action ... failing which the U.N. would be compelled to remove them if necessary by force'.[20] On 26 August O'Brien delivered the message to Tshombe and conveyed to him Adoula's invitation to go to Leopoldville, offering him U.N. transportation and protection. Tshombe's answer came a little later on Radio Katanga which announced that O'Brien 'had "ordered" Tshombe to go to Leopoldville, but that he had stood firm'.[21]

There was no alternative then to U.N. action; and the operation, code-named Rumpunch, started early in the morning of 28 August. It consisted in rounding up European officers and mercenaries in Elisabethville and in the North Katanga centres where there were U.N. garrisons. Simultaneously, certain security precautions were taken by the U.N. in Elisabethville, namely the temporary occupation by U.N. troops of the *gendarmerie* headquarters, the radio station, the post office, and the sealing off of Munongo's villa.

The operation did not meet any resistance. Tshombe was officially informed, and invited to co-operate; an offer which he accepted on condition that the precautionary measures be called off. At noon he broadcasted a statement in which he said that he bowed to the decision of the U.N. 'and had terminated the service of all foreigners in the Katangese armed forces effective that day'.[22]

The legal basis of Rumpunch

Immediately after the adoption of the February resolution, some members of the Advisory Committee suggested that the term 'evacuation' in paragraph A2 should be interpreted to mean forcible removal or expulsion, especially in view of its separate and distinct use from the term 'withdrawal', which meant voluntary repatriation by the State of origin.[23]

But the Secretary-General preferred to stick to a more restrictive

20 Urquhart, 555.
21 O'Brien, 215.
22 S/4940, 14 Sept. 1961, para. 4.
23 Advisory Committee, 24 Mtg., 22 Feb. 1961, 24–6; 28 Mtg., 1 Mar. 1961, 58; 29 Mtg., 2 Mar. 1961, 16–20.

interpretation, proposed by his legal adviser Dr. Schachter: as the resolution did not give the U.N. the power to substitute for the Congo Government, but only specific powers in the performance of specific functions, and as the use of force in the last resort figured only in paragraph A1 (prevention of civil war), but not A2 (withdrawal and evacuation of foreign personnel), the U.N. could resort only to diplomatic means in the implementation of the latter provision. The power to arrest, detain, and expel, being a particular application of the use of force, could be resorted to only in the exercise of those specific functions of ONUC in which a measure of force was authorized.[24]

Even then, it could have been argued that the very *raison d'être* of foreign military personnel *as a class*—namely to defend Katanga against the attempts of the Central Government to reintegrate it within its fold (i.e. to prepare for civil war), and to subdue those parts of Katanga which rejected secession (i.e. to wage civil war within the narrower Katanga context)—placed them squarely within the ambit of paragraph A1.

But here again the Secretary-General opted for a stricter interpretation considering that not all foreign political and military personnel as a class could be forcibly expelled on the basis of paragraph A1, but only those of them who were taken *in flagrante delicto* while perpetrating acts of civil war (or violating agreed arrangements such as cease-fires and neutral zones, or disturbing law and order); though not those merely rumoured or reported in newspapers to be associated with such activities.[25]

Yet on 26 August the Secretary-General expressed a radically different view. Commenting on press reports from Elisabethville attributing to O'Brien the statement that if Tshombe did not go to Leopoldville the U.N. would put its Force at the disposal of the Central Government, Hammarskjöld cabled Linner:

There is no change in our basic principles that we cannot serve as a military arm under the Central Government and for its specific purposes, beyond what is our clear mandate under the resolutions. Thus we cannot 'wage war' on the Katanga forces, while we can, *if necessary by force*, execute paragraph A2 of the resolution . . .[26]

24 Ibid. 63–6.
25 Ibid. The main policy consideration in adopting such a restrictive interpretation was to avoid precipitating a white exodus from Katanga and a collapse of its economy as happened in the rest of the Congo.
26 Urquhart, 555 (emphasis added).

Ordinance 70/1961 was clearly at the basis of this change of position; in the understanding of the Secretariat, it 'gave the U.N. legal rights within the Congo corresponding to the terms of the February resolution',[27] i.e. it authorized the U.N. to proceed within the Congo to the forcible apprehension and expulsion of foreign military personnel without the consent of the Katanga authorities or their countries of origin. Such action was thus considered as an extension of U.N. assistance in the maintenance of law and order and partook of police rather than military action.

However, on that theory it would have sufficed for the Central Government to legislate and to ask the U.N. to assist in applying Congolese law in Katanga and in arresting law-breakers, including secessionist leaders, for ONUC to oblige. But this was precisely what Hammarskjöld had consistently refused to do.

The explanation of these apparently contradictory attitudes lies in the principle of non-intervention as Hammarskjöld understood it. What ONUC could undertake should not only fall within the scope of the functions attributed to it, but should also avoid affecting the balance between the internal contenders. The removal of foreign political and military personnel would obviously affect that balance; but as they constituted themselves an obvious form of foreign intervention, the U.N. could go in its action as far as neutralizing this intervention, but not beyond. This is why U.N. action was presented as being directed against foreign personnel as undesirable individuals, not as an organized force or part of a force, especially not as part of the Katanga *gendarmerie*.

Limitations of Rumpunch

The initial U.N. success proved ephemeral. As a result of strong representations from the Consular corps, O'Brien acceded, during the afternoon of 28 August, to their request to suspend the operation, in exchange for a solemn undertaking from the 'Belgian Consul, who presided over the meetings ... that by arrangement with his colleagues he would undertake the responsibility for ensuring the surrender and repatriation and travel of all personnel required to be evacuated, irrespective of their nationality'.[28]

This concession, decided against the best judgment of the U.N. military Commander, proved to be a costly mistake both on the

27 S/4940, para. 2.
28 Ibid., para. 5.

military and the political levels. Militarily, signs of things going wrong started on 29 August, when the Belgian Consul said that he was overruled by Spaak, and that he could take responsibility only for Belgians and among them only for regular officers, while others could only be 'advised' to leave.[29] The suspension of the operation, followed by this *volte face*, neutralized the surprise effect of the operation for those mercenaries who were not rounded up and gave them time for concealment. Thus, by 9 September, the time-limit set for all foreign military personnel to report to a U.N. unit for evacuation, at least 104 (according to Katangese figures communicated to Colonel Egge) were missing.[30]

Politically, even with these defects, operation Rumpunch was bound to have a salutary impact on the attitude of the Katanga Government, had not the Western press and diplomatic reactions shown that Katangese resistance could expect external support. The staunchest diplomatic support came from Sir Roy Welensky (then Prime Minister of the Federation of Rhodesia and Nyasaland). In a speech to the Salisbury Parliament on 30 August he accused the U.N. of trying to subjugate Katanga and threatened that unless 'sane counsels' prevailed 'the Federation will do what is necessary and legally possible to give support to its friends'.[31] The following day the British Vice-Consul in Elisabethville, who was also representing the Federation, read the text of the speech to Tshombe in the presence of the British Consul, a presence which must have signified to Tshombe the approval of the speech by the U.K. Government.[32] This impression was confirmed by a *démarche* taken on the same day in New York by the British representative to the U.N., Sir Patrick Dean, who 'was instructed ... to ask the Secretary-General about the scope and purpose of the U.N. round-up action, to inquire whether force had been used before other means had been exhausted, and to say, in an ... echo of Radio Katanga, that in the view of Her Majesty's Government the U.N. had no mandate to remove essential foreigners and thereby cause a breakdown in the Katanga administration'.[33] Moreover, the U.K. Government decided to send Lord Lansdown, the Parliamentary Under-Secretary of State for the Foreign Office, to examine the problem *in situ*.[34]

29 O'Brien, 221.
30 S/4940, para. 10.
31 Quoted in Hoskyns, 409.
32 Ibid.; O'Brien, 228–9.
33 Urquhart, 558.
34 Ibid. 575 n.

In the same vein, the Consular corps in Elisabethville—with the notable exception of the American Consul—met O'Brien at their request, on 1 September, 'to inquire what steps the U.N. proposed to take to protect the lives and property of foreigners, both in Elisabethville and elsewhere, who were in grave danger as a result of the U.N.'s precipitate action' and to make it clear that 'they would hold the U.N. responsible ... if anything happened to any of their citizens'.[35]

Once it became clear to the Katangese, through the suspension of the operation and the escape of a number of mercenaries, and through the Western press and diplomatic campaign, that they could still get away with maintaining the secession, their resistance to the U.N. rekindled. By the end of August all signs of co-operation with the U.N. had disappeared and were replaced by hostility in word and action.

3. FIRST ROUND: OPERATION MORTHOR

The process of decision: New York–Leopoldville

Urquhart relates that after a meeting with O'Brien on 4 September, Linner and Khiary gave Hammarskjöld their assessment of the situation which required, in their opinion, urgent reconsideration of plans in view of the following developments:

(a) a large number of foreign officers and mercenaries had escaped arrest and gone into hiding and were believed to be organizing for guerrilla action;

(b) the refugee problem was reaching alarming proportions as a result of intimidation by Munongo's *Sûreté*, and imposing an untenable burden on the U.N.;[36]

(c) Tshombe was falling increasingly under the thumb of Munungo and the French officers, which rendered impossible any further progress by purely political means;

(d) Radio Katanga's inflammatory broadcasts against the U.N. and incitation to inter-tribal hatred were becoming a serious danger;

(e) tensions within the Central Government were mounting and it

---

35 O'Brien, 225–8.

36 S/4940, para. 7: 'The influx of [Kasai] Baluba refugees, who constitute the economically and educationally most advanced part of the African population of Elisabethville, began on 24 August, following the arrest of their spokesman, Mr. Bintu, and a few other leaders. By 9 September the number of refugees had reached 35,000 and created not only a very serious problem for ONUC which had to protect, feed, shelter and care for them, but also a situation likely to lead to a tribal and civil war.' Later estimates were as high as 100,000.

was learnt that the A.N.C. was preparing to launch an attack against Katanga from Stanleyville on 15 September.

On the basis of this assessment, Linner and Khiary proposed a three-stage plan of action:

[1] A campaign should be launched to persuade various governments concerned to stop their consuls in Elisabethville from encouraging Tshombe in his opposition to the U.N. One of the Secretary-General's representatives should make a brief visit to Brussels to explain to Spaak the realities of the situation ... At the same time O'Brien would urge Tshombe to put an end to inflammatory broadcasts and to arrests, terrorism and persecution organized by the Sûreté ... He would give a twenty-four-hour time limit for the expulsion of all foreign officers, after which the U.N. would, if necessary, immediately resume its rounding up operations.

[2] If none of these measures worked—and this was paragraph 9(c) of [the] plan—the U.N. would again take over the radio, arrest trouble makers and those who were inciting violence [i.e. Munongo], and at the same time take steps to prevent the Gendarmerie, the police and the Sûreté from interfering in U.N. actions [in other words, repeat Rumpunch, but more forcefully].

[3] If necessary, O'Brien and Khiary would then visit Tshombe, accompanied by a Commissaire d'État to be appointed by the Central Government, to get Tshombe's approval for Munongo's arrest and the detention of others guilty of crimes against common law. If Tshombe agreed, the U.N. would execute the warrants of arrest; if he did not agree, the Commissaire d'État would order the Katanga provincial government to conform to the laws and would in effect, temporarily take over control of the provincial administrative apparatus. It was Linner's and Khiary's belief that Tshombe would co-operate in the first and less drastic course of action and that he could be prevailed upon to announce his return to legality and to summon the Provincial Assembly, to be attended, for once, by all of its members. [They] explained that only the inevitable alternative, which was an invasion of Katanga by the A.N.C. and civil war had led them to make such drastic proposals.[37]

Hammarskjöld decided on 6 September to consult with the representatives of a number of governments (U.S., U.K., Belgium, Canada, Sweden, U.A.R., Tunisia, and Nigeria).

He concluded that most of the Governments concerned [including the U.K.] would now be prepared to assist in putting all possible pressure on Tshombe to negotiate and that they now also realized that more drastic

37 Urquhart, 559–60 (letters and numbers added).

measures could be expected if these efforts did not quickly produce the desired effect.[38]

On 7 September 'Hammarskjöld summarized his view of the U.N. position for Linner's guidance.' There were two courses of action open to the U.N.:

The first was to preserve Tshombe's legal status as provincial president and to persuade him to negotiate with Leopoldville on a new constitutional arrangement. The second was for the U.N. to take drastic measures that could lead to its exercising control in Katanga in a way contrary to the principles on which the whole Congo operation had been conducted.

In Hammarskjöld's view, the second course 'would have to be considered' only if and when two conditions obtained: (1) that a final diplomatic effort to bring Tshombe to negotiate with the Central Government was made, and failed to achieve that result; (2) that the radical course 'really seemed to be the sole alternative to civil war or to the collapse of the Adoula Government'.[39] The materialization of these two conditions was to a large extent a matter of judgment both as to substance and as to timing.

However, immediately thereafter (it must have been on 7 or 8 September) Hammarskjöld felt the necessity, according to Urquhart, 'to formulate the legal position of ONUC as he saw it' in order 'to clear his mind, and, for the guidance of Linner and O'Brien'. Urquhart's summary of this formulation is as follows:

1. The mandate of the U.N. for the protection of law and order authorized it to deploy troops to protect civilians when they were threatened by tribal war or violence.
2. Paragraph A1 of the Security Council's resolution of February 21 also authorized preventive action by the U.N. to deal with incitement to or preparation of civil war.
3. The right of U.N. troops to use force in self-defence covered attempts to overrun or displace U.N. positions. It also covered attempts to injure or abduct U.N. personnel.
4. The act of self-defence against attack could include the disarming and, if necessary, the detention of those preparing to attack U.N. troops.
5. Incitement to or preparation for violence, including troop movements and confirmed reports of an impending attack, would warrant protective action by U.N. troops, but criticism of the U.N., however pungently expressed, or peaceful demonstrations against the U.N., could not be held to justify protective action.

38 Ibid.
39 Ibid.

6. The maintenance of law and order or the prevention of civil war might justify, in certain circumstances, the closing of radio stations and airports if it was clear they were being used to foment civil war or for other unlawful purposes. The legal basis for taking such measures would be strengthened when the competent authorities of the Central or the provincial government had requested or approved such measures.

7. Arrest or detention of civil leaders was only justifiable if they were engaged in overt military action or were caught *in flagrante delicto* inciting violence. Without such justifying circumstances, the detention of political leaders would run a serious risk of violating the ban on intervention in domestic political conflicts.

8. Political leaders could be arrested by the U.N. if the U.N. was requested to do so by *both* the Central Government *and* the provincial authorities. However, it was doubtful if a warrant of arrest issued against a provincial leader by the Central Government alone was sufficient basis for the U.N. to carry out such an arrest, even if the arrest was requested by the Commissaire d'État appointed by the Central Government.

9. The appointment of a Commissaire d'État could not change the legal situation of the U.N. in conflicts between the Central Government and a provincial government, nor did it remove the obligation of the U.N. to abstain from interference in constitutional conflicts.[40]

This formulation obviously did not accommodate the radical course of action envisaged above, and it is difficult—even impossible—to include them both in a consistent set of instructions; it is not clear whether this impression of inconsistency reflects the policy itself or is due to gaps in our knowledge of what actually was decided; unless the latter formulation was considered as the guiding line, pending the elaboration of a new and more radical one along the Linner–Khiary plan. Some indications to this effect do exist. Before going to Brussels on 8 September (to inform Spaak of the real situation in Katanga) Linner had asked Hammarskjöld for authority to apply phase 2 (paragraph 9(c), the plan for more drastic action) immediately after his return from Brussels on 10 September, but in a subsequent message he suggested postponement to a later date. On 9 September Hammarskjöld cabled Khiary, who was in charge in Leopoldville during Linner's absence, 'that he had still not seen the detailed instructions for O'Brien that Khiary was formulating', and that 'with quick changes of constellations and pending your elaboration of instructions, further authority for specific action could not be given ... Although force could be used in self-defense, "very much ground may be lost psychologically at the first shot from our side, if we can be accused of acting *prematurely or in a provocative way*".'[41]

Khiary confirmed to Hammarskjöld [on 10 September] that the instructions he would give O'Brien would coincide with the Secretary-General's modifications to the plan put forward some days before by himself and Linner, namely to take over Radio Katanga if necessary and at the same time to ensure that the Gendarmerie, Sûreté, police and mercenary-led groups could not oppose the U.N.'s action or disrupt public order.

Though Urquhart does not reproduce Hammarskjöld's modifications to the Linner–Khiary plan, he does comment: 'This was, in fact, a considerable distortion of Hammarskjöld's comments on Linner's and Khiary's proposals. What he had said was that much would depend on how the plan was implemented and that the U.N. should avoid antagonizing the Gendarmerie and should, if possible, win them over to its side.' Urquhart continues: 'Khiary assured Hammarskjöld that the instructions to O'Brien were to be acted on "*avec toutefois réserve d'application après entente avec vous à Léo[poldville]*"',[42] a reference to the Secretary-General's impending visit to Leopoldville scheduled for 13 September at the invitation of Adoula which he had just received and accepted.[43]

In the meantime in Leopoldville pressure was mounting to continue to its ultimate conclusion the process begun with Operation Rumpunch. The two Chambers of Parliament met in a joint closed session on 7 and 8 September, and decided to arrest members of the Katanga provincial government (for which purpose warrants were duly issued); to send a Commissaire d'État to take over the administration and to disarm the *gendarmerie*, and to request U.N. assistance in executing these decisions; a pattern reminiscent of Ordinance 70. These decisions, though secret, reached Tshombe through the Katanga parliamentarians who had in the meantime returned to Leopoldville. As a result of this leak and of the arrival of U.N. reinforcements, tension mounted sharply in Elisabethville on 9 September. The following day O'Brien's deputy was arrested on the order of a Belgian *Sûreté* officer. After securing his release, O'Brien requested the expulsion within 48 hours of all non-Congolese *Sûreté* officers, who were largely responsible for threats and attacks against

41 Ibid. (emphasis added).
42 Ibid. 563–4.
43 S/4937 (10 Sept. 1961). Hammarskjöld had in fact asked to be invited, in order to try to deal with the situation on the spot.

U.N. personnel and installations and for the reign of terror which was the cause of the enormous refugee problem.[44]

According to Urquhart, 'Hammarskjöld strongly endorsed this demand, apparently believing that if the first steps of the plan were taken firmly, it would be unnecessary to proceed with the later and more drastic ones.' Urquhart also reveals that on that day, 10 September, Hammarskjöld did authorize Linner 'to go ahead with the plan they had discussed'; but he adds that 'Hammarskjöld certainly had no idea that any major and drastic action might be taken before he himself arrived in Leopoldville', and that although the authorization 'omitted any precise guidance on timing ... it specifically referred to Khiary's message saying that no action would be taken before consulting with the Secretary-General in Leopoldville'.[45]

The process of decision: Leopoldville–Elisabethville

It is clear that a substantive breakdown of communication occurred in the flow of instructions between New York and Leopoldville on the one hand, and Leopoldville and Elisabethville on the other. For on 11 September Khiary and Fabry (Linner's legal adviser) went to Leopoldville. According to O'Brien, that afternoon they handed him warrants of arrest (*mandats d'amener*) issued by the head of the Paraquet of Leopoldville for Tshombe, Munongo, Kimba (Foreign Minister), Kibwe (Vice-president and Minister of Finance), and Mutaka (Speaker of the House). He was instructed to arrest the last four.

As regards Tshombe [O'Brien writes], we were to arrest him only in the last resort. His residence was to be cut off, the entries and exits to be sealed, and then I was to parley with him, making it clear that his only hope lay in cooperating with the United Nations, and in peacefully liquidating the secession of Katanga. Meanwhile U.N. forces were to secure the post office and the radio studios and transmitters and to raid the offices of the Sûreté and Ministry of Information and remove the files. Europeans and senior African personnel working in these departments were to be apprehended if possible. The flag of the Republic of the Congo should be run up at the earliest appropriate moment on public buildings and on U.N. buildings ... The Central Government would send down a Commissaire d'État to take over authority, in cooperation with Tshombe if possible, in cooperation with the United Nations in any case ... Great care should be taken to avoid a clash with the gendarmerie ...[46]

44 O'Brien, 244–5; Hoskyns, 414; S/4940, para. 11.
45 Urquhart, 564.
46 O'Brien, 247–9.

As for the timing of the operation, Khiary said that it should be carried out either before 3 p.m. on Wednesday 13 September, the expected time of Hammarskjöld's arrival at Leopoldville, or after his departure from the Congo, in order to avoid embarrassing him during his stay, though he had authorized the operation. O'Brien argued that since Tshombe knew through the Katanga parliamentarians what was being planned, the sooner the action took place the better; and it was so decided.[47]

This plan was to be executed if a final effort at negotiating with Tshombe did not prove fruitful.

[O]n 12 September, U.N. representatives Khiary and O'Brien met with Mr. Tshombe and members of his government in an attempt to obtain a lessening of the tension, a withdrawal or at least reduction of the military elements from the streets of Elisabethville, an end to the inflammatory propaganda, redress of refugee grievances which would permit their return to their homes, and assurance that the evacuation of all personnel falling under Part A, paragraph 2, of the Security Council resolution of 21 February would proceed promptly. U.N. representatives also attempted to persuade the Katanga government to reconcile their political differences with the Central Government by constitutional means and gave assurances concerning Mr. Tshombe's safety if he wished to travel to Leopoldville for discussions. On all these points the answer of the Katangese government was a negative one; they refused emphatically to permit the evacuation of the foreign officers serving in the Katangese Sûreté.[48]

These requests sound like the prelude to phase 2 of the Linner–Khiary plan. As Tshombe rejected them, the operation was to be put into action—under the code-name Morthor, the Hindi word for 'smash'—at 4 a.m. on Wednesday 13 September. Khiary's last words to O'Brien, as he left Elisabethville in the afternoon of 12 September, were 'surtout pas de demi mesures'.[49]

Operation Morthor

Morthor was largely a replay of Rumpunch. It was intended to be an equally rapid and surgical military operation, based on the

47 Ibid. 251.

48 S/4940, para. 14. The report also describes the intensive deployment of heavily armed *gendarmerie* and police forces, reinforced by 300 members of Munongo's tribe in Elisabethville (para. 12). It also refers to the announcement of Kimba (Katanga's Foreign Minister') on 12 September, 'that negotiations had opened for reinforcing Katangese units with personnel and equipment from Rhodesia' (para. 12).

49 O'Brien, 246.

assumption that Tshombe, whose house would be sealed off by the U.N., would co-operate once he realized that the bases of his power were irreparably undermined; he would agree to make a broadcast declaring his acceptance of U.N. measures, renouncing secession, and inviting the *gendarmerie* to co-operate with the U.N. The African members of the *gendarmerie* would certainly follow his order, thus leaving the white mercenaries and settlers without an African screen or any semblance of legality if they decided to carry on the fight.

But events did not follow this scenario.

In the first place, the military operation did not proceed in the swift bloodless fashion that characterized Rumpunch, whether because of incompetence, lack of co-ordination between the two main contingents in Elisabethville (the Indians and the Swedes), or both. The power of the adversary was grossly underestimated. Moreover, as the operation was carried along the same lines as Rumpunch, the white officers, volunteers, and mercenaries knew exactly what to expect and prepared for it: target public buildings were heavily guarded; African soldiers were ready to fight, having been convinced that U.N. forces were out to disarm them; white volunteers and mercenaries dispersed themselves among the white population, built up arm caches in private apartments, and prepared themselves for sniping and guerrilla operations. The result was that as U.N. forces were deploying they met with heavy resistance, and serious battles (causing a number of deaths and casualties) had to be fought, especially at the post office—where heavy fighting was triggered by a sniper shooting an Indian soldier from the building where the Belgian consulate was located—and at the radio station. Although the target buildings were secured within the two hours estimated by Brigadier Raja (the Katanga U.N. military Commander), this was achieved at the expense of much bloodshed and negative propaganda in the international media. Moreover, sniping and sporadic fighting continued.

This was serious enough; but what doomed the operation irreparably was the failure of U.N. troops to seal off Tshombe's residence, thus letting him slip out of U.N. control. For the whole operation was based on the assumption that Tshombe's acquiescence was essential for the legality and political acceptability of U.N. action and consequently for the success of the operation; it would give a consensual basis to the main U.N. objective which it was not supposed, according to Hammarskjöld, to achieve by force, namely the ending of Katanga secession. Militarily, Tshombe's consent was also essential in order to deprive foreign volunteers and mercenaries

of any semblance of legality, thus leaving the U.N. forces free to deal
with them as outlaws.

According to O'Brien, Tshombe phoned him twice at 4.30 and 4.45
a.m.; he agreed to co-operate, to order his troops to cease fire, and to
declare on the radio the end of the Katanga secession in exchange for a
U.N. guarantee of his personal security; O'Brien also assured him
that he would retain his post as provincial president of Katanga. But
after that all contact with him was lost. They had arranged a meeting,
but by the time a U.N. escort was sent to accompany him to O'Brien's
residence, he had left. It transpired later on that he went first to the
British Consul's residence, where he spent an hour, before leaving for
the Rhodesian border. The U.N. force also failed to apprehend
Munongo. The only minister they managed to arrest was Kibwe. All
the same, at 8 a.m. O'Brien held a press conference in which he
declared that the U.N. operation was based on paragraph A1, that its
purpose was to prevent civil war, and that the secession of Katanga
was at an end.[50]

Hammarskjöld's decision

Hammarskjöld first heard of the fighting during a stop-over in
Accra. By the time he reached Leopoldville at 3 p.m. (13 September),
it had become clear, in Urquhart's words,

that what was supposed to have been a brief, limited, and non violent
operation, repeating the tactics of August 28, had developed into a sporadic
battle in and around Elisabethville between the U.N. forces and the
mercenary-led Katangese Gendarmerie, and that the hope of a quick end to
the fighting had vanished with the disappearance of Tshombe and the unexpectedly heavy Katangese opposition to the U.N. troops.

Urquhart adds: 'To his insistent questions as to why the operation
had gone ahead before he had been consulted, Linner replied that the
situation in Elisabethville had evidently made immediate action
necessary.'[51] Hammarskjöld had to decide on two urgent questions:
what line to follow in presenting and defending on the diplomatic level
the action already taken, and consequently what instructions to send
to O'Brien for the conduct of the operation on the terrain.

On the first point the line was set in the report—formally from
Linner to Hammarskjöld—which was prepared in the early hours of
14 September. After describing the built-up of tension and hostile acts

50 Ibid. 253–6.
51 Urquhart, 571.

on the part of the Katangese until the 13th, it describes the events as follows:

In the early hours of 13 September, the U.N. Force therefore took security precautions similar to those applied on 28 August, and deemed necessary to prevent inflammatory broadcasts or other threats to the maintenance of law and order, while the U.N. resumed carrying out its task of apprehending and evacuating foreign military and para-military personnel. At this point an alert was set since arson was discovered at the ONUC garage. As the U.N. troops were proceeding towards the garage premises, fire was opened on them from the building where a number of foreign officers are known to be staying. U.N. troops were subsequently resisted and fired at as they were deploying towards key points or while they were guarding installations in the city. U.N. troops returned fire.[52]

This paragraph clearly bases the operation on paragraph A2 of the Security Council resolution (the text given as a starting-point of the report), not on paragraph A1; it presents it as a continuation of Rumpunch having as sole objective the removal of the remaining foreign military personnel. It does not refer to the attempted arrest of Katangese leaders, which obviously goes beyond this objective.[53] The last paragraph did mention that:

In the afternoon of 13 September, the Central Government of the Republic of the Congo dispatched to Elisabethville a delegation headed by the Commissaire d'État for Katanga, Mr. E. D. Bocheley, to assist the provincial authorities in the restoration of law and order. The U.N. dispatched a team of technical experts to help in the restoration of essential utilities and public services.[54]

But it did not mention that they travelled on the same U.N. plane. This was less than a candid representation of what had taken place.[55] Whether the report reflected 'what he understood to be the

52 S/4940, para. 15.

53 The penultimate paragraph (19) of the report euphemistically states, however, that 'Mr. Kibwe is reported to be in an ONUC camp.'

54 Ibid., para. 20.

55 This was particularly the case in connection with the attempted arrest of ministers. O'Brien's dispatches to Linner had made clear, before the report was written, the military objectives they tried to secure in Elisabethville. But these objectives were consistent both with an attempt to end the Katanga secession as with a more vigorous version of Rumpunch.

O'Brien cites as evidence of an attempt to cover up what had happened, the presentation of the origin of the shooting as sniping at U.N. troops from the building of the Belgian consulate (where officers and mercenaries awaiting repatriation were

objective of the operation',[56] or what he considered the objective of the operation *should have been* according to his understanding of the situation and of the mandate, Hammarskjöld's representation had as its purpose to rectify the aim and put the operation firmly back on what he considered the right track.

The instructions finally sent to O'Brien were consistent with this line. In spite of strong prodding from Khiary, Fabry, and General McKeown to allow O'Brien to follow a more active line, Hammarskjöld insisted that U.N. troops should abstain from any new initiative and use force only in self-defence (which amounted in fact to their observing a cease-fire); O'Brien should try by all possible means to contact Tshombe and arrange for a cease-fire and to press on him the necessity of composing his differences with the Central Government. O'Brien was also asked not to take any initiative without prior authorization and to abstain from making statements.[57]

Analysis of Hammarskjöld's decision

What led Hammarskjöld to choose this course of action? To answer this question several points have to be examined.

(1) Hammarskjöld's *instructions* to his subordinates in the field were complex and rather muddled.[58] The formulation of principles he prepared for their guidance stuck to his prior interpretation of the functions and the governing principles of the operation, while his assessment of the Linner–Khiary plan gave the impression that more drastic action was not ruled out as a matter of principle, but was

---

lodged and others had taken refuge) while they were heading to the U.N. garage in which arson had been discovered. O'Brien denies having reported the arson in the U.N. garage which was presented in the report as being at the origin of the shooting (O'Brien, 264–5). Urquhart affirms, however, that there had been several reports of burning of U.N. vehicles (Urquhart, 573–4 n). In any case, the report did not need to invent such an incident to justify U.N. troops' action. For if in the process of executing one of ONUC's functions under the mandate they were fired upon, they were perfectly in their legal right to return fire in self-defence.

56 Ibid. 571.

57 O'Brien, 266; Gavshon, 136–7.

58 In their complexity and ambiguities in the face of a highly dynamic situation, these instructions bring to mind Hammarskjöld's 'irresponsible remark' to Cordier at the eve of the constitutional crisis (quoted *supra*, p. 62); as does Operation Morthor Cordier's decisions, in that the people in the field may have wanted to present Hammarskjöld on his arrival with a successful solution to a major problem, even if it meant stretching his instructions somewhat.

contingent on several factors which required in varying degrees to be subjectively assessed.

a) One major factor was time. Not only was the diplomatic method to be exhausted, *but it had to be seen to have been exhausted*, before more drastic action could be taken ('very much ground may be lost . . . if we can be accused of acting *prematurely or in a provocative way*').

b) Another factor was precisely the manner in which the action would be carried out. Legally any action which is backed by the possibility of the use of military force in case of resistance constitutes a use of force, even if force is not actually used (e.g. unopposed military occupation or maritime 'pacific' blockade). Thus, the legal nature of the action does not depend on the actual use of force, but on the means deployed in its execution. However, for Hammarskjöld, the attainment of objectives in a bloodless manner, even if it could be legally classified as use of force, was of the utmost importance. For this would signify non-opposition which could in turn be interpreted as acquiescence or acceptance. Moreover, it would have necessarily meant the swift success of the operation; and successful operations are normally less controversial than unsuccessful ones.

c) A third and related factor was that although a whole series of acts by U.N. troops did imply the use of force, they were not equally controversial.

Those acts that could be classified, even with some stretching of the interpretation, under the functions of maintenance of law and order (including the arrest of high officials taken *in flagrante delicto*), prevention of civil war (including serious preparation or incitement), and the expulsion of foreign military personnel, as well as precautionary measures ancillary to them (especially to the last, e.g. neutralization of the radio station, the *Sûreté*, and the *gendarmerie*, though in the case of the *gendarmerie*, great care was to be taken to avoid a clash with the African personnel), could be undertaken within the mandate as it stood. But acts that went beyond the foregoing functions, such as the arrest of provincial ministers or assistance in the re-establishment of the Central Government authority in the province, against the will of the provincial authorities, came close to intervention in internal affairs and were not to be undertaken except (and this was the import of Hammarskjöld's comments on the Linner–Khiary plan) in the last resort, and only as a necessary evil to avoid civil war or the collapse of the Adoula Government.

d) A fourth factor, not explicitly mentioned but doubtless assumed all along by Hammarskjöld (especially on the part of his direct collaborators who were supposed to be finely attuned to his style and way of thinking), was that whatever would be undertaken by ONUC would be properly related to, and explained in terms of, the mandate as interpreted by him up to that point.

(2) Urquhart affirms that the Secretary-General *had not authorized Operation Morthor* nor had he heard of it beforehand.[59] While this is true in the sense that he did not specifically approve the timing or the particular action which was taken, he had already given his sanction to the Linner–Khiary plan. But this was a three-stage contingency plan; and it is clear now that although there was a common understanding between Hammarskjöld and his collaborators in the field on it as a general framework for action, no such understanding existed as to priorities and pace of application. Hammarskjöld's main objective at the moment of his departure for the Congo was to get Tshombe and Adoula together,[60] but to the people in the field, especially to O'Brien, 'the last resort was almost at hand'.[61]

Thus while Hammarskjöld was still thinking in terms of phase 1, and wanted to move patiently one step at a time, demonstrating at each stage that the U.N. was doing its utmost to achieve its objectives through negotiations and diplomacy, his representatives in the field telescoped the three phases in Operation Morthor.

(3) Even then, Operation Morthor could still have been integrated into Hammarskjöld's general scheme. For phase 2 of the Linner–Khiary plan was no more than a replay of Rumpunch. It is true that it envisaged putting Munungo (and other trouble-makers) under guard, but this had been done during Rumpunch; moreover, Munungo had been publicly inciting the soldiers and the people to attack U.N. personnel and to inter-tribal and civil war, which provided another ground for taking measures against him.

The integration of phase 3 in the Secretary-General's scheme was more problematic; but it was still possible, though with greater difficulty and in a rather legalistic manner. Once phase 2 was successfully carried out, Tshombe would be faced with two alternatives: either to co-operate with the U.N. and the Central Government in order to save what he could, realizing that the balance of power had radically moved to his detriment, or to withhold co-operation. In this case, by effectively rounding up foreign military personnel,

59 Urquhart, 567, 573.
60 Ibid. 565.
61 O'Brien, 243. This describes his evaluation of the situation on 5 September.

neutralizing the radio-station, the *gendarmerie*, and the *Sûreté* head-quarters, and by putting dangerous ministers under guard, the U.N. would have paralysed the secessionist machine; it would have done so in the implementation of its specific functions under the mandate, especially the rounding up of foreign personnel, and not on behalf of the Central Government; but the ensuing paralysis would enable the Central Government to re-establish its authority over Katanga, calling on the U.N. to assist in the maintenance of law and order as it did elsewhere in the Congo.

(4) What then was Hammarskjöld's difficulty in accepting his subordinates' action? Apart from the bad preparation and the laxness in execution, which is a question of performance and results to be discussed later, it was basically a question of *legal justification*. To Hammarskjöld, if such action was to be taken at all, it could be justified within the mandate only on the basis of paragraph A2 of the February resolution, and its objective could only be to complete the rounding up of foreign personnel. Even if it resulted in the collapse of the secession, the operation was not directed against Katanga or its *gendarmerie* as such or undertaken on behalf of the Central Government or in collaboration with it.

This was a far cry from basing the action on paragraph A1 and the decisions of the Congolese Parliament. It would have gone beyond any reasonable interpretation of 'prevention of civil war' to consider that in order to prevent a probable attack by the A.N.C., the U.N. should subdue Katanga and hand it over to the Central Government. And while a serious threat of civil war or of the collapse of the Adoula Government were given as circumstances justifying *as a matter of policy* more radical action by the U.N., they did not constitute in themselves the legal basis of this action, which could only be found in the mandate.

The same applied to the execution of the warrants of arrest issued by the authorities of Leopoldville. Here it was no longer a question of instruments of municipal law enabling ONUC to execute its international mandate (as was the case of Ordinance 70 in relation to Rumpunch), but rather of ONUC acting as an executive agency of the Central Government, and the action directed not against a form of foreign intervention (again as in Rumpunch), but against an internal contender.

Thus, though the material components of Morthor could have been integrated, perhaps with some stretching, into Hammarskjöld's patiently built design for the mandate, it was basically the justification given by O'Brien that he could not accept. He did, however, try to integrate O'Brien's declarations within his scheme, by presenting them as statements of fact and not of purpose or of legal basis of U.N. action. Thus the reference to civil war was not one to paragraph A1 nor to the threat of an A.N.C. attack, but to the on-going inter-tribal strife within Katanga resulting from intimidation and molestation of the Baluba in Elisabethville and the punitive campaign against them in the north.[62] As to the declaration that the Katanga secession was at an end, he explained it in a cable to Bunche on 14 September in the following terms:

We do not know what O'Brien may have said ... but my best guess would be that he said, *as a statement of fact*, that with the alleged flight of Tshombe and Munongo ... obviously secession had ceased. If he did, this was diplomatically imprudent but decently intelligent readers should be able to distinguish between a statement of fact concerning result of a specific operation and a statement concerning immediate aim of this same operation ...[63]

This distinction between the immediate aim (i.e. formal objective) of the operation and its outcome (especially when this outcome is close to its policy objective) must have seemed too legalistic and artificial to O'Brien.[64] But it was real enough in Hammarskjöld's way of thinking.

(5) Hammarskjöld's decision was determined not only by legal considerations, but also, and perhaps in the first place, by the *results* of the operation. It was said in explaining his choice that he abhorred the violence and bloodshed that had just occurred through U.N. action and that he also realized that the U.N. was in no position to carry on a drawn-out war in Katanga.[65] These are *a posteriori* considerations, which would not have been relevant had the operation succeeded. But the operation was clearly not a success, and the course Hammarskjöld chose was the most conducive to bringing it to an end; in O'Brien's words, it 'lowered the price of peace'.[66]

62 Gavshon, 131.
63 Urquhart, 576.
64 O'Brien (270) described Hammarskjöld's attitude as seeking 'consistency with previous words at the expense of consistency with present action. This might have cost him less of a struggle than it would have cost anyone who delighted less in ambiguity. The successful wielder of ambiguity has a certain high imperiousness in his attitude to facts and inclines to a magician-like confidence in the overmastering power of language. This confidence is unfortunately contagious.'
65 Hoskyns, 422.
66 O'Brien, 268.

O'Brien considered that Hammarskjöld should have either disowned Morthor as *ultra vires*, or pursued it to its ultimate conclusion,
but that the course he chose was the least tenable for ONUC.[67] But
here again—as in his policy of non-recognition in the aftermath of
Cordier's questionable decisions—Hammarskjöld chose what was
seemingly the most difficult practical course of action in order to
safeguard both the principles and the fate of the Operation.

4. THE ROAD TO THE CEASE-FIRE

Western pressures

To Hammarskjöld, Operation Morthor was precisely what he had
warned against, both 'premature' and 'provocative'; and though it
had failed in securing its immediate military objectives, it was saddled
with much wider aims and a 'wrong' legal justification; all of which
made for its very controversial character (which in turn had a great
bearing on Hammarskjöld's ensuing decision). In this respect, the
reactions of member States, especially permanent members of the
Security Council, were of the utmost importance. This is why the
urgent request of the new British Ambassador to meet Hammarskjöld
as soon as he arrived in Leopoldville was of a great significance.
Ambassador Riches did meet Hammarskjöld on the day of his arrival,
just after dinner (which Hammarskjöld had with the members of the
Central Government) and before the report was prepared and the
instructions sent to O'Brien. According to Gavshon, the crux of the
meeting was a formal *démarche* amounting to this:

Her Majesty's Government was serving notice, with the greatest emphasis at
its command, that Britain would have to consider withdrawing *all* support
from ONUC's mission unless:
1 – Hammarskjöld could provide an acceptable explanation for what had
happened in Katanga; or
2 – Hammarskjöld could provide an assurance that the fighting would
swiftly be ended.[68]

The importance of this *démarche* cannot be overestimated. Hammarskjöld had already lost the confidence of two of the four effective
permanent members of the Security Council, the U.S.S.R. and
France; if the U.K. also withdrew its support—apart from aggravat-
ing the financial crisis—this would leave him completely dependent

67 Ibid. 263–4.
68 Gavshon, 130.

on the U.S., a very dangerous position for a Secretary-General who wanted to preserve the independence of the Secretariat and of the Operation. An indication of the existence of such a danger was given the following day, 14 September:

Bunche reported that President Kennedy and Dean Rusk were 'extremely upset' that there had been no consultation with the U.S. Goverment, which provided the largest share of the financial and logistical support for the U.N. operation in the Congo. Rusk had urged that Hammarskjöld bring Adoula and Tshombe together and warned that U.S. support would evaporate if the Gizenga line was to become dominant. Hammarskjöld was infuriated by this 'extraordinary démarche'. 'It is better', he told Bunche to tell Rusk, 'for the U.N. to loose the support of the U.S. because it is faithful to law and principles than to survive as an agent whose activities are geared to political purposes never avowed or laid down by the major organs of the U.N. ...'[69]

Thus when it came to the Western Powers, the challenge to the Secretary-General's conduct of the operation did not take the form of contesting his interpretation of the mandate in the Security Council (as with Lumumba and the U.S.S.R.), but that of direct overt or covert pressure on him.

There was also the threat of direct intervention from Rhodesia. In Parliament, Sir Roy Welensky declared that 'nothing so disgraceful in the whole history of international organization had happened as this latest action.' He alerted all Federal forces and dispatched troops to the border in view of 'the serious threat' to Rhodesia's security and pledged aid 'to anyone from Katanga who is endangered because of his democratic belief'. In fact Tshombe and other Katanga leaders were regrouped in the border town of Kipushi, under the effective protection of the near-by Rhodesian forces, and in close contact with the Rhodesian Government.[70]

These pressures were accompanied by a vicious campaign, especially in the Belgian, Rhodesian, and British press, against the U.N. in general, and O'Brien in particular, the whole peppered with stories of 'atrocities' committed by U.N. Indian troops.

On the military front, if on 13 September the Katangese thought the game was up, by the 14th the apparent discomfiture of the U.N. authorities and the inconsistency between their declarations in Elisabethville and in Leopoldville, the publicity given to the British

69 Urquhart, 575.
70 Hoskyns, 426; Gavshon, 124. O'Brien (274–5) provides detailed indications of Rhodesian intervention.

Ambassador's *démarche*, the strong support from Rhodesia, and press criticism of U.N. action made it clear to them that once again all was not yet lost and that if they manoeuvred cleverly, they could still achieve a cease-fire on the basis of the *status quo ante*. As a result, they intensified military action to prove that Katanga was fighting back. In this they were helped by two main factors: the passivity imposed on U.N. troops by the new instructions and the fact that the Katangese were in possession of a single jet Fouga plane, which went unopposed to bomb and strafe U.N. objectives. U.N. troops were subjected to land and air attacks in Elisabethville and around the Kamina base. But most critical was the position of the Irish company which had been surrounded in Jadotville since 12 September and which was now under heavy fire and short of food and water. A relief column was stopped at a bridge 20 km from Jadotville and strafed by the Fouga.

On Friday 15 September Hammarskjöld decided to delay his return to New York. He also instructed Bunche, on the latter's and also O'Brien's suggestion, to make urgent requests for a small number of jet fighters from Ethiopia, India, and Sweden, to defend the U.N. troops against the Fouga, and to get clearance from the U.K. for the transit and over-flight of the planes through Kenya and Uganda. Ethiopia accepted at once, but the U.K. invoked 'technical difficulties' to refuse to give the clearance.[71]

By the end of the day, it became clear to Hammarskjöld that what was most urgently needed was a cease-fire and that he had to negotiate it himself, for as Gavshon put it, 'only the Secretary-General could take the responsibility of signing a truce that part of the world would consider to be an appeasement, almost a surrender'.[72] In consequence, he proceeded with his aides to draft a note to Tshombe laying down the lines along which talks between them could take place. This note was not to be sent right away, but at the first opportunity.

On Saturday 16 September the event that most attracted attention was the meeting between Hammarskjöld and Lord Lansdowne, who had advanced his fact-finding trip (decided upon after Rumpunch) and had arrived in Leopoldville the day before. There was much speculation about what went on between the two. According to Lansdowne's own version, which agreed with that of Urquhart, when the meeting took place, Hammarskjöld had already reached a decision to seek a meeting with Tshombe and had already drafted the note

71 Urquhart, 577.
72 Gavshon, 151.

outlining the bases of discussion, which he showed to Lansdowne, adding that he considered Ndola in Rhodesia as the most suitable place for the meeting.[73]

As far as Hammarskjöld was concerned, the talks with Lansdowne were in reality little more than a matter of 'courtesy and information' and an additional source of irritation ... [But he] clearly foresaw the interpretation that was likely to be put on Lansdowne's visit. 'I am certain', he cabled Bunche ... that every paper will take for granted, if and when the approach to Tshombe is made known, that this is the result of 'constructive proposals' made by Lansdowne for Western Powers. Both groups of governments would rather like this interpretation. (For the record it may be said that the approach was decided upon and the message written before I received Lansdowne).[74]

In the same embarrassing vein was the American Ambassador's *démarche*, undertaken later in the day on behalf of 'President Kennedy, Dean Rusk, and Lord Home, the British Foreign Secretary, asking Hammarskjöld to remain in the Congo as long as hostilities continued, in order to show the "seriousness with which the responsibilities of the Secretary-General under U.N. resolutions are being carried out." Once again', Urquhart comments, 'the Western Powers were pushing an open door and compromising the Secretary-General's position by appearing to suggest a course of action he himself had already decided on.'[75]

The approach to Tshombe

The Secretary-General was thus waiting for an opportunity to suggest to Tshombe a meeting at Ndola. The initiative came surprisingly from Tshombe, who sent a message to O'Brien through the British consulate declaring that he was 'prepared' to meet him at 11.30 a.m. the following day, Sunday 17 September, in Bancroft, Rhodesia, to discuss a cease-fire.[76] In Gavshon's words: 'It seemed very much like a victorious general's summons to a defeated foe.'[77]

In cabling Leopoldville for instructions, O'Brien advised against accepting a meeting in Rhodesia which 'might be tantamount to

73 Urquhart, 579. Lansdowne's version was given a month later in the House of Lords, and is reproduced *in extenso* in Gavshon, 164–7.

74 Urquhart, 579, who describes the considerable embarrassment caused by Landsdowne's visit and the resentment is provoked both in Hammarskjöld's staff who regarded it as 'a blatant example of attempted great power pressure' and in the Congolese Central Government and Parliament.

75 Ibid. 580.

76 S/4940/Add. 4, 17 Sept. 1961, para. 4; Urquhart, 582.

77 Gavshon, 172. Cf. O'Brien, 284; Hoskyns, 429.

accepting something resembling the arbitration of Sir Roy Welensky'.[78] Instead he was instructed to relay Hammarskjöld's message to Tshombe suggesting a meeting in Ndola at a later hour of Sunday 17 September.

The message—after recalling the mandate, especially the first two paragraphs of the February resolution and the affirmation therein that the solution of the Congo problem could be reached only through conciliation among the Congolese themselves, without interference or imposition from outside—went on to state:

(3) A principle of the United Nations which is absolutely binding upon all is the maintenance of peace and, to that end and in order to protect human life, they are bound to cease all hostilities and to seek solutions to the conflict by means of negotiation, mediation and conciliation.

(4) You have yourself accepted the objectives of the United Nations mission as defined in paragraph (1), that is to say, the maintenance of public order, the prevention of civil war and the evacuation of all the personnel referred to by the Security Council. There should therefore be no difference of opinion between the Organization and you as to the framework within which ways must be sought of putting an end to the present armed conflict.

(5) As regards the idea that a solution to the problem of the Congo should be sought through reconciliation which would naturally have to be achieved within the framework of the constitution of the Republic you have several times given us clear indications that you also accepted this point of view. I am therefore convinced that you do not share the opinion of certain elements who reject the idea of reconciliation, which leads me to the conclusion that your views and those of the United Nations are identical with respect to the principles on which the attempt to find a solution to the political problem should be based.

Hammarskjöld then recalled Tshombe's request for a cease-fire on 13 September and the subsequent U.N. efforts to arrange for a meeting for this purpose, before adding:

(7) I have been informed of the message received by Mr. O'Brien from Mr. Dunnet, the British Consul, inviting him to meet you tomorrow at 11.30 a.m. at Bancroft in Northern Rhodesia. I suggest that I should meet you personally, so that together we can try to find peaceful methods of resolving the present conflict, thus opening the way to a solution of the Katanga problems within the framework of the Congo [i.e. 'within the framework established by the Security Council and already accepted by you']. The proposed meeting obviously requires that orders should be given beforehand for an immediate and effective cease-fire ... before I leave I must have your reply to this

78 O'Brien, 284.

message, including your decision regarding the cease-fire. The cease-fire will occur automatically on the United Nations side, in view of the fact that according to the instructions given and the rules followed by the Organization, it only opens fire in self-defence.[79]

This message, reminiscent of the 'Memorandum on Implementation' issued by Hammarskjöld before meeting Tshombe in August 1960, had the same ingredients that reflected Hammarskjöld's style of diplomacy. It reiterated the principles in a way that made them acceptable to the recipient, by emphasizing the limitations they imposed on U.N. action in his regard, thus making room for agreement. Proceeding from an assessment of the balance of power between the U.N. and its adversary at that juncture, Hammarskjöld was seeking to achieve what was possible (in the event saving the military and diplomatic situation), even at the expense of postponing or abandoning some immediate tactical objectives, as long as the principles and the final aims were safeguarded.

Tshombe's answer was given to O'Brien by the British Consul at 10 a.m., Sunday 17 September. He agreed on the principle of an immediate cease-fire, provided U.N. troops were confined to their camps and all troop movements and reinforcements were stopped. He also agreed to go to Ndola and indicated that he would be accompanied by 'his Minister of Finance, Mr. Kibwe, his Minister for Foreign Affairs, Mr. Kimba, and the Secretary of State for the Common Market, Mr. Mwenda-Odilon'.[80]

This 'arrogant' answer was unacceptable to Hammarskjöld and he replied sharply to it, stating that there could be 'no question of anything but an unconditional cease-fire and an agreement of both parties to meet together, all other modalities obviously to be discussed in the course of the meeting.' However, when O'Brien contacted the British Consul at approximately 2 p.m. to ask him to convey this reply to Tshombe, he was told that the latter had already chartered a plane and intended to travel to Ndola at 3 p.m. In the absence of further word from Tshombe, Hammarskjöld decided to go to Ndola all the same.[81]

Hammarskjöld's fatal trip

Hammarskjöld had seen Lord Lansdowne in the morning. He turned down his offer to accompany him, in order to avoid any

79 S/4940/Add. 4, para. 7.
80 Ibid., paras. 10–11.
81 Ibid., paras. 12–13.

semblance of British mediation. But as it was necessary to check on the arrangements for the meeting before his arrival, they decided that Lansdowne would precede him in another U.N. plane, it being understood that he would not talk to Tshombe and that he would leave Ndola before the arrival of Hammarskjöld.[82]

Lansdowne left Leopoldville about 4 p.m. followed by the Secretary-General's party just before 5 p.m., local time. The Secretary-General's plane did not file a complete flight plan and followed a roundabout itinerary to avoid possible interception by the Fouga. At 12.10 p.m., Rhodesian time, the pilot informed the Ndola control tower that the airport lights were in sight, and that he was descending, but that was the last heard from the plane. After some time, the officials waiting for the Secretary-General reached the conclusion that he must have changed his mind about landing in Ndola. It was not until the following morning that a search party was organized; and it found the wreckage of the plane in the afternoon.[83]

The news of the tragic death of the Secretary-General caused a shock wave all over the world. It was immediately and widely assumed that it was due to foul play, attributed to the British, the Rhodesians, Tshombe, Munongo, the mercenaries, and last but not least to the fanatical French officers. Two commissions of inquiry were set up; the Rhodesian one concluded that the crash was caused by a human error on the part of the pilot, while the one established by the General Assembly inconclusively reported that there was not enough evidence to establish the exact cause of the crash, but did not rule out the possibility of sabotage or of an external attack.[84]

The cease-fire agreement

The death of the Secretary-General left the Secretariat in a state of deep shock; but his efforts to reach a cease-fire had to be continued. After further exchanges, Khiary went to Ndola where he met Tshombe on 19 September. On the afternoon of the 20th they signed the following provisional agreement:

82 Urquhart, 585; Gavshon, 180–1.
83 Ibid. 7–25; S/4940/Add. 5, 19 Sept. 1961.
84 A/5069 and Add. 1, 24 Apr. 1962. A lengthy analysis of the two reports is provided by Gavshon, 208–43.

1. An immediate cease-fire shall be ordered;

2. The cease-fire shall come into force on 21 September 1961, at 00.00 hours, throughout Katanga;

3. A joint commission consisting of four members having full powers shall immediately be set up to supervise the application of this agreement and to seek ways of placing the relations between the United Nations and Katanga authorities on a basis of mutual understanding and harmony, and also to fix the respective positions of each side's troops;

4. No movement of troops to reinforce a garrison or position shall be allowed. This prohibition applies to all means of warfare, arms, ammunition and other military devices;

5. The two parties shall be free to supply their troops with provisions in the usual way;

6. The exchange of prisoners shall be carried out at the direction of the commission mentioned in article 3;

7. This agreement shall be made public simultaneously by the United Nations and the Katanga government.[85]

Though the provisional agreement was to come into force at 00.00 hours on 21 September, its preamble provided that it 'will not become final until it has been approved by the Secretary-General'. But as soon as it became known, it was heavily criticized by the Afro-Asians as being at variance with the Security Council resolution of 21 February; they also expressed their apprehension lest it would be construed as an act of recognition by the U.N. of Tshombe's secessionist regime, and a prohibition on reinforcing U.N. troops by men and weapons (especially aircraft) even outside Katanga.[86] In consequence, in communicating its final approval to Tshombe on 24 September, the Secretariat Headquarters 'formally transmitted' with it 'the express conditions, as understood during the negotiations' (though not included in the text), which were:

The conclusion of the agreement shall in no way affect the resolutions of the Security Council, including that of 21 February 1961, and of the General Assembly.

The agreement is of a strictly military nature and applies solely to the U.N. Force in Katanga and to the armed forces of Katanga. It has no political intention or aim.

The agreement does not apply outside Katanga.[87]

85 S/4940/Add. 7, 20 Sept. 1961, para. 6.

86 Advisory Committee, 56 Mtg., 21 Sept. 1961. This was the first meeting of the Committee since 17 August, i.e. since before Rumpunch.

87 S/4940/Add. 10, 6 Oct. 1961, para. 2. These clarifications are reminiscent of those included in the Secretary-General's message to Kasavubu ratifying the agreement of 17

At this juncture what counted most for ONUC in the cease-fire was to get back the some 190 U.N. prisoners, mainly the Irish company captured in Jadotville. Tshombe, on the other hand, convinced that he had won the battle, wanted to use the cease-fire agreement as a means not merely of re-establishing the *status quo ante*, but also of neutralizing ONUC militarily in such a manner as to rule out the threat of any future offensive action on its part. Once this was done, he could engage in negotiations with the Central Government from a position of strength, with a view to reaching or rather dictating the terms of a settlement with them, along the lines of the Tananarive agreement.

Thus when the joint commission (provided for in article 3 to supervise the implementation of the agreement) met on 26 and 27 September, the Katangese members started by requesting the withdrawal of U.N. troops from Katanga or their confinement to their camps, and the roads between the camps and airports; proposals which were obviously unacceptable to ONUC's representatives. Again on 28 September a joint subcommission was created to visit the garrisons in order to 'fix the respective positions of each side's troops' according to article 3; it visited the areas controlled by U.N. troops in North Katanga, but when it came to continue the agreed itinerary by visiting the strongholds of the *gendarmerie* in the south, Jadotville, Kolwezi, and Kipushi, the Katangese refused them access.[88] And all the while, the Katangese were procrastinating on the question of the exchange of prisoners.

The Protocol of implementation

On 2 October Khiary changed tactics by proposing the conclusion of a Protocol of implementation of the cease-fire agreement. Once more, the Katangese resorted to their dilatory tactics. They presented a number of proposals which were obviously unacceptable to Khiary, being incompatible with the Security Council resolutions. It was only under pressure from Britain and Belgium and after Khiary had fixed a time-limit for his return to Leopoldville, that an agreement was reached on 13 October.[89]

April (see *supra*, p. 112) and another reaffirmation of the principle of the non-negotiability of the mandate.

88 Ibid., paras. 7–10.

89 S/4940/Add. 11, 23 Oct. 1961, and Annex I for the text of the Protocol. Cf. Hoskyns, 437.

For the U.N. this Protocol secured two important objectives, both of which already included in the cease-fire agreement: (1) the fixing of a definite and clear date and place for the exchange of prisoners (art. 1); and (2) the creation of three joint subcommissions to supervise the application of the cease-fire agreement, with 'full liberty to visit any part of Katangese territory at any time at the request of either of the two parties' (art. 2).

The Katangese, on their part, made the utmost use of their U.N. hostages to exact new concessions. It is true that their extremist demands—such as the undertaking that ONUC would keep only a 'symbolic' military contingent in Katanga, that it would never mount a police action there, that it would not authorize the entry into Katanga of other forces than its own and Katanga's—were rejected as being incompatible with ONUC's mandate. But the Protocol went beyond the cease-fire agreement in several respects. The latter was basically a stand-still agreement, which is usually understood as the freezing of the positions of the parties as they stand at the time it enters into force. However, the Protocol fixed 12 September, the day before fighting broke out, as the critical date for determining the positions of the parties, which meant the re-establishment of the military *status quo ante*. This led to the reintroduction into North Katanga, from which they had been ousted, of 'the same number of [Katangese] troops to hold the same garrison points as on the earlier date' (art. 3) (though this did not undermine the U.N. firm control in these areas). Moreover, several strategic points and installations occupied by U.N. troops in Elisabethville were restored to the Katangese, including the post office and the radio station, against the Katangese undertaking to maintain their neutrality, to ensure the freedom and immunity of ONUC communications, and to refrain from inflammatory attacks and from acts such as interrupting U.N. water or electricity supplies (arts. 5, 6, 8). The U.N. also guaranteed the Katangese the right to use ONUC-held airports for civil transport and for the provision of troops, and allowed them to maintain the same force of fifty-two as on 12 September, in the Elisabethville airport, with an undertaking not to disarm them (arts. 7, 11).

These were sizeable concessions, but the most controversial (and the one on which the negotiation risked a rupture) did not deal with the situation on the terrain. Khiary had wanted to include a 'without prejudice' clause safeguarding the continued application of the Security Council resolution, especially paragraph A2, but the Katangese insisted that as this question fell outside the scope of the Protocol, it should not be dealt with therein. On the other hand, they insisted on the inclusion of an article 10, providing that 'the representatives of ONUC shall not consider that the cease-fire had been violated in the event that the Katangese gendarmerie counters an attack from the outside'. Though the gist of this provision was inherent in the nature of the agreement, politically it amounted to an explicit recognition by the U.N. of Tshombe's right to repulse by force any attempt by the Central Government to send the A.N.C. into Katanga, and was thus bound to draw the strong reactions it did (from the U.S.S.R.,[90] the Afro-Asian members of the Advisory Committee,[91] and from the Central Government[92]).

When the Protocol was finally approved by Headquarters on 23 September, the three conditions on the basis of which the cease-fire agreement was first approved were reiterated and supplemented by the following:

2. This protocol of agreement is limited to relations between ONUC and Katanga armed forces in Katanga. Approval of it involves no derogation of the unity, territorial integrity or independence of the Congo, affirmed and reaffirmed by resolutions of the Security Council and the General Assembly, of the sovereignty of the Republic of the Congo (Leopoldville), or of the authority of its Central Government.

3. Further, note is taken that it was acknowledged in the discussions between the two parties to the negotiations which led to the formulation and signing of the protocol, that full compliance with the requirements of part A, paragraph 2, of the Security Council resolutions of 21 February 1961 is a condition essential to the effective application of the protocol.

4. This approval is given, finally, on the understanding that the exchange of prisoners will precede the execution of all other provisions of the protocol.[93]

As to the execution of the Protocol, Tschombe failed to proceed to the exchange of prisoners on the agreed date of 16 October, and tried to take over the public buildings before the exchange. Finally, as the U.N. stood firm, it took place on the 25th and the buildings were then

90 S/4962, 16 Oct. 1961.

91 Advisory Committee, 58 Mtg., 16 Oct. 1961; 58 Mtg, 18 Oct. 1961. It was there that an interpretation by Khiary of the controversial article 10 of the Protocol was mentioned to the effect that the words 'attack from outside' in that article referred to an attack from outside the Congo and not one from the Central Government!

92 S/4964, containing a communication from Adoula of 15 Oct. 1961, in which he expressed his 'deepest apprehensions as to the political implications—affecting the very continuation of all U.N. operations in the Congo ...'

93 S/4940/Add. 11, Annex II.

handed over. This was but a foretaste of things to come. For Tshombe's violations of the cease-fire and the Protocol came thick and fast and all ONUC officials could do was to make representations for their cessation.[94]

Most dangerous of these violations was the Katangese military build-up in disregard of the cease-fire both in arms (especially aeroplanes) and men. Expelled mercenaries were filtering back via Rhodesia, which was openly helping Tshombe in every way, and were given cover as civilian employees. The U.N. could only expel, but neither detain nor punish them, a situation which posed a serious problem to ONUC.[95]

The Central Government campaign against Katanga

The failure of Morthor considerably weakened the position and the cohesion of the Central Government. On 4 October Gizenga went back to Stanleyville ostensibly for private business, then refused to return, and started to consolidate his position there, thus raising the spectre of counter-secession unless something was done about Katanga. In despair of U.N. action after the cease-fire and the Protocol, the Central Government decided to launch a two-pronged campaign against Katanga. The first involved troops under Mobutu's command moving, in October, from Kasai towards Katanga. But as soon as they were struck by Tshombe's 'airforce'—which was considerably strengthened in the meantime in violation of the cease-fire—they beat a disorderly retreat attacking in the process the European population of Luluabourg (the capital of Kasai) during the first days of November, and causing difficult problems of maintenance of law and order for U.N. troops there, before the bulk were eventually repatriated to Leopoldville. The other campaign was launched by troops under General Lundula from Orientale and Kivu into North Katanga during the first half of November, and although the north was controlled by pro-Central Government administrators and U.N. troops, there too the A.N.C. elements terrorized the population, creating similar problems for U.N. troops. This culminated in the massacre of Kindu (in Kivu) where, on 11 November, elements of the Stanleyville A.N.C. captured and savagely massacred eleven Italian ONUC aircrew.[96]

94 S/4940/Add. 12, 2 Nov. 1961, paras. 1–15.
95 Hoskyns, 447.
96 S/4940/Add. 13, 15 Nov. 1961; O'Brien 310–13.

5. THE SECURITY COUNCIL RESOLUTION OF 24 NOVEMBER 1961

In New York the sixteenth General Assembly met under the shadow of the tragic death of Dag Hammarskjöld and the threat of a serious constitutional crisis, in case the Russians seized this opportunity to revive their troika proposal of the previous year. It was on 3 November, after intensive negotiations, that the Security Council unanimously recommended U Thant's appointment as Acting Secretary-General until the end of Hammarskjöld's term in 1963, a recommendation approved by the General Assembly the same day.[97]

Attention turned once again to the Congo. The Afro-Asians were critical of the cease-fire and Protocol agreements and apprehensive of the consequences of the resulting stalemate in Katanga upon ONUC and the Central Government, especially as the fighting between the A.N.C. and the Katanga *gendarmerie* was then going on. On 3 November Ethiopia, Nigeria, and Sudan requested the convening of the Security Council 'to consider the situation prevailing in the province of Katanga, Republic of the Congo (Leopoldville), caused by the lawless acts of mercenaries'.[98] The Council met on 13 November, and on the 14th an Afro-Asian draft resolution was submitted by Ceylon, Liberia, and the U.A.R.[99]

A lengthy discussion ensued. The U.S. proposed several amendments particularly with a view to widening the scope of the condemnation of secessionist activities and the new powers of ONUC to deal with them beyond Katanga to eventual similar activities by Gizenga in Stanleyville.[100] The U.S.S.R. rejected—and finally vetoed—most of them as diverting attention from the real problem of Katanga. Significantly, one of the amendments vetoed by the U.S.S.R. was an explicit reiteration of the mandate of the Secretary-General under Security Council resolutions. The draft resolution was finally adopted on 24 November, by 9 votes with 2 abstentions, the U.K. and France. The resolution reads:

The Security Council,
Recalling its resolutions s/4387, S/4405, S/4426 and S/4741,

---

97 S/4972, 3 Nov. 1961; G.A.Res 1640(XVI) 3 Nov. 1961.
98 S/4973. The reference to mercenaries was intended to emphasize the foreign element in the situation.
99 S/4985 and Rev. 1, 20 Nov. 1961.
100 S/4989, 20 Nov. 1961; Rev. 2, 24 Nov. 1961.

Recalling further General Assembly resolutions 1474 (ES–IV) 1592(XV), 1599(XV), 1600(XV) and 1601(XV),

Reaffirming the policies and purposes of the United Nations with respect to the Congo (Leopoldville) as set out in the aforesaid resolutions, namely:

(a) To maintain the territorial integrity and the political independence of the Republic of the Congo,

(b) To assist the Central Government of the Congo in the restoration and maintenance of law and order,

(c) To prevent the occurrence of civil war in the Congo,

(d) To secure the immediate withdrawal and evacuation from the Congo of all foreign military, paramilitary and advisory personnel not under the United Nations Command, and all mercenaries, and

(e) To render technical assistance,

Welcoming the restoration of the national Parliament of the Congo in accordance with the 'Loi fondamentale' and the consequent formation of a Central Government on 2 August 1961,

Deploring all armed action in opposition to the authority of the Government of the Republic of the Congo, specifically secessionist activities and armed action now being carried on by the provincial administration of Katanga with the aid of external resources and foreign mercenaries, and *completely rejecting* the claim that Katanga is a 'sovereign independent nation',

Noting with deep regret the recent and past actions of violence against United Nations personnel,

Recognizing the Government of the Republic of the Congo as exclusively responsible for the conduct of the external affairs of the Congo,

Bearing in mind the imperative necessity of speedy and effective action to implement fully the policies and purposes of the United Nations in the Congo to end the unfortunate plight of the Congolese people, necessary both in the interests of world peace and international co-operation, and stability and progress of Africa as a whole,

1. *Strongly deprecates* the secessionist activities illegally carried out by the provincial administration of Katanga, with the aid of external resources and manned by foreign mercenaries;

2. *Further deprecates* the armed action against United Nations forces and personnel in the pursuit of such activities;

3. *Insists* that such activities shall cease forthwith, and *calls upon* all concerned to desist therefrom;

4. *Authorizes* the Secretary-General to take vigorous action, including the use of a requisite measure of force, if necessary, for the immediate apprehension, detention pending legal action and/or deportation of all foreign military and paramilitary personnel and political advisers not under the United Nations Command, and mercenaries as laid down in part A, operative paragraph 2 of the Security Council resolution of 21 February 1961;

5. *Further requests* the Secretary-General to take all necessary measures to

prevent the entry or return of such elements under whatever guise and also of arms, equipment or other material in support of such activities;

6. *Requests* all States to refrain from the supply of arms, equipment or other material which could be used for warlike purposes, and to take the necessary measures to prevent their nationals from doing the same, and also to deny transportation and transit facilities for such supplies across their territories, except in accordance with the decisions, policies and purposes of the United Nations;

7. *Calls upon* all Member States to refrain from promoting, condoning, or giving support by acts of omission or commission, directly or indirectly, to activities against the United Nations often resulting in armed hostilities against the United Nations forces and personnel;

8. *Declares* that all secessionist activities against the Republic of the Congo are contrary to the 'Loi fondamentale' and Security Council decisions and specifically *demands* that such activities which are now taking place in Katanga shall cease forthwith;

9. *Declares* full and firm support for the Central Government of the Congo, and the determination to assist that Government, in accordance with the decisions of the United Nations, to maintain law and order and national integrity, to provide technical assistance and to implement those decisions;

10. *Urges* all Member States to lend their support, according to their national procedures, to the Central Government of the Republic of the Congo, in conformity with the Charter and the decisions of the United Nations;

11. *Requests* all Member States to refrain from any action which may, directly or indirectly, impede the policies and purposes of the United Nations in the Congo and is contrary to its decisions and the general purpose of the Charter.[101]

The resolution and the mandate

The Security Council debates took place while ONUC was labouring under a triple handicap: As a result of the failure of Morthor and the subsequent cease-fire and Protocol, it was militarily on the defensive in Katanga; the collapse of the A.N.C. campaign, apart from the troubles it caused, was threatening the unity and continued existence of the Adoula Government; at the same time, Katanga's military potential was being continuously reinforced and its relative political position proportionately strengthened, so much so that its leaders were starting to speak overtly of self-determination. The resolution purported to face up to these adverse circumstances by taking a firmer stand *vis-à-vis* the Katanga secession and strengthening ONUC's mandate to facilitate its effective implementation in spite of them. In

101 S/5002.

this respect, several points in the resolution (and the discussions surrounding it) are worth noting.

(1) Though no member tried to convene the Security Council or *challenge* Morthor there (as did the U.S.S.R. and Lumumba on earlier occasions), the Western Powers, as we have seen, applied direct pressure on the Secretary-General while the crisis was going on.[102]

However, during the debates leading to the adoption of the resolution, the French and British delegates as well as Spaak criticized Morthor (and to a lesser extent Rumpunch) as using excessive force and being *ultra vires*.[103] Moreover, Spaak accused ONUC in general and O'Brien in particular of discrimination against the Belgians.[104] These criticisms were put forward not so much to reopen the debate on the legality of past action as to caution against following a similar course in the future, especially against allowing for the use of force in the resolution which was under discussion.

In his closing statement, after the adoption of the resolution, U Thant did admit that mistakes were made, but strongly refuted the charge of discrimination.[105]

(2) One of Stevenson's amendments vetoed by the U.S.S.R. was a reaffirmation of the *Secretary-General's mandate*.[106] But unlike the February resolution which did not mention the Secretary-General at all, paragraphs 4 and 5 of the new resolution entrusted him with specific tasks. This led Stevenson to declare that 'this new resolution can in no way be a diminution of, but only an addition to, authority previously granted ...'[107] To which Zorin retorted:

---

102 The objections and reservations of some Afro-Asian members (*supra*, pp. 155, n. 86; 158, n. 91), the U.S.S.R. (*supra*, p. 158, n. 90), and the Central Government (*supra*, p. 158, n. 92) to the cease-fire and Protocol agreements were not taken to the Security Council either (though the Central Government communication did reserve such a possibility). The objections of the Central Government and the U.S.S.R. took the form of written and legally motivated communications, which were published and thus constituted a more legal and institutionalized form of challenging the Secretariat implementation of the mandate.

103 Berard (France) SCOR, 974 Mtg., 15 Nov. 1961, paras. 69–73; Sir Patrick Dean (U.K.) SCOR, 976 Mtg., 17 Nov. 1961, paras. 164–6.

104 SCOR, 974 Mtg., 15 Nov. 1961, paras. 84, 114–22.

105 SCOR, 982 Mtg., 24 Nov. 1961, para. 109.

106 S/4989 and Rev. 2. The proposed paragraph 13 referred specifically to the Secretary-General's diplomatic role in seeking to achieve the unity of the Congo (with a view to reducing the emphasis on the use of force).

107 SCOR, 982 Mtg., 24 Nov. 1961, para. 97.

... the main task which now confronts the Acting Secretary-General and the United Nations Command is that of scrupulously and consistently implementing the specific provisions of the newly adopted resolution and of refraining from interpreting them in some particular way of their own. They must act in accordance with the decisions as adopted, and not with any of the proposals that have not been adopted.[108]

In other words, the Russians were trying to reinterpret the role of the Secretary-General as being limited to the fulfilment of specific tasks, specifically mentioned in the resolutions, and not of a general mandate; while the Americans were reiterating the interpretation which had been followed until then, and which seemed to be more appropriate as long as the earlier resolutions which conferred a general mandate on the Secretary-General were not repudiated by the Security Council.

In his closing statement, U Thant indirectly reaffirmed the second interpretation, while putting the emphasis on the specific responsibilities entrusted to him in the new resolution.[109]

(3) The resolution itself went further than its predecessors in several respects. Prominent among them was its definition of *the powers of the Secretary-General in dealing with foreign military personnel and material* in Katanga.

Not only did it explicitly authorize the Secretary-General to use force in the implementation of paragraph A2 of the February resolution (thus settling retroactively the controversy over Rumpunch and especially Morthor); but it also authorized him to deal with foreign personnel after capture[110] and to control the movement of persons and goods across the borders to prevent the entry of foreign military personnel and material into the Congo.[111]

---

108 Ibid. para. 151; see also para. 152.

109 Ibid. paras. 104, 102.

110 This was one of the vexing problems facing ONUC, because it legally could neither detain nor punish the captured mercenaries but merely hand them to their consuls for evacuation. But this was not a sufficient deterrent and there were clear signs that many of them found their way back, especially via Rhodesia. The question was debated in the Advisory Committee, and on a U.N. suggestion, the Central Government promulgated Ordinance 83, of 13 Nov. 1961, for the punishment of mercenaries, and requested the U.N. to hand them those who are captured for legal action (S/4940/Add. 14). The resolution permitted ONUC to detain those captured pending such action or deportation.

111 This was one of the powers Hammarskjöld (and the Western members) objected to, during the debates in the Security Council and the General Assembly, in December 1960 as implying direct exercise of sovereignty and overriding that of the Congo (*supra*, p. 93). But in November 1961, it was adopted without any serious objection from any quarter.

Objections were raised by France, Belgium, and particularly the U.K., on the grounds that the resolution put too much emphasis on force and not enough on conciliation, that force was not conducive to a solution but to escalation, and that it was contrary to the Charter and would set a dangerous precedent for the future, putting the U.N. 'at the beck and call of any state faced with the problem of a dissident minority within its own borders'.[112] These criticisms intimated that the new resolution was *ultra vires*, going against the principles of the non-use of force and non-intervention.

(4) As concerns *the authorization to use force*, the question of its being *ultra vires* or not revolved on its legal basis in the Charter. And here we are clearly, in fact much more clearly than in the case of paragraph A1 of the February resolution, within the ambit of Article 42 of the Charter.[113] Such an authorization is within the powers of the Security Council; hence there is no room for accusation of *ultra vires* here.

In the same vein, though the resolution did not reiterate paragraph A1 of the February resolution, the prevention of civil war was on everybody's mind, in view of the recent A.N.C. campaign. In his closing statement, U Thant declared:

... everything possible must be done to avert civil war, even by the employment of force, should this prove necessary as a last resort. This, I believe, necessarily implies a sympathetic attitude on the part of ONUC toward the efforts of the Government to suppress all armed activities against the Central Government and secessionist activities.[114]

In both cases the relevant legal question was not whether the use of force as such had a legal basis in the Charter or not, but whether in case of the use of force by ONUC, a *differential treatment* between the parties to an internal conflict would not be *ultra vires*, as a violation of the principle of non-intervention in internal affairs.

(5) As far as the *principle of non-intervention* is concerned, a simple

112 Sir Patrick Dean (U.K.), SCOR, 976 Mtg., 17 Nov. 1961, para. 165; SCOR, 982 Mtg., 24 Nov. 1961, para. 118; Berard (France) ibid., para. 60.

113 That is unless we consider (a) that the resolution authoritatively determined that the mere presence of mercenaries constituted a threat of civil war, hence automatically falling within paragraph A1 of the February resolution (an interpretation which had been considered too extensive by Hammarskjöld) and that paragraph A1 was not based on article 42 (but see the contrary argument *supra*, p. 103ff.); or (b) that the new powers fell within the function of maintenance of law and order extensively redefined.

114 SCOR, 982 Mtg., 24 Nov. 1961, para. 104. This was saying aloud what Hammarskjöld had said in the privacy of the Advisory Committee after the constitution of the Adoula Government.

answer would be that as long as the use of force was based on article 42, then according to article 2, paragraph 7, ONUC was not bound by the principle of non-intervention. But if we consider that that was not the case, it becomes necessary to distinguish between two aspects of ONUC's attitude and action: (a) its position of principle *vis-à-vis* the Katanga secession; and (b) the means it was allowed to use in giving effect to this position of principle.

Concerning the position of principle of the U.N. on the controversy between Katanga and the Central Government, the previous resolutions indirectly repudiated the Katanga secession by reaffirming the unity and territorial integrity of the Congo. But in spite of the Russian efforts from the beginning to establish the direct responsibility of ONUC in this respect,[115] this was not explicitly included in any of the Security Council resolutions[116] before the November one, which for the first time provided in its preamble as one of the 'policies and purposes' (i.e. functions) of the U.N. in the Congo: 'To maintain the territorial integrity and the political independence of the Republic of the Congo.'

And again for the first time the resolution did not limit itself to exhorting all the Congolese factions to settle their differences within a united Congo and to propose conciliation to that end, but condemned in no uncertain terms the Katanga secession as such (paragraph 1), demanding that it cease forthwith (paragraphs 3 and 8) and declaring it (as all secessionist activities in the Congo) illegal and contrary to the *Loi Fondamentale* and the Security Council decisions (paragraph 8).[117]

What is the reason for this change of emphasis? The previous line was set on the basis of the two assumptions laid down in Hammarskjöld's second Report and reflected in the resolution of 9 August: (a) that Tshombe did not want to secede from the Congo but merely to have a different constitutional arrangement, hence the controversy was purely constitutional and internal; and (b) that the Katanga problem 'did not have its root' in foreign intervention, an assumption which again emphasized the predominantly internal character of the problem. On the basis of these two assumptions, the formulation of the principle of non-intervention included in the August resolution

---

115 e.g. Zorin, SCOR, 879 Mtg., 21 July 1960, para. 121.

116 But see G.A.Res. 1474 (E.S. IV), 20 Sept. 1960, second operative paragraph.

117 Paragraph 8 was added by the sponsors as a concession to the U.S., which wanted the resolution to cover an eventual Gizengist secession in the east as well as Katanga's.

was adopted. However, both assumptions were revealed in practice to be wrong.

During the November debates in the Security Council, Tshombe addressed a message to the Secretary-General invoking Katanga's right of self-determination.[118] He thus clearly invalidated the first assumption; and the strong condemnation of the secession in the resolution was in no small part in response to this claim. But the belated discovery of a real secessionist intent on the part of Tshombe was not in itself a sufficient legal ground for the U.N. to take a position against secession. For here the consideration of propriety intervenes: the U.N. should not act as a holy alliance between the established governments to maintain the *status quo*.

The strong rebuttal of Tshombe's claim, which amounted to a finding by the Security Council that the conditions of self-determination did not apply in the case of Katanga, was based on two main considerations. The first was that Tshombe's regime was not representative. Not only were the Baluba of North Katanga opposed to him, but even in the south the black élite, almost exclusively composed of Kasai Baluba, were also in opposition and largely reduced to refugees in U.N. camps.[119]

But the main objection to Tshombe's regime was that it merely served as a façade for foreign interests, that it was made possible and maintained through foreign intervention, though the forms of intervention changed over time. This was the rebuttal of the second assumption and the basic legal ground permitting the U.N. to take a stand on secession. It is true that the condemnation was directed to the secession itself and not to its foreign mainsprings. But once the identification between the secessionist movement and its foreign roots is made (as it was clearly done in paragraph 1 of the resolution), this comes down to the same thing.

The distinction becomes important, however, in relation to the second aspect of the U.N. attitude which is the means that ONUC was allowed to use in pursuing its position of principle. For although secession was condemned, force was not allowed in order to put an end to it as such, but only for the purpose of eliminating its foreign props, i.e. foreign military personnel and material.[120] This means that

118 S/4988, 17 Nov. 1961.

119 See *supra*, p. 133, n. 36; p. 7, n. 13.

120 This distinction corresponded to Hammarskjöld's interpretation of the mandate (obviously before the adoption of the November resolution). Thus in a cable of 26 August to Linner he wrote: 'We cannot "wage war" on the Katanga forces, while we

the U.N. was not simply acting at the 'beck and call' of a member with internal difficulties, but in order to eliminate a form of foreign intervention aiming at the dismemberment of a member state; and after all the elimination of foreign intervention was the basic *raison d'être* of the Operation from the beginning.

It can thus be said that the resolution did not depart from the interpretation of the principle of non-intervention as such, but from the prior interpretation of the factual situation.

6. SECOND ROUND: THE DECEMBER BATTLE

From incidents to battle

The new Security Council resolution was considered by Tshombe and his government as a 'declaration of war' and a prelude to a military offensive by the U.N.; an interpretation encouraged by the mercenaries who were convinced that they would win a second round, and were thus seeking confrontation. As a result, the situation rapidly deteriorated and the anti-U.N. campaign was highly intensified. On 25 November, the day following the passing of the resolution, Tshombe delivered a fiery speech in which he called on the Katangese to be prepared to take up whatever arms they could find, including poisoned arrows, spears, axes, and picks; and threatened to resort to a scorched-earth strategy. The mounting tension and the continuous incitement of the Katangese troops led to a series of assaults against U.N. personnel; the most serious took place on 28 November, when commandos broke into a private house and took away George Ivan Smith and Brian Urquhart (the two high Secretariat officials replacing O'Brien during his stay in New York for the Security Council meetings), who were brutally beaten up and released only after the intervention of the American Consul and Kimba and Munongo.[121]

In spite of the efforts of the U.N. representatives to convince Tshombe that the U.N. was not planning aggressive action against Katanga, but that it was the continuation of the attacks on its personnel that would oblige the U.N. to exercise its right of self-

---

can, if necessary by force, execute paragraph A2 of the resolution' (Urquhart, 555); and in another to Bunche from Leopoldville on 14 September: 'To my knowledge, all members of the U.N. are for the cessation of Katanga separatism as established U.N. aim, although an aim not to be achieved by the initiative of offensive action against Katangese forces' (ibid. 576).

121 S/4940/Add. 15, 30 Nov. 1961. Cf. Hoskyns, 448.

defence,[122] the anti-U.N. campaign did not abate, rendering a wider clash inevitable.

The incident which triggered the fighting occurred in the Elisabethville airport in the afternoon of 2 December.

Drunken Katanga *gendarmes* molested some airport workers and a woman. For the sake of maintaining order, Indian Derga troops of ONUC ... disarmed the *gendarmes* who were misconducting themselves. Thereupon the remaining *gendarmes* and police jumped into trenches and opened fire on the ONUC troops. As a result, the Indians were compelled to disarm and detained them all.[123]

The *gendarmerie* interpreted this incident as the beginning of the expected U.N. offensive and immediately started patrolling the town and established two road-blocks, one on the road between the airport and the town and the other in a strategic tunnel under the railway line commanding the road between the Swedish contingent camp and down-town.

The *gendarmes* arrested in the airport were handed over to the Katangese authorities in town, around midnight, in exchange for a promise from Kimba (who was replacing Tshombe, on his way to Europe to attend a Moral Rearmament Conference in Switzerland) that Katangese patrols would withdraw from town and the road-blocks would be dismantled. However, during the night, several additional U.N. personnel were abducted and on the morning of 3 December the *gendarmes* returned to patrol the town and to man the two road-blocks.

It thus became apparent that Kimba did not control the *gendarmerie* and that he was simply trying to buy time for the launching of a general Katangese offensive against the U.N., of which the outlines were clearly emerging. They included the abduction of as many U.N. personnel as possible— civilian as well as military—to secure U.N. hostages (the Irish example was still vivid in their minds), and controlling and cutting the lines of communication between the several U.N. troop concentrations in the Elisabethville area, and between them and the outside, with a view to pinning them down and dealing with them one by one. Indeed the camps of the different contingents as well as the airport were on the outer ring of the city. In

122 e.g. Linner's letter of 28 November to Tshombe (S/4940/Add. 15, Annex I).

123 S/4940/Add. 16, 6 Dec. 1961, para. 9. It must be remembered that a clause in the Protocol specified that the *gendarmes* in the airport should not be disarmed. But in the circumstances, the U.N. troops were in a position of self-defence, and what they did was a minimal riposte to the fire, which seemed completely justifiable.

order to communicate with each other and with ONUC headquarters which were in the residential part (at the north-western edge) of town, they had to pass through the centre, and it was clear that the road-blocks intended to cut them from the centre, hence from headquarters and from each other and from the airport, with the exception of the Indian detachment which was already there.[124]

After all the solemn warnings of the U.N. had gone unheeded (and Kimba's undertakings unfulfilled), on 5 December the U.N. troops, with the authorization of U Thant, undertook a limited military action to dismantle the road-blocks. This led in turn to generalized attacks by the Katangese against the different U.N. positions and U.N. headquarters. The U.N. Command decided, however, to follow a restrained defensive policy limited to holding their positions on the outer ring of the city and ensuring freedom of movement between them until reinforcements were completed.

But in order to prevent the Katangese from reinforcing their positions, which could have tipped the balance in their favour, the U.N. airforce, which had been built up around Katanga, entered into action, destroying several Katangese planes on the ground in Kolwezi, stopping an armoured column on the road from Jadotville to Elisabethville, attacking the radio transmitter and other objectives, but always with much restraint and avoiding the civilian population. In the meantime, the road to the airport remained insecure; the U.N. headquarters in the residential area were intermittently (and very inaccurately) shelled and shot at from near-by villas. Sniping was rampant in the centre of town, the mercenaries and *gendarmes* using civilian populations as a shield, and firing from hospitals, ambulances, and private houses, probably to draw U.N. fire on civilian objectives, for propaganda purposes. The U.N. troops only returned fire on private houses from where they were fired upon and they held their fire when civilian casualties were probable. All the same, the anti-U.N. propaganda was at a zenith and stories of brutality and atrocities abounded.[125]

On 14 December the reinforcement of U.N. troops in Elisabethville was completed. As they could not mount a frontal attack on the town without inflicting heavy damage on civilian lives and property, 'it was decided to move around Elisabethville, eliminating all Katangese positions on the edges and establishing control around the perimeter

124 Ibid. in general; Hoskyns, 449 (for a map of the town with U.N. and Katangese positions).

125 S/4940/Add. 16; Add. 17, 9 Dec. 1961; Add. 18, 20 Dec. 1961.

[outer ring].'[126] Thus that night and on the following day, U.N. troops completely cleared the areas along the road to the airport, and around ONUC's headquarters. On the 16th three strategic objectives 'which had been much used to impede ONUC's freedom of movement'[127] were secured: the Ethiopians gained control of the Lido area and the road to Kipushi and the Rhodesian border; the Irish took over the tunnel under the railway bridge and the Swedes attacked and captured Camp Massart, the main *gendarmerie* camp in Elisabethville. Sniping continued, however, from private houses as well as mortar and small-arms fire from the Union Minière buildings, where it appeared that the main body of Katangese forces in Elisabethville had concentrated. Finally, the Ethiopians occupied the compound in the early morning of 19 December and the unilateral order of cease-fire was issued to U.N. troops, beginning at 7 a.m. of that same day.[128]

U Thant's decision

At this juncture, the U.N. was faced with the choice between moving in on the centre of the town for a complete take-over, risking many more casualties among its own troops and the civilian population (basically the Europeans, as the African part of Elisabethville known as the *Cité* was rather calm during the whole period and was almost untouched by the fighting) or using its superior military position to bring Tshombe to his senses.

Two developments on the diplomatic level must have influenced U Thant's decision. The first was the severe criticism of U.N. action formulated by a number of countries; they obviously included Belgium, South Africa, Rhodesia, and Portugal, but also Madagascar, Greece, and more significantly France and Congo–Brazzaville; the latter two went as far as denying the U.N. transit, overflight, and other facilities over their territories.[129] The U.K. was silent at the beginning, but the announcement on 8 December that the Government would supply a limited number of bombs for the Indian planes in Katanga caused a flurry in the House of Commons and on 13 December the Government reversed its decision to supply the bombs and called for a cease-fire.

U Thant's strong stand in the face of such criticism can be

127 Ibid., para. 20.
128 See in general ibid., paras. 17–28; S/4940/Add. 19, 22 Dec. 1961; S/5038, 21 Dec. 1961, para. 2.
129 For the exchanges between the President of the Congo (Brazzaville) and the Secretary-General, see S/5035, 19 Dec. 1961. For the French measures, see *Le Monde*, 17 Dec. 1961.

explained by two reasons: in the first place, the U.N. legal position was based on the very firm ground of self-defence. The other was the unreserved backing of the U.S., which was openly associated with the operation by sending several Globemaster planes for U.N. troop transport. But the military position was at that juncture reaching a limit beyond which self-defence would be difficult to justify. And the U.S. was also in favour of a negotiated solution from this position of strength rather than dealing the death-blow to Katanga with all the legal, political, and military risks it would entail.

The other important factor bearing on U Thant's decision was the radical reversal in Tshombe's attitude, once he realized that in spite of the mercenaries' assurances the situation was turning to his disadvantage. On 15 December, he sent a cable to President Kennedy, indicating his desire to negotiate with Adoula various aspects of the Congo problem and asking for the President's assistance in this respect. Tshombe's aim was to obtain a stand-still cease-fire before U.N. troops went too far; he must have been made to understand that the advance of U.N. troops would not be stopped until he engaged in serious negotiations with Adoula. But even then, U Thant declared, with U.S. approval, that the operations would not be stopped until the minimum objectives of the U.N., namely securing freedom of communications and the security of U.N. personnel, were achieved; he added that there would be no cease-fire agreement, but only a unilateral order to U.N. troops to hold their fire for the duration of the negotiations.[130]

The Kitona Agreement

Arrangements were made for a meeting in the Kitona military base in the Lower Congo. The U.S. President sent his private plane with the U.S. Ambassador to the Congo, Edmund Gullion, as his personal representative, to pick up Tshombe at Ndola and bring him to Kitona—which was done on the morning of 19 December; while Adoula and his party flew in from nearby Leopoldville. Ralph Bunche and Robert Gardiner were also there as representatives of the Secretariat. Negotiations began on the 20th and started exclusively between the representatives of the Central and provincial governments. But as difficulties emerged, positions polarized, and deadlocks developed, the role of Bunche and Gullion in search of a mutually acceptable solution became much more important (as did the

130 S/4940/Add. 19, para. 2; see also U Thant's cable of 15 December, to Spaak (S/5025/III).

pressure they exerted on the parties). Finally, 'after a good deal of difficulty, an agreement was arrived at outside the meeting room on 21 December 1961 at approximately 2.30 a.m.'[131]

It was a suggestion from Bunche concerning the last contentious point that saved the day. Indeed, Tshombe insisted on including in the agreement a reservation concerning its ratification by the Katanga Assembly. But Adoula, remembering the use of the same pretext to denounce the earlier agreement (signed by Tshombe before his release in June), categorically rejected such a reservation. Finally, at Bunche's suggestion, Tshombe made the following unilateral declaration, which did not include the reservation:

The President of the Government of the Province of Katanga:

(1) Accepts the application of the *Loi fondamentale* of 19 May 1960;

(2) Recognizes the indissoluble unity of the Republic of the Congo;

(3) Recognizes President Kasa-Vubu as Head of State;

(4) Recognizes the authority of the Central Government over all parts of the Republic;

(5) Agrees to the participation of representatives of the province of Katanga in the Governmental commission to be convened at Leopoldville on 3 January 1962 with a view to study and consideration of the draft constitution;

(6) Pledges himself to take all necessary steps to enable deputies and senators of the province of Katanga to discharge, from 27 December 1961, their national mandate within the Government of the Republic;

(7) Agrees to the placing of the Katanga *gendarmerie* under the authority of the President of the Republic;

(8) Pledges himself to ensure respect for the resolutions of the General Assembly and the Security Council and to facilitate their implementation.[132]

This declaration was communicated to Bunche with a covering letter carrying the reservation:

I have the honour to communicate to you herewith the text of a declaration that I propose to make following the conversations just held by my delegation with the delegation of the Central Government.

I would however draw your attention to the fact that the haste with which my journey was made did not allow me the time to consult the competent authorities of Katanga so as to be authorized to speak on their behalf.

I accordingly propose to do this on my return and to inform the Central Government of the steps to be taken with a view to the application of the enclosed declaration.[133]

---

131 S/5038.
132 Ibid., para. 7(a).
133 Ibid., para. 7(b).

Bunche in turn communicated the declaration to Adoula with a covering letter which did not refer to the reservation.[134]

Freedom of movement and the limits of self-defence

By resorting to aggressive action (on the basis of an erroneous evaluation of the military situation) first against individual U.N. personnel, then on a wider military scale, the mercenaries provided ONUC with a perfect opportunity to achieve its military objectives, without being open to the charge of taking the initiative in the use of force or of violating the cease-fire, basing itself on the unassailable ground of self-defence.[135]

The emphasis was put on two concrete applications of the right of self-defence. The first—which could also be covered by the maintenance of law and order—was to ensure the security and physical protection of U.N. personnel against assault and abduction. The other concrete application constitutes also an independent right of its own, based on the principle of the autonomy of the Force and the Operation, namely the right of freedom of movement. This right was recognized by the 'Basic Agreement' of 27 July 1960 between the U.N. and the Central Government,[136] and the more detailed 'Status Agreement' of 27 November 1961.[137] But it equally derived from the right of self-defence; for if the Force had a right to hold and defend positions occupied under orders, the exercise of this right necessarily implied the defence of the freedom of movement and communication between these positions, and between them and the outside.

The purposes of the operation, according to U Thant, were

to regain freedom of movement, restore law and order, and assure that for the future the United Nations Force and officials in Katanga would not be subjected to attacks. These operations were in this sense . . . an exercise of the right of self-defence; they were moreover, pursued up to such time, that the indicated objectives were achieved; that there were satisfactory guarantees in

---

134 Ibid., para. 7(d).

135 When taken to task by Spaak for exceeding the limits of use of force authorized for the apprehension of mercenaries by the November resolution (S/5025/AII, 8 Dec. 1961), U Thant firmly answered that the U.N. 'was obliged to use force in self-defense' (S/5025/BI, 8 Dec. 1961).

136 S/4389/Add. 5.

137 S/5004. Article 30 provides: 'The Government shall afford the members of the Force and the officials serving under the United Nations in the Congo full freedom of movement throughout Congolese territory and to and from points of access to Congolese territory. This freedom shall extend to the operation of vehicles, aircraft, vessels and equipment in the service of the United Nations.'

this regard for the future, not only in Elisabethville but over the whole of Katanga; and that the United Nations was satisfied that it would be able to proceed with the implementation of the Security Council and General Assembly resolutions without obstruction from any source.[138]

There may be some doubt whether the latter part of the statement—concerning the satisfactory guarantees for the future not only against the repetition of such violations, but also for the implementation of U.N. decisions all over Katanga—did not exceed the limits of self-defence. It is necessary, however, to recall that, in actual fact, that part of the statement was not followed through. ONUC, for example, did not use force to enter the South Katangese strongholds of Kipushi, Jadotville, and Kolwezi. It did not consider that either freedom of movement or self-defence authorized it to use force *to occupy new positions*.[139]

Could it be said that by making his unilateral order of cease-fire conditional on Tshombe's consent to negotiate with Adoula and by limiting it to the duration of the negotiations, U Thant went beyond self-defence, and a long way towards imposing a political solution by the threat of force?[140] Here again, it is necessary to recall that in tracing the limit of self-defence (which is the bringing to an end of the aggression or attack against oneself), the attitude of the adversary is determinant; thus to have required a serious proof of Tshombe's peaceful and co-operative intentions was not completely alien to self-defence in that context. In any case, the link between the negotiations and the defensive operations was not absolute: the operations continued even after Tshombe had left for Kitona, until ONUC achieved its minimal objectives consistent with self-defence in the Elisabethville area; on the other hand, it did not try to secure by force its freedom of movement nor the implementation of the November resolution beyond that area; which shows that in practice the limits of self-defence were clearly observed.

Could it be said, on the other hand, that in the face of the criticism of the adversaries of U.N. action and the pressure of his staunchest ally, the U.S., U Thant baulked and stopped the operation short of full implementation of the mandate? If this were the case, 'then

138 S/5078/I, 16 Feb. 1962; see also S/5035 (statement of U Thant of 10 Dec. 1961).

139 For earlier controversies on that point—at the time of the initial deployment of the Force in Katanga and of the Matadi crisis—see *supra*, p. 33, n. 37; p. 108.

140 Hoskyns, 456; A. Burns and N. Heathcote, *Peace-Keeping by U.N. Forces* (1963), 147.

Security Council resolutions appear to be less determinative and the Secretariat more responsive to pressures from powers acting outside the Council than the Charter warrants'.[141] Such a criticism does not seem justified, however; for at the time, ONUC did not command sufficient military resources to consolidate its position in the Elisabethville area and at the same time to launch a military offensive against South Katangese strongholds, even if it wanted to.[142]

The challenge to the Secretary-General's action and interpretation of his mandate did not take place in the Security Council, but directly through formal protests (Belgium, Congo–Brazzaville), denial of facilities and resources (Congo–Brazzaville, France, U.K.), appeals for a cease-fire (U.K.), and informal pressure; but it was counter-balanced by the strong and open support of the U.S. (an attitude which was largely determined by the fear of a Gizengist counter-secession in Stanleyville), in addition to the Afro-Asian and Socialist States. Congo–Brazzaville did request a meeting of the Security Council,[143] but no such meeting took place, probably because the majority, including the permanent members, were not in favour.

Even stronger resistance was manifested when the U.S.S.R., dis-satisfied with the 'diplomatic' course the events were taking after Kitona, of 'negotiating' with Tshombe, called, on 25 January, for 'an urgent meeting of the Security Council to consider the question of the implementation of the Security Council resolution of 24 November 1961'.[144] Both Adoula[145] and the Conference of Heads of African and Malagasy States and Governments, which was then meeting in Nigeria,[146] regretted, and protested against, the Russian initiative at a time when the intervention of the Security Council could disturb the on-going efforts towards a settlement. The meeting, which took place on 30 January, was short lived. A draft resolution to adjourn *sine die* was adopted by 7 votes to 2 (U.S.S.R. and Romania), with 2 absten-tions (U.A.R. and Ghana), this being a procedural matter.[147]

Gizenga in Stanleyville

Parallel to developments in Katanga, and since 4 October, when Gizenga returned to Stanleyville—ostensibly to spend a week on

141 Ibid. 146.
142 Advisory Committee, 65 Mtg., 9 Jan. 1962, 6–10.
143 S/5026, 15 Dec. 1961; S/5027, 15 Dec. 1961.
144 S/5064.
145 S/5066, 28 Jan. 1962.
146 S/5069, 29 Jan. 1962.
147 SCOR, 989 Mtg., 30 Jan. 1962, para. 75.

private business, but subsequently refusing to go back to Leopoldville in spite of the appeals and visits of members of the Central Government—the situation there was also degenerating. Gizenga was consolidating his hold on the Oriental province, including the A.N.C., without, however, officially declaring the constitution of a rival government. On 13 November two events took place which helped to check his progress; the first was that General Lundula—the most senior military officer in the east, and a firm supporter of the Stanleyville regime until the emergence of the Adoula Government—went to Leopoldville and swore allegiance to the Central Government. The same day, the Kindu massacre was committed by military elements theoretically loyal to Gizenga. On 8 January, Parliament summoned Gizenga to return to Leopoldville within 48 hours. On the 13th the President of the Oriental province made a broadcast asking Gizenga to go to Leopoldville and reiterated the allegiance of the provincial government to the Central Government. At that, fighting erupted between Gizenga's private militia, consisting of about 300 former members of the *gendarmerie*, and the A.N.C. soldiers under General Lundula. General Lundula requested ONUC's assistance in re-establishing law and order and disarming the *gendarmes*. Adoula confirmed the request, which was immediately accepted by U Thant 'who confirmed that the assistance requested by the Prime Minister could be afforded within ONUC's mandate to assist the Central Government in the maintenance of law and order and in the prevention of civil war'.[148] ONUC's participation in the disarming of the *gendarmes* was rather limited and was done without firing a single shot. On 14 January Gizenga informed Adoula of his intention to go to Leopoldville and asked for U.N. transport. The following day, Parliament adopted a motion of censure against Gizenga removing him from his position as Vice-Prime Minister. On 18 January Adoula, Lundula, and the provincial President asked for ONUC's help to transfer Gizenga to Leopoldville; a transfer which took place on the 20th. Gizenga asked for U.N. protection in Leopoldville; this was extended to him, with Adoula's consent, but after one day, he relinquished U.N. protection and was moved to a villa put at his disposal by the Government. In fact, from that moment he was under house arrest and was eventually sent to an island at the mouth of the Congo river.[149]

148 S/5053/Add. 1, 20 Jan. 1962, para. 16.
149 S/5053/Add. 2, 23 Jan. 1962, paras. 1–4; Add. 3, 29 Jan. 1962, paras. 9–16; Add. 5, 30 Jan. 1962; Add. 8, 19 Feb. 1962, para. 30; Add. 11, 20 Aug. 1962, paras. 62–3.

The decisions of ONUC during this episode raise several legal questions. The first is whether the participation of the Force in disarming the *gendarmerie* elements loyal to Gizenga was consistent with the mandate, in view of earlier stands and precedents. In this respect it should be recalled that Gizenga had not declared a rival government in Stanleyville nor taken over the provincial government. These elements were thus not covered by any *de jure* or *de facto* 'authority exercising governmental functions';[150] they constituted a purely private militia, and could be dealt with as renegades who had broken loose from their command (which they had done in fact), under the function of maintenance of law and order.

By adding to this sufficient legal justification 'the prevention of civil war', however, U Thant introduced an unnecessary legal complication; for if the situation could be characterized as one of potential civil war, then the U.N. was not supposed to side with one party against the other. In any case, we have seen that after the formation of the Adoula Government, ONUC did not consider hostilities arising from Central Government action against secessionist movements as constituting civil war in the meaning of paragraph A1 of the February resolution.

Another question concerns the transport of Gizenga to Leopoldville in a U.N. plane and the limits of U.N. protection extended to him there. Once again, if this transport took place exclusively at the request of the Central Government (together with Lundula and the provincial government), it would have gone against the earlier ruling; as it would have if the transport had taken place at the exclusive request of Gizenga. But in the case at hand, all parties requested the transport, which left no reason for the U.N. to refuse it. The same applies to U.N. protection of Gizenga in Leopoldville. He had requested it and it was granted to him, with the consent of Adoula, even before he left Stanleyville. But after one day in Leopoldville, he preferred to relinquish it (probably considering that it was setting a limit to his freedom of movement and action); the Officer-in-Charge of ONUC drew his attention to the consequences of this step, and obtained a written acknowledgement from Gizenga before he left the U.N. premises.[151] In consequence, it cannot be said that ONUC acted improperly or against precedent in this respect.

---

150 O. Schachter, 'Preventing the Internationalization of the Internal Conflicts. A Legal Analysis of the U.N. Congo Experience', *1963 Proceedings ASIL*, 221.

151 S/5053/Add. 3, paras. 9–13.

7. ATTEMPTS AT CONCILIATION

Negotiations between Tshombe and the Central Government

After Kitona, Tshombe started by sending the rest of the Katanga parliamentarians to Leopoldville to participate in the work of the national Parliament, as well as three representatives to take part in the discussions on the revision of the *Loi Fondamentale*. He convoked the Katanga Assembly to meet for discussions on the Kitona declaration; after six weeks and lengthy debates, it adopted a cautious (and almost non-committal) resolution, by which it accepted 'the *draft* declaration of Kitona ... *as a potential basis of discussion* ...', while reserving 'its right to ratify the final agreements which may be concluded ...[152]

Before agreeing to go to Leopoldville to negotiate personally with Adoula, Tshombe required and obtained, in a long exchange with the U.N., formal guarantees not only of his security and freedom (and those of his party), but also of his right to return at any time to Katanga; and this even in the following contingencies:

in case the Government of Mr. Adoula were to change its attitude; the Leopoldville Parliament were to take a decision which would prejudice his security; the Head of the State ... were to take measures against him; the judicial authorities were to institute proceedings; hostilities were to be assumed in any part of the Congo, and particularly in Katanga; any event were to occur, or any person were to take action, for any reason whatever, which would endanger his person.[153]

The negotiations started in Leopoldville on 15 March and were conducted in two rounds. During the first, which lasted from 15 March until 16 April, the two parties negotiated alone, but Mr. Gardiner, the Officer-in-Charge of ONUC, extended his general assistance to them. The two basic points discussed were: the powers of Tshombe, who insisted that any agreement reached would be final only after the ratification of the Katanga Assembly—a thesis rejected by Adoula; and the immediate applicability of the *Loi Fondamentale* in Katanga. Adoula considered that the Katanga Assembly resolution implied the immediate application of the *Loi Fondamentale* to Katanga until agreement was reached on a new constitution; while Tshombe considered it as superseded by events, hence a transitional regime based largely on the *status quo* should be agreed upon, pending the

152 S/5053/Add. 8/Annex I (15 Feb. 1962) (emphasis added).
153 S/5053/Add. 9 (5 Mar. 1962).

adoption of a new federal constitution. Positions remained polarized. On 6 April Tshombe presented a series of proposals to Adoula, and on the 16th Adoula gave him his counter-proposals in the form of 'draft conclusions' to the Leopoldville meetings, in which he accepted the idea of a federal constitution and proposed the division of mineral proceeds, 70 per cent for the Central Government and 30 per cent for the provisional government and a transitional regime on the basis of the *Loi Fondamentale*. He also informed Tshombe of his leaving for Coquihatville for a short visit until 21 April; thereupon Tshombe also decided to leave for Elisabethville.[154]

Though he several times reiterated his intention to return to Leopoldville, Tshombe kept postponing the date. In the meantime, after discussing with Adoula, Gardiner elaborated a revised version of the former's 'draft conclusions' which was accepted by Adoula; then moved on to Elisabethville to discuss it with Tshombe. After further negotiations Gardiner prepared a 'final' text of the 'draft conclusions', which served as a basis of discussions during the second phase of the negotiations (which started, after Tshombe's return to Leopoldville, on 25 May and went on until 26 June).

The U.N. representatives Gardiner and Rolz-Bennet (the new U.N. representative in Elisabethville) took an active part in this phase of the negotiations. Four commissions were established: military, monetary, economic and fiscal, and transport and communication. Much of the negotiations were devoted to the elaboration of the terms of reference of these commissions. However, when the discussion moved to 'specific decisions concerning consolidation' which included the type of new constitution and the transitional steps, no agreement could be reached. On 25 June negotiations moved to the last item, the preparation of the final communiqué. Each delegation submitted a draft which was not acceptable to the other. Finally, Gardiner prepared a compromise text, which was not accepted either, because of the insistence of the Katangese on including in it para-graph 6 of their own draft, providing for the maintenance of the secession pending the agreement on a transitional regime. The last meeting went on until 5.30 a.m. on 26 June, and the Katanga deleg-ation left immediately afterwards.[155]

In the face of this discouraging result of the negotiations and Tshombe's diplomacy of attrition—seemingly co-operative on pro-cedural questions such as the creation of mixed commissions, and

154 S/5053/Add. 10, 27 June 1962, paras. 1–15.
155 Ibid., paras. 16–34.

making goodwill gestures (e.g. the transfer after his return of 100 million francs to the Central Government), but stalling on substantive issues—the patience of U Thant (and the Central Government) was wearing thin; the more so that two factors were pressing for an early conclusion: the fast-evolving financial crisis of the U.N. and the military build-up in mercenaries and arms in Katanga.

The U Thant Plan

In consequence, U Thant, in consultation with the Advisory Committee,[156] and after a trip to European capitals to solicit their collaboration, devised a new and more vigorous approach, aimed at bringing maximum—mainly economic—pressure on Tshombe, short of the use of force, with the help of member States. It consisted of a package deal which was not negotiable but had to be accepted or rejected as a whole. This 'Plan of National Conciliation' which came to be known as the 'U Thant Plan', included a series of substantive proposals, basically a federal constitution, the division of the foreign-exchange proceeds on a fifty–fifty basis, the reintegration of the *gendarmerie* in the A.N.C., and a general amnesty. It included also a time-table, which if not respected would lead to four successive phases of increasing economic pressures, leading to a boycott of Katanga products and interrupting all economic relations and communications with it.[157]

On 20 August the Plan was presented to Adoula, who accepted it on the 23rd. It was then notified to Tshombe (on the 24th), who was asked to give his answer in ten days. On 3 September he signified his acceptance, though protesting against the time-limit which he considered as an ultimatum. On 10 September the Secretary-General sent the two parties an identical letter enclosing a detailed programme for the immediate implementation of the Plan. It included the drafting of the new constitution, the creation of three joint commissions with the participation of U.N. experts, to establish the

156 S/5053/Add. 11, 20 Aug. 1962, para. 68: 'In consulting the Advisory Committee on the Congo, I raised the question . . . of the necessity or advisability of a meeting of the Security Council . . . with a view to formulating a new mandate for the United Nations operation or to clarifying and strengthening the existing mandate. I made it clear, in this connexion, that at present there was, in my opinion, no mandate for the United Nations to take any initiative in the use of force to achieve the political objective of ending secession. The consensus of the Committee was that the present mandate was adequate, and that there seemed to be no necessity at this juncture, for further Security Council action.'

157 Ibid., paras. 64–91.

administrative details of implementation of military, monetary, and revenue provisions of the Plan, and several transitional steps to be taken by the parties leading to the final reintegration of Katanga into the Congo—particularly, on the part of Katanga, the taking of an oath of allegiance to the President of the Republic by all *gendarmerie* officers and the dissolution of the Katangese Foreign Ministry and withdrawal of representatives abroad; and for the Central Government, the proclamation of a general amnesty and an offer to assign a number of ministries to Tshombe's Conakat party.

The draft federal constitution was prepared with the assistance of international experts, and was submitted to the two Chambers of Parliament, then to a Conference of Provincial Presidents, which met from 16 to 23 October, but which Tshombe refused to attend. The Commissions were established but again a preliminary controversy broke out over their mandate: the Central Government's position was that their mission was to apply the Plan, while the Katangese delegates claimed that it could only serve as a basis for discussion. In consequence, they did not achieve much progress on substantive issues.[158]

By the middle of November, the date that U Thant considered as the limit of Phase I of his Plan based on persuasion, it became clear that Tshombe was again using dilatory tactics, playing for time in the hope of an early withdrawal of the U.N. from the Congo under the strain of the financial crisis.

The military situation

On the military level, tension had never abated since the end of hostilities. After Tshombe's return from Kitona in January, discussions with the U.N. took place for the return of the *gendarmerie* to the city, and especially to Camp Massart. ONUC insisted, however, that the return should be simultaneous with the deployment of the Force, in application of the principle of freedom of movement throughout the Congo, in the southern strongholds of Jadotville, Kolwezi, and Kipushi. Negotiations stalled on that point and the situation remained as it emerged after the fighting, i.e. the main buildings and Camp Massart remaining in the hands of the U.N. In time, the *gendarmerie* established road-blocks beyond those of the U.N. on the outer periphery of town, thus blockading the roads to their own strongholds.

The U.N. pressed hard for the elimination of foreign military

158 S/5053/Add. 13, 26 Nov. 1962.

personnel and mercenaries. Tshombe suggested the creation of mixed commissions with guaranteed freedom of movement to check on foreign personnel anywhere and at any time. This device proved, however, to be completely ineffective, as the Katangese members of the Commission tipped the mercenaries and garrisons off before the visits. After much insistence, the Katangese furnished the U.N. with fragmentary and dated information on mercenaries, but ONUC managed to gather documentary evidence proving the existence of 300 to 500 mercenaries. Tshombe, however, continued to deny and tergiversate and did not take any action in this respect.[159]

The U.N. also tried to check the inflow of arms and mercenaries into Katanga by soliciting the co-operation of the U.K. and Portugal, especially with a view to stationing U.N. observers on selected routes and airports in Rhodesia and Angola, on the basis of paragraph A5 of the November resolution, but neither government accepted the Secretary-General's proposal. In due time, Katanga resumed its military build-up in mercenaries and arms, especially aeroplanes.[160]

Military incidents did occur, their number and gravity increasing with the deterioration of the situation. The first serious one took place on 17 July in the aftermath of the Katangese celebration of 'Independence' on 11 July, another on 12 September, and a still more serious one on 24 September, causing two deaths and several casualties in a U.N. patrol.[161]

In the meantime, after the failure of the negotiations between Tshombe and Adoula in Leopoldville, the Central Government launched a military campaign in early August against the remaining Katangese garrisons in North Katanga. The U.N. attitude—already assumed by Hammarskjöld after the constitution of the Adoula government and explicitly stated in U Thant's declaration after the adoption of the November resolution—was that they could not intervene on the basis of paragraph A1 of the February resolution against the efforts of the legitimate government trying to reassert its authority over a secessionist movement. This provision was invoked, however, against Katanga to request it to halt its bombardments and troop movements 'otherwise ONUC would be forced to intervene with all the means at its disposal'.[162]

159 S/5053, paras. 11–15; Add. 1, paras. 32–4; Add. 3, paras. 1–8; Add. 4; Add. 6; Add. 7; Add. 8, paras. 17–29.
160 S/5053, para. 16; Add. 12, paras. 1–36.
161 Ibid., paras. 51–4.
162 S/5053, Add. 11, para. 61.

The military commission, which was established to examine the modalities of applying the military clauses of the U Thant Plan, managed to agree on a cease-fire and the halting of all military movements on 16 October. But Adoula rejected it the following day, because it would have amounted to a recognition of Katanga's authority over the north which had been established as a separate province and because the draft called for the institution of observation groups only in North but not in South Katanga. Gradually it became clear that the A.N.C. was gaining the upper hand in the fighting. The Katangese accused ONUC of supporting the A.N.C. in its operations and resorted to indiscriminate bombings and scorched-earth tactics in their retreat; actions which drew vigorous protests from ONUC and warnings to Tshombe that the U.N. would not remain inactive in the face of the bombing of civilians.[163]

At the same time in Elisabethville, since early July U.N. personnel both military and civilian, had been subjected to increasing harassment. On 22 September two Tunisian soldiers were abducted, soon to be followed by others in spite of the vigorous protests of ONUC and reiterated promises of their release by the Katangese. The anti-U.N. campaign was extended early in December to the consular representatives and nationals of member States backing the U Thant plan, such as the U.S., Italy, and even Belgium. Moreover, the Katangese seized several wagon-loads of ONUC goods valued at nearly 1 million dollars at the Rhodesian border in July, and in spite of repeated promises by Tshombe to release the goods, it later transpired that they were sent to Kolwezi and distributed to the *gendarmerie*.[164]

The activation of the last phases of the U Thant Plan

By October, and especially after 15 November, the date he considered to be the limit of phase I of his plan, U Thant had reached the firm conviction that Tshombe had no real intention of abandoning secession and was merely playing for time; this led to the decision to switch ONUC's strategy from one of persuasion to one of maximum pressure short of use of force. It consisted of the activation of phases II to IV of the U Thant Plan. But other measures implying a more vigorous posture on the part of ONUC were contemplated as well. These fell into two categories: the first included measures to imple-

163 S/5053, Add. 14, 11 Jan. 1963, paras. 12–15.
164 Ibid., para. 10.

ment decisions favouring reintegration, whether Tshombe accepted them or not, such as the protection of the Union Minière installations once it had decided to stop paying royalties to Tshombe, and the protection of Central Government immigration and customs officers who would come to exercise their functions in Elisabethville. The other category of action contemplated was that ONUC which had been withstanding a great amount of harassment and provocation would assume a more vigorous role in removing *gendarmerie* road-blocks, eliminating onerous restraints on its freedom of movement, and stopping interference with the flow of its supplies. Both these types of measures (especially the first) were likely to draw a forcible reaction from the Katangese; but if they started the fighting, ONUC could then hit back to the full extent of its capacity in self-defence.[165]

8. THIRD ROUND: THE FINALE (OPERATION GRANDSLAM)

Events started on the morning of 24 December, when *gendarmes* opened fire on U.N. troops in the area of the Union Minière compound. The troops did not return fire. An hour later an unarmed U.N. observation helicopter was shot down by the *gendarmes*, and one wounded officer later died of his wounds. After repeated demands the helicopter and its badly treated passengers were returned to the U.N. Sporadic firing against U.N. positions continued, with U.N. troops holding their fire. Finally, on 28 December, after lengthy negotiations between the U.N. representative in Elisabethville and Tshombe, in the presence of the U.S. and the U.K. consuls, Tshombe agreed to stop the firing by the *gendarmerie*, and, in principle, to the removal of the road-blocks and the withdrawal of the *gendarmerie* from areas in the vicinity of Elisabethville from where they had been attacking U.N. troops. But when asked to sign a declaration to that effect, he refused, on the pretext that he needed the prior approval of his cabinet. Finally, he was formally notified that ONUC would have to take the necessary action to remove the road-blocks. Tshombe left the residence of ONUC's representative at 4 p.m., and 15 minutes later, action started to clear the road-blocks. In general the *gendarmerie* offered no resistance, but dispersed at the sight of U.N. troops. On 29 December Tshombe issued a statement accusing the U.N. of

---

165 Advisory Committee, 70 Mtg., 12 Oct. 1962, 7–17; 72 Mtg., 13 Dec. 1962, 3. There are indications that this policy was tried even earlier. See S/5053/Add. 12/Annex XVIII (letter of Tshombe, dated 25 September, concerning the incident of 24 September).

attacking Katanga and threatened to destroy Katanga's whole economic potential and to follow a scorched-earth policy. Also on 29 December U.N. Swedish jets undertook several sorties against Kolwezi military airport destroying most of the Katangese planes on the ground and rendering the airport unusable. By the end of the day, all road-blocks had been cleared and ONUC forces were in effective control of an area extending 20 km around the city. On 30 December the Irish contingent occupied the nearby city of Kipushi and U.N. troops in Kamina base occupied the adjacent town of Kamina-ville.[166]

On 31 December U Thant issued a long statement, declaring that the operation undertaken on 28 December to remove the *gendarmerie* road-blocks in the Elisabethville area had been completed. He reiterated that the U.N. was not waging war on anyone and did not use force for political ends. He declared that Tshombe had left of his own volition and was free to return to Elisabethville and called for a speedy implementation of the provisions of the Plan by both parties, explaining that by 'speedy' he meant a fortnight.[167]

The 'breakdown of communication' and the crossing of the Lufira river

Though U Thant did mention as one of the U.N. demands that 'ONUC personnel must have full freedom of movement throughout Katanga, which would necessarily mean freeing the Jadotville road and establishing ONUC presence in Jadotville, Kolwezi and Kipushi', the tone of the statement made it clear that he considered that military action was terminated and that these demands would not be pursued by military means. At the time that U Thant made his statement, however, Indian troops were advancing on the terrain along the Jadotville road, a thrust culminating in their entry and occupation of Jadotville unopposed on 3 January 1963. This was the result of the famous 'breakdown of communication' for the investigation of which U Thant sent Bunche to the Congo on that very day.

From Bunche's report,[168] the episode can be reconstructed as follows: A contingency plan was prepared during Bunche's visit to the Congo in October 1962 (and later approved by the Secretary-General) for 'military entry' into the South Katangese strongholds 'to

166 S/5053/Add. 14, paras. 30–61.

167 Ibid., Annex XXXI; see also Annex XXXII for his clarification of this statement, on 2 January.

168 Ibid. Annex XXXIV, 10 Jan. 1963.

achieve freedom of movement for ONUC throughout Katanga', 'if all non military efforts finally failed'[169] (code-named by the Indian officers 'Operation Grandslam'). The entry into Jadotville, to be followed by Kolwezi, constituted the second and third phases of that plan, the first being the re-establishment of security and freedom of movement in and around Elisabethville.

The first phase was unexpectedly activated on 28 December, after a week during which U.N. troops had been subjected to *gendarmerie* fire, which they did not return. It was quickly and successfully completed in two days. The following day (31 December) the move along the Jadotville road started, leading to the 'abrupt telescoping of the first and second phases' of the plan and the 'breakdown of communication'. There were two contributory factors. The first was the considerable transmission delays compounded by heavy use of code, between New York and Leopoldville, Leopoldville and Elisabethville, and Elisabethville and the active units. The other contributory factor was a misunderstanding arising from two successive cables sent from Headquarters to Elisabethville on 30 December. The first specified 'that any further military action in Katanga other than ... in self-defence, should only be undertaken after clearance with Headquarters'. But it 'was quickly recognized that this directive was too restrictive, in that it would unduly limit and handicap the patrol, probing and perimeter expanding actions normal and necessary in military field practice'. The subsequent cable was designed to soften the restrictiveness of the first; it advised the military 'to exploit their road-block success, to extend their Elisabethville perimeter and to keep the gendarmerie and mercenaries off balance and on the run'. It may have been understood by the Commander as ushering the second phase (though Bunche did not say so, but merely that he had 'found in Elisabethville a broader interpretation [of the cable] ... than had been intended by it'). At least it was understood as authorizing probing and extension of control as far as possible. It was probably on that basis that probing patrols entered Kipushi and Kamina-ville on 31 December.

The ONUC company which moved out of Elisabethville on the Jadotville road, on the evening of 31 December 1962 also started out as a probing patrol:

169 Bunche significantly adds two other objectives of the plan to the achievement of freedom of communication, to 'ensure the elimination of mercenaries and assist national unity'.

[A]fter overcoming the first resistance at Lubumi, not far from Elisabethville, they encountered much less opposition thereafter than had been envisaged in the plan. They continued to press forward, therefore, and were able to cross the Lufira river [considered as the main obstacle to Jadotville] by a bridge which had not been completely demolished and to establish [by night fall of 1 January] a bridgehead on the western bank without meeting any formidable opposition beyond the destruction of bridges.

It was only 'after the Lufira had been crossed' that 'the Secretary-General's statement of 31 December . . . on the end of the fighting and on United Nations intentions was . . . received in Elisabethville', and consequently that an 'order of the Force Commander . . . was received that the advance should be halted and the river should not be crossed'.

To have withdrawn from the west bank by night and under enemy fire might well have been costly in ONUC lives and material. To have halted at the bridge-head would have left the troops exposed to the *gendarmerie* and mercenary fire from high ground not far from the river, and would have caused very serious supply problems.

The commanding officer in the field decided that militarily, at any rate, he had no choice but . . . to move ahead and clear out the sole remaining pocket of resistance . . . In this decision he had in mind, particularly, his military training; the security and moral of his troops; the 'scorched earth' threats of Mr. Tshombe; the information obtained from two captured mercenaries that Mr. Tshombe had just been exhorting them to hold up the ONUC advance for three days 'after which world public opinion would force the U.N. to withdraw', and the mercenaries' assurance that there would be no opposition ahead.

From both a military and practical standpoint [Bunche concluded], I believe that there can be no question that the action taken along the Jadotville road and the entry into Jadotville were entirely sound.

Beyond self-defence?

According to Ralph Bunche, 'the Katangese troops, led by mercenaries, played into the hands of the United Nations Force by launching an attack on United Nations positions in Elisabethville',[170] thus opening the way to a heavy riposte based on the unassailable ground of self-defence.

But if self-defence, as interpreted by ONUC until then, clearly applied to the dismantling of the Katangese road-blocks on the outer

170 R. Bunche, 'The United Nations Operation in the Congo', in Cordier and Foote (eds.), *The Quest for Peace* (1965), 132.

periphery of Elisabethville, it was equally clear that it could not cover the entry into Jadotville. In this respect, it was necessary either to invoke a new ground for the use of force, or to reinterpret the limits of self-defence. Indeed a new ground was repeatedly invoked, namely the right of freedom of movement of ONUC throughout the Congo, on the basis of article 30 of the Status Agreement of 27 November 1961 between the U.N. and the Central Government.[171]

If all that was needed, however, for the U.N. to enforce its right of freedom of movement, even in the face of local resistance, was the consent of the Central Government, then it could have done so from the very beginning of the Operation. For this right was implied in the initial consent of the Congolese Government, and was 'ensured' by it in the Basic Agreement of 27 July 1960. In any case, the Status Agreement came into force before the second round. All the same, the U.N. did not invoke it on that occasion as a legal basis for deploying troops into new positions, by force if necessary, but only for defending the freedom and security of movement and communication between the positions it already held (which was after all a mere application of the right of self-defence).[172]

The new element then was not so much the right as the modalities of enforcing it. The entry into Jadotville, on the basis of the right of freedom of movement implied the adoption of a more extensive interpretation of self-defence, which allowed U.N. troops to use force to defend themselves not only while holding positions occupied under orders, but also during the initial stage of taking hold of such positions. It may be recalled that this was the interpretation proposed by the U.S.S.R., Poland, and Tunisia during the debate in the Security Council on the entry of the U.N. Force into Katanga, an interpretation which was strongly resisted by Hammarskjöld.[173]

Did the entry into Jadotville on that basis mean that the U.N. was using force to bring the Katanga secession to an end, in violation of the principle of non-intervention? The entry into Jadotville was justified as an exercise by the U.N. of its right of freedom of movement throughout the Congo. The clashes with the Katanga *gendarmerie* were not aimed at ending the secession, but at overcoming the resistance to the exercise by the U.N. troops of that right. But once the U.N. Force was stationed in the South Katangese sanctuaries, it would have had

---

171 Ibid.; S/5240, 4 Feb. 1963, paras. 7–8.
172 *Supra*, p. 174.
173 *Supra*, p. 33, n. 37.

to implement its mandate of rounding up foreign military personnel and mercenaries, by force if necessary. Without those foreign elements, however, the Katangese *gendarmerie* would have ceased to exist as a fighting force. Though this would inexorably have led to the collapse of the secession, the U.N. Force would have acted within its mandate and exclusively against the foreign elements which made the secession and its continuation possible, and which constituted the latest form of foreign intervention in the Congo. The fact that the effective elemination of the foreign element was enough to bring about the collapse of the secession, far from being an argument against U.N. action, provided a clear evidence of the all-pervasive nature of foreign intervention and of the secession being a mere façade for the foreign interests behind this intervention.

The Katangese secession comes to an end

Tshombe had left Elisabethville on 28 December for Kolwezi, after a short visit to Salisbury.

Even prior to United Nations entry into Jadotville [probably just after the Secretary-General's statement of 31 December] he had shown some interest in returning to Elisabethville for discussions aimed at reaching a basis for ending the secession of Katanga and expressly authorized the director of the 'National Bank of Katanga' to proceed to Leopoldville for discussions on the question of the foreign exchange proceeds of the Union Minière.[174]

But in his clarification of 2 January, the Secretary-General considered that it was 'too late for negotiations', and that the only discussions required were 'on technical matters involved in implementing certain provisions of the Plan'.[175]

During the following days in Kolwezi and then after his return to Elisabethville on 8 January, Tshombe's mood alternated between co-operation with the U.N. in the hope of reopening another drawn-out round of negotiations, and threats (very serious in view of the extent of damage already done) of pursuing a scorched-earth policy.

On 12 January, he precipitately left for Kolwezi via Rhodesia, and it was learnt that the Union Minière installations at Kolwezi (which were the largest) and the near-by bridge, dam, and power-station, had been thoroughly mined and would be blown up if ONUC approached that town. Strong diplomatic pressures were exerted on Tshombe by his traditional friends to refrain from wanton destruction

174 S/5053/Add. 15, 30 Jan. 1963, para. 5.
175 See *supra*, p. 186, n. 167.

and to control his extremist lieutenants. In consequence, late in the afternoon of 14 January the Secretary-General received through Belgian Government channels a statement from 'Mr. Tshombe and his ministers meeting in council in Kolwezi', announcing their readiness to end secession, to allow U.N. troops freedom of movement throughout Katanga, and to return to Elisabethville to arrange for the complete implementation of the U Thant Plan. But they requested that the amnesty included in the Plan should be put immediately into effect. On that basis, Tshombe returned to Elisabethville on 17 January and concluded an agreement with the acting representative of ONUC there, which provided *inter alia* for the immediate clearance of mines and explosives in Kolwezi and for ONUC's peaceful entry there on 21 January. Thus, by that date 'the U.N. Force had under control all important centres hitherto held by the Katangese ... The Katangese *gendarmerie* had ceased to exist as an organized force';[176] and with it the Katanga secession.

176 S/5053/Add. 15, para. 37. Tshombe and his associates continued to hold their provincial positions. On 16 January Ileo was appointed by President Kasavubu as Minister of State resident in Elisabethville, where he arrived on the 23rd. The maintenance of law and order remained the over-all responsibility of ONUC, working in co-operation with the Katangese police. In order to avoid incidents, it was decided, by agreement with Adoula, that A.N.C. troops would be gradually introduced in Katanga, and would be placed there under the operational command of ONUC (ibid., paras. 42–52).

EPILOGUE

WITH the ending of the Katanga secession, a major phase in the activity of the U.N. in the Congo came to a close. But the task was not yet completely achieved, in view of the tenuous capacity of the Congolese Government in the field of maintenance of law and order. The Security Council had not fixed a time-limit for the Operation, but the fourth Special Assembly had allocated funds until the end of 1963, which thus constituted the limit.[1] But on 22 August Prime Minister Adoula asked for the maintenance of a reduced Force until the end of the first semester of 1964. There was a strong argument for a quick withdrawal, namely the U.N. financial crisis, but an equally strong one for granting the Prime Minister's request. Finally the General Assembly decided to maintain the Force until 30 June.[2]

The political situation degenerated once again after the suspension of Parliament by President Kasavubu on 29 September 1963. As a result the Lumumbists fled to Brazzaville—which had witnessed in the meantime the overthrow of Youlou and the installation of a revolutionary regime—where they established the 'Committee of National Liberation'. An armed uprising started soon thereafter in the Kwilu Province, under the leadership of Pierre Mulele, Lumumba's former Minister of Education; and another in Kivu in February 1964 under Gaston Soumialot.

These were clear situations of civil war. But ONUC, with much reduced troops, and in the process of phasing out, was in no position to intervene effectively, except through participation in humanitarian activities usually in conjunction with the Red Cross, such as bringing relief and evacuating the wounded, foreigners, and U.N. and specialized agencies' personnel from threatened areas.

The final withdrawal of the Force started in May and the last U.N. soldiers left the Congo on 30 June 1964.[3]

1 G.A.Res. 1876 (ES–IV), 27 June 1963.
2 G.A.Res. 1885 (XVIII), 18 Oct. 1963.
3 S/5784, 29 June 1964, para. 259.

CONCLUSIONS

THE purpose of this study has been to demonstrate and analyse the variety of roles played by law in the shaping and evolution of the U.N. Congo Operation; more specifically the ways in which law influenced the major decisions taken, mainly by the Secretariat, in the carrying out of this Operation. These can be classified as follows:

THE INSTRUMENTAL USES OF LAW

1. *Social engineering: designing the Operation*

The frequent recurrence of terms such as 'mandate', 'principles', and 'interpretation' clearly reveals that the Operation was conceived and cast from the beginning into the legal and constitutional framework of the Charter. Indeed one of the main purposes for the Operation was to contain the Congo crisis and internalize it within the U.N., thus subjecting it to both the substantive terms of reference (the principles and purposes) and the institutional procedures of the Organization.

The Operation itself was conceived and mounted from scratch by Dag Hammarskjöld, in a brilliant exercise of social engineering, with the double purpose of facing up to the immediate crisis, but also of expanding the role of the U.N. in world affairs. We have seen in detail how he tailored the mandate to be granted to him by the Security Council to the needs of the situation as he perceived them, in the light of this double purpose.

The mandate was thus a legal translation of political purpose into specifically defined *functions*. But it was not a purely enabling instrument. For these functions had to be performed within certain limitations (apart from their definitional boundaries) set by the *principles*, which represented the constraining facet of the mandate.

2. *Legal strategy: the interpretation and implementation of the mandate*

The tension between the pursuit of political aims through the vigorous fulfilment of the functions on the one hand, and the constraining effect of the principles on the other, was at the basis of all the controversies to which the Operation gave rise. They thus took the form of legal controversies over interpretation.

As the implementation of the mandate was entrusted to the

Secretary-General, he detained the power of initial interpretation both in day-to-day implementation and in his dealings with the contenders. We have seen how effectively Hammarskjöld used this power in pursuing his general strategy of distributing roles among the contenders according to a general plan of action which, if accepted by all, would open the way to a solution of the crisis. The power of interpretation was used first in devising a plan of action on the basis of a substantive interpretation of the mandate which—apart from being legally sound—provided at least minimal satisfaction to all the contenders and hence stood the greatest chance of being acceptable to all.

Legal argument—based on his power of interpretation—was also used by the Secretary-General, both as a sword and as a shield, in dealing individually with the contenders, trying to persuade them to accept his rules of the game. As a sword, he used it as an objective basis for his claims *vis-à-vis* the contenders to bring them to do, or to acquiesce in ONUC doing, what was required for the implementation of the mandate. In this respect, it was used as a stick as well as a carrot, by emphasizing not only the illegal posture of the recalcitrant party but also occasionally the limits of U.N. action or of what was required from him. Legal argument provided the Secretary-General also with a shield against exaggerated claims and demands for U.N. action which, according to his interpretation, could not be accommodated within the confines of the mandate.

3. *Institution-building: constitutional development*

Hammarskjöld's interpretation was not final, however. It could be, and soon was, challenged. Here again Hammarskjöld had thought from the beginning of a distribution of constitutional roles between the deliberative and the executive organs, and envisaged the Operation as an opportunity for enhancing the constitutional development of the Organization.

Hammarskjöld's constitutionalist outlook comes out clearly in his systematic elaboration of a process of interpretation, which was intended initially to leave him much leeway in implementing the mandate, while formally submitting his interpretation to constitutional surveillance. Under attack, however, he moved from this doctrine (of 'tacit approval' by the Security Council) to one seeking more active participation, first by establishing the Advisory Committee, and later by asking for more guidance from the deliberative organs, which was not forthcoming, and for a parliamentary standing body, which did not materialize either. Finally, in the face of an all-out Russian attack on the office of the Secretary-General and on him personally, he elaborated a theory of political responsibility of the Secretary-General similar to the constitutional doctrine of 'vote of confidence'.

LAW IN DECISION-MAKING

These considerations describe a wide, all-pervasive role of law, but one which emphasizes its enabling character. At the concrete level of decision-making, however, though these considerations are ever present in the mind of the decision-maker, it is the constraining rather than the enabling role of law which forces itself on his immediate attention. In other words, it is the role of law as a parameter of action rather than as a variable which claims priority, in terms of urgency if not necessarily in terms of importance; the more so the higher the level of controversy surrounding the decision.

In these circumstances the executive organ may seek guidance from, or be challenged before, the deliberative organs, following the constitutional process of interpretation. But this may prove to be to no avail, if the controversy over the interpretation polarizes the members of the Security Council or the General Assembly in a manner that prevents the organ from taking a decision. In such cases, Hammarskjöld considered that it was still possible 'to resolve controversial questions on a truly international basis', namely the purposes and principles of the Charter and the practice and precedents of the Organization. He admitted, however, that 'problems of political judgement still remain' but considered that 'the elements of purely personal judgement' could be minimized by seeking 'the representative opinion of the Organization' through continuous contact with *permanent missions* and the creation of *advisory committees* for major operations.[1]

Still these elements reduce but do not eliminate the margin of judgement of the decision-maker. The study reveals that two factors particularly affect the ways in which law bears on the decision-making process in such circumstances.

1. *The decision-maker's concept of law*

With all these preoccupations with law and the process of interpretation, there remains a margin of subjectivity deriving from

1 'The International Civil Servant in Law and Fact' (Oxford Lecture), reproduced in Foote, op. cit. 329 at 346.

conscious or unconscious factors such as one's own initial perception and understanding of the standards of legality, one's evaluation of factual situations which may be highly complex and dynamic, and one's own background, ideology, and sympathy with, or antipathy to, causes and persons involved in a situation.

What was the concept of the two Secretaries-General of the role of law in the Operation?

(a) *Hammarskjöld*

Because of his awareness of working within an evolving constitutional structure, and contributing by his action to its evolution, Hammarskjöld was very conscious of the importance of the legal propriety of such action. This consciousness was reflected both in his method of proceeding and in his stands and statements.

For instance, when discussing, in the Advisory Committee, the proposed steps which he intended to take, he always commented at length on their Charter basis and related them in legal terms to the mandate, thus revealing meticulous prior legal preparation. In this he collaborated closely with Dr. Oscar Schachter, the then Director of the General Legal Division, who was asked by the Secretary-General more than once to elaborate on certain legal points in the Committee. Furthermore, on several occasions he dismissed certain suggestions without going into their merits on the grounds that the U.N. was not legally empowered to implement them.

Among Hammarskjöld's numerous statements on the fundamental importance of strict observance of law, and on its role in the U.N. in general, the most revealing was one made in the Advisory Committee:

This Organization will, I hope, survive the Congo crisis. What is done on this point and that point in the Congo crisis creates precedents. If those precedents are in contravention of international law, of the Charter, of the decisions of the organs—even if they may follow the views of some members of those organs—we have ... impaired the prestige of the United Nations, and perhaps irreparably. Because, do remember one thing. It is not only the success of this or that effort which will count in the final evaluation of the United Nations; it is also the way in which the success was achieved ... the United Nations just as much as any government—and I would say more than any government—cannot easily brush aside legal considerations so that the United Nations itself can be accused of lawlessness ... Therefore, let us try to find solutions which achieve the political aim, but let us try to find them in forms which we shall not regret later on.[2]

2 Advisory Committee, 29 Mtg., 2 Mar. 1961, 81.

Hammarskjöld's concept of law was—as often in the case of non-lawyers—formal and rather legalistic. In general, and as a matter of legal policy, he was more inclined towards adopting a strict interpretation of the mandate, considering that a more liberal interpretation had to come from the deliberative organs, just as a change in the mandate would. Occasionally he even resisted the adoption of such a liberal interpretation or the enlargement of the mandate because, although this would have provided him with a legal basis for more drastic action, it would have violated his concept of the political role that the Organization should play in the crisis. In one or two cases he went as far as invoking the Charter limitations on the powers of the Assembly and the Council in order to deter them from adopting such an enlargement of the mandate.

(b) *U Thant*

It has been alleged that U Thant was less worried about legal considerations, that he even departed from the standards of legality and impartiality set by Hammarskjöld. To what extent are these allegations verified by this study?

It is true that in the declarations and reports of U Thant on the Congo one finds much less legal justification than in Hammarskjöld's, and then mainly in terms of statement of principle rather than of detailed reasoning and analysis. It is also true that U Thant resorted less often to the Advisory Committee and not at all to the Security Council after the adoption of the November 1961 resolution in the wake of his election.

This can be explained in part, no doubt, by the difference in the natural disposition of the two Secretaries-General. U Thant was more intuitive, less expository, and less worried about external representation, and hence legal justification, than Hammarskjöld. His concept of law was less legalistic and procedural, more substantive and teleological. But this is no more than a partial explanation. The great difference was in the context within which each operated. Hammarskjöld's was the constitutive and the most controversial period. By the time U Thant took over, the pattern had settled, as had the acrimonious controversies over the Operation and the role of the Secretary-General. A large consensus, including the two Super Powers and the Third World, was achieved on a comprehensive and liberal redefinition of the mandate in the November 1961 resolution, with only the European colonial powers in (relatively mild) opposition. All this called for much less legal justification and indicated clearly that what was expected from U Thant was to finish off the job and bring the Operation as quickly as possible to a successful conclusion. It is true that some of his declarations in relation to the objectives of the second round and to action in Stanleyville were so widely phrased as to create an ambiguity in this regard. But, as we have seen, the action itself did not trespass the limits of the mandate.

It can thus be said that U Thant may have given less attention to legal justification, though not necessarily less weight to legal considerations. He obviously did not possess Hammarskjöld's analytical mentality or his talent for exposition and precision; and he may not have had the benefit of legal advice of the same quality.

2. *The complexity of the decision-making process*

Decisions can be analytically reduced to two elements: (a) the *determination* (French: *constatation*) of facts, of events or generally the elements of a situation at issue; and (b) the *decision* properly speaking, which is the specification of the consequences of the determination, of what should be done to face up to the situation which has been determined. These two elements are not always operated by the same person or organ within complex organizations such as the U.N.

The more complex the process of decision-making and the more persons are involved in it, the greater the risk of conflicting views over determinations and the legal consequences to be drawn from them, and the more probable are the breakdowns of communication creating situations in which different participants in the decision-making process act on different understandings, assumptions, or interpretations leading to internally inconsistent decisions.

The study of the major decisions taken in the course of the Operation bears witness to the fact that even within the Secretariat, which is an integrated organ with a neat hierarchical structure leading to a single locus of authority, such risks and dangers are not totally absent.

LAW IN INTERNATIONAL ORGANIZATION

What general conclusions can be drawn from these considerations, particularly as concerns the role of law in international organization?

The current view of law as a mere constraint is true but incomplete and rather simplistic. For law bears on the actions and shapes the expectations of its subjects in many other ways as well. Prominent among them is its role as a *facility*,[3] ranging from simple enabling

3 Cf. H. L. A. Hart, *The Concept of Law* (1961), 27.

devices to the most complex structures of collective action which enable the subjects to achieve collectively what they cannot undertake individually (either because of limitations of resources and time horizon, or because of the lack of legitimacy of individual action or, finally, because the collective action requires the simultaneous co-ordination of the activities of a large number of subjects). It is in the latter case that law comes nearest to a tool of social organization and management, i.e. of social engineering.

One of the complex facilities on the international level is the international organization, which provides the legal framework for collaborative efforts with a view to achieving common ends. But in this context, the role of law as a facility begets its role as a constraint. For international organizations are entities of a secondary order, in the sense that they are created by, and their powers devolve from, the states which are the primary actors on the international level. Consequently, the powers of international organizations are limited by the extent of devolution, as reflected in their constitutive instruments.

Thus, in view of the constitutional structure of international organizations, law is called upon to play a greater role within their context than in a purely inter-state setting. This role is further reinforced for reasons pertaining to the political environment in which these organizations function. If the organization is nearly universal, its membership reflects deep political cleavages and conflicts of interests and ideologies, and hence a low degree of consensus, which makes it imperative to fall back on, and to justify both individual behaviour and collective action in terms of the only objective standards accepted by all, i.e. the constitution and fundamental principles of the organization and of general international law. In other words, the extreme heterogeneity of the political environment makes legal justification more imperative.

An indirect consequence of this heterogeneity which further enhances the importance of legal justification in international organizations, is the open character of their process of decision-making, which contrasts with the standard practices of national governments. This is because the protagonists are represented within the organization, which makes it very difficult, if not impossible, to withhold information or defend decisions and acts by mere assertions of international (by analogy with national) interest.

In sum, it can be said that law plays a much greater role, both quantitatively and qualitatively, in shaping the interactions and decisions within international organizations than outside: quantitatively, because the structure and environment of these organizations multiply the occasions where detailed legal justification is required; qualitatively, in consequence, because formulating positions, interests, and claims in terms of law is bound largely to condition their substance.

INDEX